THE HUMAN MIRROR

THE HUMAN MIRROR

Material and Spatial Images of Man

Edited by
MILES RICHARDSON

Louisiana State University Press   *Baton Rouge*

ISBN 0–8071–0074–9
Library of Congress Catalog Card Number 73–90872
Copyright © 1974 by Louisiana State University Press
All rights reserved
Manufactured in the United States of America

Designed by Dwight Agner. Set in Linotype Baskerville
by Heritage Printers, Inc., Charlotte, North Carolina.
Printed on Warren Olde Style paper and bound by Halliday
Lithograph Corp., West Hanover, Massachusetts.

Published with the assistance of the Council on Research,
Louisiana State University

To *Australopithecus,*
who first caught a glimpse
of the human soul
in a piece of rock

Contents

List of Maps

List of Figures

List of Tables

Preface

Several years ago, when I first thought about editing an anthology on material culture, I knew that a critical question would be about the scope of the book. Should the scope be narrow, focused on a single theme or on one sociocultural stage; or should it be broad, covering several concepts and crisscrossing a number of sociocultural types? I opted for the broad perspective. I wanted the volume to make this statement: Here is a field worthy of study that has a long history in anthropology and in related disciplines. The material culture field has had its ups and downs as interest has moved from the external aspects of culture to the mental and social. But today students of mankind are climbing out of the mind and unhooking from the social in order to see the things that they have stumbled on while trying to reach their informants. Here under one cover is the entire range of what scholars are doing in the field of material culture.

To voice this statement I felt that the volume had to include (1) chapters that continued in the tradition of using material culture as a means of reconstructing history counterbalanced with those that put material traits to new tasks, (2) chapters that treated material culture as a thing in itself and ones that related things to the society that produced them, (3) chapters that considered the material expression of bands and tribes weighed against those that analyzed the material confines of villages and cities, and (4) chapters with viewpoints primarily from ethnography, but also from archaeology and, particularly, from cultural geography, the spatial sister of anthropology.

The audience to which this statement would be directed was to be a specialized one, composed of individuals from the various disciplines with an interest in material culture. These individuals should find several chapters that spoke to them about various aspects of the field. Upon reading the book, the individuals in the scholarly audience would leave with an idea to explore or, if the entire statement came to them clearly, with a desire to lay out the directions that future studies in material culture might take.

With the idea of the book fixed in my mind, I began looking for contributors. William Fenton, because of his long familiarity with the field and his work with the Committee on Anthropological Research in Museums, was able to suggest several excellent people. Several of my colleagues at LSU suggested names, as did friends in other departments. To each potential contributor I sent a letter explaining the volume and suggesting what his role might be.

The responses from the potential contributors varied considerably. Some immediately turned down the invitation, either because they were overcommitted (a response typical of several established scholars) or because they could not meet the suggested deadlines; others hedged their bets by accepting but then pulled out for one reason or another. One individual, a respected scholar, agreed on the telephone to write a chapter, but that was the last I heard from him. But gradually the list grew, as scholars saw in the invitation a way of expressing their ideas on material culture.

As the manuscripts from the contributors began to arrive, I read each carefully and then returned it to the author with my suggestions for revision. One debate that I continually had with myself was about my role as editor. What was I supposed to do? Upon reading a manuscript that I thought should have more attention, I would at times shrug my shoulders and tell myself, "Well, it's that person's manuscript. He should know what he wants." Other times, feeling a surge of power, I would proclaim to myself, "No, it is my volume and my responsibility." Do other editors of anthologies feel the same way? I don't know, but I still haven't resolved the argument.

The contributors and I also exchanged suggestions about the illustrations. After several years of watching geographers at work, I began to develop an appreciation for maps, photographs, and line drawings. Since a theme of the volume was that to analyze culture you have to begin with what you can see, the volume demanded illustrations. Thus, I encouraged the contributors to illustrate their articles. The art historians and the cultural geographers, by and large, replied with ample illustrations; the anthropologists, with notable exceptions, answered with less enthusiasm. Fortunately, through the School of Geoscience at LSU, I had access to excellent draftspeople and a professional photographer; with their aid I was able to equip each article with at least a location map.

The final revision made and the last illustration drawn, this volume, the work of several years and several people, appears with its plan and purpose intact. It speaks to a specialized audience about the range of studies that are going on today in material culture. The contributions move from Neanderthal child care to behavioral adjustments in crowded spaces, from the contributions of an individual artist to the imprints of total societies, from a consideration of a single object to a view of the complete cultural landscape, from mural paintings in Mexican prehistory to a beam press on a Greek island, and from transoceanic diffusion in pre-Columbian times to modernization in contemporary Africa. I regret the absence of a contribution by a theorist from the arrogant but immensely refreshing group professing the new archaeology. I regret even more the absence of a study of the material culture of contemporary urbanites. I would have loved to include a chapter along the lines of Oscar Lewis' inventory of items that the poor in Mexico City had gathered around them.

Each chapter in the book has an abstract, illustrations, and references. The decision to have abstracts with each chapter goes against the advice of my colleagues and initially of the Press. Aside from my stubbornness, I wanted each chapter accompanied by an abstract so that the chapter would be self-contained and available to the specialist, whose particular interest may limit him to two or three contributions, and to the instructor, who may want to assign certain ones to his class. On the other hand, individuals with wide interests and a ranging curiosity may read the book as a whole because I have grouped the chapters so that they complement each other and progress to form a complete book. Perhaps among the readers of this volume—the specialist, the generalist, the instructor, and the student—there will be one who, intrigued by what he finds here, will go on to construct a more refined, more elegant statement about man and his works. I hope so.

Acknowledgments

Several people have helped me in the editing of this book. I deeply appreciate their assistance. Doye Wood expertly typed the entire manuscript while she was also busy keeping me from making too many errors when I was departmental chairman. Her colleagues, Maudrie Monceaux, Darleen Wade, and Linda Watson, kindly helped with the revision. Philip Larimore, Clifford Duplechin, and Carolyn Martin of the cartographic section and Donald Nugent of the photographic section of the School of Geoscience did excellent work in preparing for publication nearly all of the illustrations. Dr. Bob F. Perkins, Acting Director, School of Geoscience; Lewis Nichols, Assistant to the Director; and Dr. Donald Vermeer, Chairman, Department of Geography and Anthropology, openly gave their support and the resources of their offices. In addition, Don and I have chatted about this volume on several occasions, and I have always come away with a helpful insight.

Charles East, Director; Leslie Phillabaum, Associate Director; Dwight Agner, Production and Design Director; and Marie Carmichael, Editor, Louisiana State University Press, have been helpful, pleasant people to work with. I am especially grateful to Mr. Phillabaum for his sympathetic, intelligent support. The outside readers of the manuscript made several constructive suggestions about content and organization. The LSU Press Committee and Dr. William G. Haag, its chairman, also passed on helpful advice.

The occasion for revising the manuscript occurred while I was on sabbatical leave, and I thank Dr. Irwin A. Berg, Dean of the College of Arts and Sciences, for his warm support and the administration of Louisiana State University for granting the sabbatical. The leave provided time for reflection that, otherwise, would not have been possible. My interest in material culture goes back to the days when I took Dr. Fred Kniffen's "proseminar" on cultural geography. I hope that he can recognize his influence and ideas in this book. On a personal level, Valerie Richardson encouraged me with both praise and criticism, and we are beautiful together.

Part One

Introduction

Chapter 1

Images, Objects, and the Human Story

Miles Richardson

One theme that stands out in the often murky record of human progress is the close association between the biological evolution of man and the evolution of his material culture. At the beginning of the Pleistocene period (that critical geological time during which a bipedal hominid became the life-form that we are) a small-brained, large-jawed primate scraped together an existence on the African savanna with a single, all-purpose tool, the flaked pebble. At the end of the Pleistocene a large-brained, small-jawed primate exploited most of the world's ecological zones with a material inventory that included the spear, the spear-thrower, the harpoon, probably the bow and arrow, beautifully chipped knives and scrapers, tools for making other tools (like the burin), awls, clothing, shelters, the controlled use of fire, and in the caves of western Europe delicate portraits of magnificent beasts. Written in straightforward archaeological prose, the story is clear: man's biological evolution is the result of his adaptation to culture as a way to exploit the environment. At sometime during the Pleistocene, human genes ceased to respond directly to the natural environment and began to change frequency in accordance with the requirements for the more effective use of culture. Man began to adapt to being man.

3

Man's adaptation to being himself began when he successfully interjected culture between himself and the natural environment. The intrinsic symbolization that lay within him became extrinsic (Hallowell 1968). Man took the material of his mind and projected it onto his behavior and onto natural substance; he molded behavior and substance to fit the mental images that sparkled within him. The results are there to see, in the starkly plain archaeological account that reads from crude pebble tool to delicate Solutrean point.

Man's ability to mold the substance of nature to fit the images of his mind—to make tools—made him a biological success. As devices for manipulating the environment, tools allowed man by the end of the Pleistocene to move from a single ecological niche in Africa to the distant regions of the world. However, the importance of tools lies not solely in their being substitutes for nature's claws, teeth, and fur. Early tools are also indicators that early man was using symbols in his speech and in his behavior, for toolmaking "and language are concordant. Selection favored the cognitive structures dependent on brain organization and social structure which resulted in both language and tool-making" (Holloway 1969, p. 404). Language expresses "the reification by the human mind of its experience, that is, an analysis into parts (including actions and properties) which, as concepts, can be manipulated as if they were objects" (Bronowski and Bellugi 1970, p. 673). The reification of experience into concepts may have been joined with the solidification of ideas into stone.

THE MIRROR OF MATERIAL CULTURE

Tools, concepts, and language are all made of the same stuff; all are symbols taken out of the mind and impressed onto material, behavior, or sound waves. Tools, or more broadly, material culture, have an additional impact. Because the material through which it achieves an empirical reality is more durable than behavior or sound waves, material culture continues to have an existence, as it were, apart from the drift and flow of opinions, attitudes, and ideas. Material culture is at the final point in the process of extrinsic symbolization; it represents the fullest expression of man's efforts to objectify his concepts. Once this objectification takes place, material culture becomes a mirror that man may view to find out about himself—not only about his technical ingenuity, but also about how he, the symbol user, came to be, about the awful mystery of being human.

The mirror of material culture is made of things—chalice, altar, and statue—and their systematic interrelations displayed across space —church, plaza, town, and region. Human domesticated space—yards, parks, and fields—is as much a part of the mirror as are the tools that man holds in his hands. Wherever man has gone, wherever he sees that he is going, from Antarctica to Jupiter and beyond, the magic of culture transforms these places into mirrors that reflect his image.

Material culture is a mirror *of* humans. To the student of human ways it provides glimpses of other people. To the archaeologist, material culture yields information about peoples now dead. Apart from natural remains, such as pollen and bones of wild animals, artifacts are the only source that the archaeologist has to work with. He has no informant to teach him the use of an ax or to explain the intricacies of kinship. With such a handicap, his task would seem impossible. And until recently the archaeologist has felt so constrained by his data that he has limited his analysis chiefly to erecting chronologies, of proving that a certain ceramic style preceded another, that Tchefuncte Incised may be earlier than Tammany Pinched. Now, a more daring, confident spirit is moving through archaeology, and the archaeologist is demanding from material culture information about sexual division of labor, activity areas within a site, and even forms of kinship. The archaeologist is pushing his data and his mind to their limits. If this effort at times results in exaggerations, it is also opening new ways of interpreting past societies through their material remains.

Material culture is also a mirror of the ways of contemporary peoples. To the ethnographer (and to his partner, the cultural geographer) material culture is the point where he must begin his quest for understanding. Through its material expression, a foreign culture confronts the ethnographer and makes him aware of where he is and what to expect. When the ethnographer finds himself in a community with streets laid out in a grid pattern and with a central plaza bounded on one side with a church and on another with a governmental building, he is told in no uncertain terms that he is in a traditional Spanish-American community. The ethnographer makes the necessary adjustments and prepares to talk (in American Spanish) to his informants about medicinal remedies that restore the body's equilibrium, about the fictive kinship system of god-parenthood, about the values of dignity, respect, and honor, and about how Christ taught us the way to die.

Because material culture is the vehicle through which social structures and cultural categories achieve sensory existence (Sorokin 1964, pp. 125–28), the material form of a community provides the ethnographer with direct data on nearly every aspect of local life. The regional configuration of settlements tells him the position of his community in the larger society: a vibrant nucleus centered in a network of communication links or a small dot off on a dirt road. The different structures and activities indicate the function of the community: a market to which people come or a dormitory that ex-peasants leave to work in the nearby city. The size and location of religious structures in the community express the relative power of churches and the number of their members: the massive Catholic church, confidently erect in the town's center and the flimsy Protestant chapel, struggling for a foothold on the edge of town. And the inequality of social class appears in the domestic architecture: the large mansion that bestows the blessings of status and the small shack that does not keep out the rain.

The material imprint that social structure and cultural category make varies according to the level of technological development. The imprint may be the delicate trace of leaf hut, hunting net, and elephant spear that the pygmy makes as he moves through the tropical forest; it may be the spreading stain of diseased forest, foul air, and cruddy water that the industrialist leaves as he rapes the earth. The material imprint also varies according to the type of ideology that people pursue. Some religious groups, such as the Hutterites of the northern Great Plains, believe that "life in this world is transient, temporary, and of no consequence where it is lived" and severely limit the expression their society makes on earth (Hostetler and Huntington 1967, p. 21). Others, such as the Baptists of the southern United States, while agreeing that happiness is not in this world, are less sensitive to the danger of accumulating material goods and are constantly raising money to build a new church or to increase the minister's salary. But no matter the technology and no matter the ideology, societies cannot escape, even in extinction, from impressing themselves on material substance, from forming a mirror of their ways.

To the student of humanity, material culture is a mirror of people's lives. To people, as they move about the social stage, material culture is a mirror *for* their behavior. They read in the objects displayed around them information concerning the plays they act in. The objects cue them as to which part they must select from their behavioral repertoire in order to produce a successful performance. House, church, store, and bar—like mother, priest, merchant, and drinking buddy—are sets of instructions for ordering behavior. Like all culture, material culture has a communications function (Richardson 1974*a*).

The Pleistocene paradox of an animal domesticating itself, of man emerging as a series of adaptations to being human, continues to haunt us. As genetically wired symbol users, we see each other darkly, through the distortions of culture, and our efforts to touch one another are forever failures. Only in good science fiction and in poor social science do humans meet mind to mind. In the real world we are isolated from our own kind, eternally so. We must guess what others are intending. To help us in our guesswork we read the other's behavior and look at the material objects surrounding us. With hints from mental images, with external data from behavior and objects, we then act, perhaps together. Cut off from the governing control of external data, as in a sensory deprivation experiment or in solitary confinement, our minds spin out of control and generate horrible scenes that for a time drive us mad (La Barre 1970, pp. 51–54). Placed in a foreign culture where the external input of strange behaviors and exotic objects crashes against our familiar mental images, we go into culture shock and become paranoid. For all of our bluster, we are fragile creatures, in delicate balance with each other. We need the reassuring information found in material culture that we truly exist together in an orderly world.

A SPANISH-AMERICAN SOCIAL PLACE

As a mirror containing reassuring information for appropriate action, material culture orders our world into discrete social places. Social places, or "sites" (Kuper 1972), are familiar areas within a community's space where people meet—homes, schools, hospitals, churches, stores, bars, police stations, and even streets, wherever people regularly come together. Each social place has attached to it a distinctive set of concepts and a distinctive array of behavioral elements. Each is further segregated from all others by a highly visible material pattern. As people in the community move from place to place they ready themselves for action based on the information contained within their minds, in the behavior of others, and in the material objects before them. At each place, people think and act in accordance with the material expression of that place. Consider the market and the church in a traditional Spanish-American community (Richardson 1974b).

The existence of a Spanish-American town or small city stems from its market and its church. They are its reason for being and are the basis for all other activities. Located in the center of town, they willingly share each other's clientele. People, particularly those from neighboring villages, will choose to celebrate God and buy groceries at the same time. Only on the most sacred days of Holy Week—Thursday and Friday—does the market bow to the church and shut its doors. The presumed antagonism between commerce and religion in traditional Anglo-American communities is all but missing.

To the local community a busy market is a sign of its dominant position in the regional hierarchy of settlements and of its progressive urbanity. It is a secular place, with a degree of freedom from the customary restraints on activities. It is not immoral, but slightly amoral, full of clever people who may take advantage of the ignorant or the foolish. Its physical structure is a large, rectangular building with its floor partitioned into small stalls. It has few ornamentations, but because it is in Spanish America, a large statue of the Sacred Heart of Jesus stands in the middle. The items for sale run through the list of local products and more. Vegetables and fruits are offered here; over there are fish, cheese, and sausage; the stalls there, where the dogs are, sell meat; here is one with various kinds of canned and packaged goods, Del Monte peaches and Kellogg cornflakes among them; in that section in the corner are shoes, clothes, baskets, leather goods, hardware, machetes, and a parrot; and here is a stall full of pictures in bright tones of the Virgin of Carmen, of Saint Martin of Porres, of Jesus in the Garden, of the crucified Christ, bleeding on the cross, and a black and white photograph of a physician long dead but whose spirit continues to cure the faithful.

Each stall is a packed nest of carefully arranged goods. In the middle of the nest is a man or frequently a woman. He is constantly in motion, jumping from one side of the nest to the other, and he shouts at the shoppers going past him, "Look! Lettuce a peso a head. Potatoes five pesos a pound." If one of the crowd slows as if to stop, he rushes toward the person, "In order to serve you, señor! What pleases you?" If the customer buys an item, the merchant quickly completes the sale. Before the shopper has finished counting his change, the merchant is off to the other side of his nest, "Look! Beans. Carrots. At your service, *caballero*" (Fig. 1.1).

FIG. 1.1   "A Peso Each, Señora"

The physical and social boundaries of the market are not tight. Around the peripheries of the building are open-air stalls or simply spots on the pavement where the produce is a little cheaper and where the seller is more aggressive and less careful with the change. Here in the peripheries nonmarket activities appear. Shoeshine boys and beggars stake out favorite spots. Lottery vendors optimistically shout, "What number? What number? Tomorrow it plays." Gradually the market disappears into small clusters of men, lined along the sides of the street, idly watching the scene before them and chatting about this and that.

To the local community the church is also a sign of urbanity and of civilization. The church is a place for worship, but in the act of worshiping the people demonstrate their attainment not only of grace but also of *cultura*, a level of education, a display of proper behavior, a manifestation of dignity that only truly urban, civilized people have. Represented in the more traditional churches as a life-sized figure stretched in agony on a cross located above the altar, the central figure of Christ teaches men how to suffer and how to die—composed, with restraint, with dignity, with patience, with *cultura* (Richardson, Bode, and Pardo 1971).

Clearly the most imposing structure in the community, the church is also the most sacred place, traditionally dark, full of statues and pictures, with every nook and corner full of meaning. Within, the movements of the small family groups that make up the large congregation are orchestrated by the priest. As he moves through the mass, the people (more or less together) cross themselves, kneel, stand, sing (sporadically), pass coins to the collector, and (relatively few of them) walk to the communion rail and eat the flesh of God. Actions are tightly controlled, and behavior flows predictably to the end.

Departures from the stereotyped pattern creep in. Each individual has his own style of crossing himself, and for some the hands flutter about the face and body in intricate movements that seemingly have no end. Along the edges of the congregation, an old woman and a retarded young man sell the parish news and raffle tickets for a television set. Outside the church at the main entrance, another woman sells small pictures of saints. Near her a beggar has momentarily escaped the eye of the parish priest, and to the person who has just dropped a peso in his hand, he graciously wishes, "May God pay you."

Because they are both part of the Spanish-American tradition, the two social places of market and church share characteristics, but clearly they are different. The market is a place of rapid-fire, two-party exchanges. The semiprivate exchanges occur in an environment of conflicting demands, noise, and the crush of uncaring people. Physically, the market has a minimal structure, with few ornamenta-

FIG. 1.2   A Set of Behavioral Cues

tions and informational restraints, for its communications task is
relatively easy: provide for a continuous sequence of quick interactions between two people. Neither physically nor behaviorally is
the market sharply bounded; instead it gradually loses itself in the
surrounding streets. Conversely, the church is a place for lengthy,
public, carefully orchestrated interplays between the priest and the
members of the congregation. While elements, such as prayer, occur
in places other than the church, the entire behavior sequence is
unique to that place. Seen from the perspective of secular behavior,
the sequence of church behavior is peculiar, it is monotonous, it is
bizarre, it is ritual (Rappaport 1971). Such behavior requires the
support of a material environment that is full of informational con-
straints; redundant instructions of statues, pictures, crosses, and ornate
altars must reassure the participants of the correctness of their actions
(Fig. 1.2). Departures from the dominant pattern of ritual are minor;
both physically and behaviorally the church is a tight unit.

The market and the church are familiar places within the space of the traditional Spanish-American community. Each has attached to it a distinctive set of concepts and a peculiar array of behavioral elements. Concept and behavior are empirically expressed in unique material structures. Guided by the cues they read in the material mirrors, people in the community find each other and together perform the social act appropriate to the place. Only to the brash, uncultured stranger does the market appear chaotic and the church bizarre. To the townspeople, they are places of order where people are reassured, in the trivia of buying lettuce or in the complexity of taking communion, that *we* exist.

CONCLUSION

The theme of the Pleistocene is man evolving in response to the use of culture as a means of exploiting the environment. Back at its beginnings, a human creature walked across the African savanna with the image, the word, and the tool. Some two million years, past the end of the Pleistocene and into the present, man has spread throughout the world and beyond. But the secret of tools lies not solely in their ability to exploit the natural environment, for unlike the twigs that some chimpanzees use to feed on termites, human tools are made of the same stuff as mental images and spoken words. As material culture, tools are the final objectification of intrinsic hopes. As imprinted thought and as engraved behavior, material culture becomes a mirror in which man can see himself.

The images reflected in the human mirror explain much about man's ways and about what kind of creature he is. Vanity is one of man's traits, and when men allow the seductive permanency of material culture to deceive them, that too appears in the material record.

> I met a traveller from an antique land
> Who said: Two vast and trunkless legs of stone
> Stand in the desert. Near them, on the sand
> Half sunk, a shattered visage lies, whose frown,
> And wrinkled lip, and sneer of cold command,
> Tell that its sculptor well those passions read
> Which yet survive, stamped on these lifeless things,
> The hand that mocked them and the heart that fed:

And on the pedestal these words appear:
"My name is Ozymandias, king of kings:
Look on my works, ye Mighty, and despair!"
Nothing beside remains. Round the decay
Of that colossal wreck, boundless and bare
The lone and level sands stretch far away.

(Shelley 1903, p. 211)

If the interaction between man and his tools during the Pleistocene brought about his very existence, then might not new tools, new settings, and new structures result in new men? We may become flabby appendages of mighty machines and end the human story with a whimper; or we may well blow ourselves up and punctuate our final chapter with a real bang. And it may be that in the future, in the distant future, another poet will contemplate the ruins of our civilization, the interstate highways, domed stadiums, supersonic aircraft, missile silos, and pentagon buildings—our vanities—and be moved to write that here was earth and here was man. In the meantime, those of us whose task it is to tell the human story look for understanding in the works of men: in ancient burials, in carved masks, in murals, and in archaic oil presses; in traditional objects in a modernizing country and in familiar chickens in strange places; in Amazon hammocks, in Louisiana landscapes, and in the material adjustments to endemic violence, crowded spaces, and changing and not-so-changing social structure. We gaze into the human mirror seeking after the mystery that is man. That's what this book is about.

REFERENCES CITED

Bronowski, J., and U. Bellugi
    1970   Language, Name, and Concept. *Science* 168:669–73.

Hallowell, A. Irving
    1968   Self, Society, and Culture in Phylogenetic Perspective. In M. F. Ashley Montagu, ed., *Culture: Man's Adaptive Dimension*. New York: Oxford University Press.

Holloway, R. L., Jr.
    1969   Culture: A *Human* Domain. *Current Anthropology* 10:395–412.

Hostetler, John A., and Gertrude Enders Huntington
    1967   *The Hutterites in North America*. New York: Holt, Rinehart, and Winston.

Kuper, Hilda
  1972   The Language of Sites in the Politics of Space. *American Anthropologist* 74:411–26.

La Barre, Weston
  1970   *The Ghost Dance: Origins of Religion.* Garden City, N.Y.: Doubleday.

Rappaport, Roy
  1971   Ritual, Sanctity, and Cybernetics. *American Anthropologist* 73:59–76.

Richardson, Miles
  1974*a* The Spanish-American (Colombian) Settlement Pattern as a Societal Expression and as a Behavioral Cause. In H. J. Walker and W. G. Haag, eds., *Man and Cultural Heritage.* Vol. 5 of *Geoscience and Man.* Baton Rouge: School of Geoscience.

  1974*b* The Material Expression of a Small City in a Developing Society. *Annals of the South Eastern Conference on Latin American Studies,* Vol. 5. (In press) Carrollton, Ga.: West Georgia College.

Richardson, Miles, Barbara Bode, and Marta Eugenia Pardo
  1971   The Image of Christ in Spanish America as a Model for Suffering. *Journal of Inter-American Studies and World Affairs* 13:246–57.

Shelley, Percy Bysshe
  1903   *Poems.* London: Blackie and Son.

Sorokin, Pitirim
  1964   *Sociocultural Causality, Space, and Time.* New York: Russell and Russell.

Chapter 2

The Advancement of Material Culture Studies in Modern Anthropological Research

William N. Fenton

ABSTRACT   Despite living in a gadget, thing-oriented culture, American anthropologists since at least 1920 have written relatively little about material culture. This decline in interest is related to the reduced status of the research museum in ethnological investigation. Most modern ethnologists in the United States have never collected for a museum or worked with museum specimens. Yet studies of material culture have not vanished, and a surprising number appear under such rubrics as technology, primitive art, and cognition.

Theoretical treatment of material culture goes back at least to the works of O. T. Mason who wrote about the origins of invention before the turn of the century. Also at this time Franz Boas was beginning his important and voluminous writings on the material culture of the Eskimo and of the Northwest Coast. This early tradition was continued and amplified by Wissler and Dixon. Other important works that came before World War II were those of Leslie Spier, Peter Buck, Ralph Linton, and Cornelius Osgood. Although the research began in the thirties, Kluckhohn and Hill's important work on Navaho material culture was not completed until 1971. Among other works appearing since World War II are those of Weltfish, Sayce, and Robert Spier.

In 1965 the Committee on Anthropological Research in Museums (CARM) was appointed by the American Anthropological Association. This committee, with financial support from the Wenner-Gren Foundation for Anthropological Research, has recommended endowing nearly forty museum research fellowships. Partially supported by CARM, several guides to collecting and inventorying museum objects have appeared recently.

15

The future of material culture studies is linked to the future of the museums of man. Anthropological museums will have to break from the Victorian mold of the natural history museum and identify more closely with history and art. Museums will need to expand from being places designed to preserve objects to being centers where men, through the study of artifacts, can better understand other men.

A decade ago several of us who had museum connections became concerned about the decline in material culture studies generally and set out to put museums back into the mainstream of anthropological research. We were particularly aware that the ethnographical collections for which we were responsible were not being consulted by our colleagues and their students, that the few students who came to look at collections were devotees of primitive art, and that, while collecting was proceeding in Africa and Melanesia where native cultures were rapidly disappearing, these activities were not resulting in documented collections. We knew too that documentation was poor on older collections in our care, and with few exceptions the same situation prevailed in European museums where much of the best of older North American material is to be found. We decided that the best way to improve a bad situation and to accomplish our aims was to train a new generation of scholars who would use collections as resources for research both in the museum and in the field. Our representations to the Executive Board of the American Anthropological Association (AAA) resulted in the appointment of the Committee on Anthropological Research in Museums (CARM) in 1965, which has been supported entirely by the Wenner-Gren Foundation for Anthropological Research. The program and accomplishments of CARM have been summarized in the annual reports of the AAA (Frantz 1968, *et seq.*) and in the 1969 annual report of the foundation (Wenner-Gren Foundation 1969 [and subsequent years], pp. 22–24). In the words of one of its members, this ongoing program of research fellowships represents "a response to the conviction that hope lies in the increase of quantity, quality, and prestige of ethnological research based on museum collections" (Sturtevant 1969, p. 637). Examples of CARM's accomplishments will be discussed subsequently.

THE PRESENT STATUS OF MATERIAL CULTURE STUDIES

The present minimal participation by anthropologists in studies of material culture is paradoxical when one considers that a principal theme in American culture is the dominance of technology. In a society that turns out and accepts eight million automobiles per year, there is a definite relationship between our technology and the artifacts that it produces and which the society accepts and incorporates into daily life. These artifacts require for their production a certain know-how of assembly, supporting skills for their maintenance and repair, and a complete understanding, if not created demand, for the place of the artifact in the cultural activity in which it is employed.

But somehow the American tradition of mechanical ingenuity has not reached anthropology as a profession. If it has, it operates at a level other than research. What has happened to the American handiman whose motto was: "Don't buy it, if you can make it!" Most of us have been touched in some way by the how-to-do-it mania, which has swept the country in recent years, and evidence of our participation in it always amazes and sometimes alarms colleagues visiting from abroad. I am at a loss to explain this seeming paradox between anthropologists and their culture, unless most of the object-minded individuals have gone into archaeology.

Material culture studies, nevertheless, have stayed alive at a generally consistent level during the present century. The hue and cry of a decade ago, when several of us contributed some ten papers to the literature deploring the decline in such studies since 1900, is evidently not warranted according to Sturtevant's recent findings (1969, pp. 623, 625, 632). Such studies have never bulked very large in the literature of anthropology, so they have never really died, although fewer individuals proportionately contribute them. Considering the whole profession, relatively fewer anthropologists are employed in museums. Most of the jobs are now in universities. Anthropology, nevertheless, still has a huge responsibility for collections, although the rewards for taking care of them enjoy a priority beneath teaching and publishing. Ethnology, which is the central field of cultural anthropology, is the least dependent on collections for its researches and therefore enjoys an ambiguous relation to museums.

Indeed, as Sturtevant maintains, research on material culture has always been less important in ethnology than research on social and mental culture. This is not as it should be, since true material culture studies seek to identify cognitive patterns. At any rate only 8.6 percent (five out of sixty-five) of the papers published in the journals of the United States, England, and France in 1967 dealt with material culture, and several of these could have been done without reference to museum collections (Sturtevant 1969, p. 632).

In recent years there has been a noticeable trend away from research responsibilities in museums having major collections. In several instances collections are separated widely from curatorial staff— a move that was begun years ago in New York by George Heye when he built the annex to the Museum of the American Indian at Pelham Bay at a considerable distance from Broadway and 155th Street. Where the staff are university professors who do not use collections to illustrate their teaching and do no research on them, the objects take up valuable space. Where the emphasis is on exhibits which can be justified for educational purposes (although no one knows how effectively the exhibits teach) and where public relations become the predominant interest of the director, research collections are bound to suffer and become less important. They cease to illustrate concepts worthy of modern anthropology, and when the director succumbs to the temptation to sell important pieces on the art market, first-rate curators leave and second-rate curators are hired. By this time the museum has ceased to encourage field collection of documented specimens and takes in undocumented collections which are useless for research purposes and which only compound the problem.

The gloomy picture that I have painted of the crisis now faced by our ethnographic museums is illuminated by a few bright spots, which have recurred about once in a decade during the past seventy years, suggesting that interest in material culture studies has not always been at such a low ebb and that our major museums may survive for the next generation. Hope for material culture studies lies in studies now only beginning; the solution to the plight of museums having research responsibilities awaits massive federal and state aid, which is not likely to be forthcoming for a decade at least. Meanwhile they must hold out as best they can. History affords some perspective on these trends.

HISTORICAL TRENDS

It is now commonplace to observe that anthropology was nurtured in museums and has matured in universities. The *rite de passage* occurred after World War I. Until then jobs were in museums or in research bureaus (Bureau of American Ethnology) connected with institutions having museums. Early teaching posts—at Harvard, California, and Pennsylvania—were conducted in museums or were split appointments between curatorial and teaching duties. For a few years Boas divided his time between the American Museum of Natural History and Columbia University before relinquishing the former, and afterward Wissler went the other route. Since much teaching went on in museums, students grew up with ethnographic collections and did their first research on problems in material culture; and their fieldwork was commonly supported for the purpose of increasing the museum's collections with documented specimens. Field notes were demanded for the accession records and for the museum catalog, and the need for this documentation often led to the exploration of other topics related to the specimens.

Gradually interest shifted away from objects and problems of invention and diffusion to topics and problems less amenable to museum treatment. Kroeber's early work was on the decorative arts of the Arapaho and their neighbors; Wissler's early work on the material culture of the Blackfoot and the Dakota Sioux pioneered a series of historical and distributional studies; but Lowie concentrated on kinship and age grades, and Leslie Spier wrote his dissertation on the Sun Dance (Kroeber 1900, 1902; Wissler 1904, 1910; Lowie 1916, 1920, 1929; Spier 1921). As anthropology ceased to be object minded, anthropologists no longer felt compelled to care for collections. They lost interest in putting up exhibits to fulfill some systematic plan, to illustrate some ecological concept, or for teaching purposes. Wissler alone retained his original interest (stemming from psychology) in the museum as an educational instrument. Others, like Lowie, who first lectured at the American Museum and afterward went to the University of California at Berkeley, drifted away from museum responsibilities. Sapir, long before teaching at Chicago and Yale, first built up the collections of the National Museum of Canada, where one finds pages of catalog entries in his meticulous hand. He directed a major program of field research, which sponsored both Speck's work on northeastern Algonquian art (Speck 1914), and Waugh's studies of Iroquois subsistence, technology, and medicine (Waugh 1916, and ms. field notes). It was then that he wrote what is undoubtedly the most famous methodological paper in American ethnology (1916) and his widely known book on language (1921).

Articles and monographs devoted to material culture topics were quite popular in the United States at the turn of the century. W. H. Holmes, O. T. Mason, and Frank H. Cushing were contributing papers to the *American Anthropologist* on decorative arts, the origins of inventions, on basketry, and on weapons treated systematically. Studies of this genre, which reflect the theoretical interests of the day, fall off sharply after Wissler's landmark paper in 1914 on the material cultures of the American Indian. Indeed, Wissler then lamented that "for some years the study of material culture has been quite out of fashion" (1914, p. 447; de Laguna 1960, pp. 801, 519–20). Wissler's remark set me to wondering just when the break had occurred. Apparently, the decline commenced in 1900, leveled off in 1910, and fell off sharply after 1920 (Sturtevant 1969, p. 626).

The decennial indices of the *American Anthropologist* tell the story. For the years 1928–1938, there are nine entries to articles under "material culture" and sixteen under "technology." For the next decade, 1939–1948, Greenman's article, "Material Culture and the Organism" (1945, pp. 211–29), stands alone, and there is one reference under "technology." At the mid-century (1949–1958), "material culture" has become "technology," under which perhaps better indexing discloses thirteen entries ranging from canoe-making on Truk to textiles. Of promise is "Implications of Technological Change for Folk and Scientific Medicine" (Gould 1957, pp. 507–16), which portends a search for system. In the most recent cumulative index, 1959–1969, I note in Volume 66 an exchange of views between Amesbury and Ehrich on the validity of "material culture" as a concept. (To the former it is totally unacceptable, since "all culture is nonmaterial.") One finds an encouraging number of articles on technology in relation to some systematic exploration of cultural ecology, such as "Material Culture and Cognition" (Robbins 1966, pp. 745–48), and as material for cross-cultural comparisons.

But as Sturtevant points out, most of these articles seem unrelated to the existence of ethnographic museum collections, and he concludes: "Most modern ethnologists have never studied museum specimens, have never collected for a museum, have never been in a museum storage area. Yet I suppose that at least 90 percent of museum ethnological specimens have never been studied" (1969, p. 632).

As a control I looked at the *Southwestern Journal of Anthropology*, which was founded in 1945 by Spier. Inasmuch as he gave material culture a high priority in his own ethnographic fieldwork, it is not surprising that he rounded up four articles, which are indexed under "material culture," including Foster's important study of Mexican mold-made pottery (1948, pp. 356–70). Other titles occur under topical headings—blow gun, cloth, textiles, etc.

To summarize, although material culture studies are not what they once were, studies of technological subjects have never really gone out of fashion and they persist in new guises and serve different ends. The commonplace that one hears in the profession—"there isn't much interest in material culture studies any more"—really says that fewer anthropologists proportionately are involved with materials per se; but the remark overlooks the important fact that other anthropologists are interested in the ideas that lie behind the objects and are searching for data to analyze systematically and to treat statistically. Material culture offers them the longest sequence and the broadest distributions, and as an area it is most amenable to evolutionary inference.

THEORETICAL INTEREST

Technology and its artifacts, inventions, and subsistence comprised much of the earlier theoretical works in ethnology. Between 1894 and 1904, Otis T. Mason of the U.S. National Museum was turning out his great monographs: "North American Bows, Arrows, and Quivers" (1894), *The Origins of Invention* (1966, first published 1895), and "Aboriginal American Basketry" (1902). His approach was systematic, analytical, and he foresaw the idea of the culture area, which was utilized by Boas in arranging exhibits, first in Chicago in 1893 and afterward at the American Museum—an idea which Wissler later developed into a theoretical concept.

No one, however, was more problem oriented than Boas. From his first fieldwork among the Eskimo (1888), and afterward on the Northwest Coast, he observed, sketched, collected, and described a vast array of materials both as technology and as art. Of all his writings the most succinct statement of his views on technology is contained in the chapter, "Invention," in his *General Anthropology* (Boas *et al.* 1938, pp. 238–81). The stress is on mechanical principles—gravity, the lever, torsion, disturbance of equilibrium, the resisting power of hard surfaces, the roller, the pulley—and the application of these to implements—the hammer, weighted projectiles, centrifugal force (bola), increasing the velocity by lengthening the arc (atlatl), the spring (snare), propulsion (blow gun), fire by friction (drill), float, and others. I might add that the mechanical knowledge required in canoeing—the leverage of paddling versus poling—can only be appreciated by learning to handle small boats in different ethnographic settings, and yet these motor techniques are nowhere described. They are most amenable to motion picture techniques.

Wissler, between 1904 and 1914, when he was conducting field and museum studies that produced a series of landmark monographs on the material culture of the northern Plains (1904, 1910, 1914, and 1934), was keenly aware of motor habits as they related to productive processes of material culture (1914, p. 123). As a trained psychologist he distinguished between psychological and cultural phenomena and concluded that "culture differentiation and psychological differentiation run in relatively independent cycles" (1914, p. 130). Wissler is perhaps better known for bringing a system to listing data, for mapping distributions, locating culture centers, defining areas, noting trait associations, inferring history where direct history failed, and for discovering a common denominator for all cultures—his "universal culture pattern" (1923).

Dixon wrote *The Building of Cultures* (1928) in criticism of Wissler's environmentalism, especially the age and area hypothesis. Dixon himself had done important work on the elaborate basketry of the Indians of northern California (1902) and was thoroughly familiar with the ethnographic collections at the Peabody Museum at Harvard. In his critique of Wissler he makes a valuable distinction between discovery and invention, the latter being "purposeful discovery" (1928, p. 34).

No one made better use of this argument than Leslie Spier, who in a few brief years produced important comparative ethnographies on the Wisslerian model, but with great sophistication, on the Havasupai (1928), Klamath (1930), and the Yuman tribes of the Gila River (1933). In Spier's fieldwork, material culture received detailed consideration, as he believed that the ethnographer's drawings and his explanations should enable the reader to reconstruct the objects.

Of comparable virtuosity are the studies, *Samoan Material Culture* (1930) and *Material Culture of Kapinga-Marangi* (1950), by Peter H. Buck (Te Rangi Hiroa), who brought into his Yale seminar examples of the objects he was analyzing and describing and then projected his field observations to the search for older specimens that navigators had carried off to museums in Europe. The dividends of that seminar have appeared in strange guises among the Navaho and the Iroquois. Those of us who knew the late Ralph Linton are aware of how deeply he identified with the world of artifacts from his early fieldwork on the material culture of the Marquesas (1923), his long association with the Field Museum, and his sustained interest in primitive art (1955).

We see the influence of Malinowski in the H. S. Harrison article on material culture in the 1930 edition of the *Encyclopaedia Britannica*. Harrison wrote about invention, environmental influences, diffusion, and the implications for cultural evolution. In his treatment, he revealed himself to be an "instrumentalist," like Malinowski, and favored the "opportunist" factor in innovation. Thirty-eight years later, in 1968, George Quimby rewrote the article and made the discussion fit the system of L. A. White, for whom evolution is the dominant theory of development. In this view, "material culture consists of tools, weapons, utensils, machines, ornaments, religious images, clothing, and any other ponderable object produced or used by humans." These objects have an enduring quality and they often outlast the societies and cultures that produce them. And the instrumental character of much of man's material culture, to the extent that it satisfies primary needs of subsistence, shelter, clothing, etc., posits a functional relationship of technology to environment, and of man to a secondary environment which his culture creates. Indeed, as Harrison reminds us, "a great part of man's material culture is directly associated with his primary need . . . of procuring food." It follows that studies of subsistence embrace much of material culture (Parker 1910; Waugh 1916).

The "materialistic" view of material culture by White and Quimby contrasts with the "idealistic" definition of objects. Thoreau was possibly the first to question whether objects themselves are really part of culture when he characterized an arrowhead as a "fossil thought" (Journals, March 28, 1859, in Shepard 1927, p. 318). Cornelius Osgood, in his work on the northern Athabaskan cultures, defines the field as comprising *ideas* "about objects external to the mind resulting from human behavior as well as ideas about human behavior required to manufacture these objects" (1940, p. 26). Perhaps Osgood's conceptualizations of material culture remain better known than the definitive character of the monographs. In themselves, they are important landmarks in the field of material culture studies.

The last person whom most students of anthropology would identify with material culture studies is the late Clyde Kluckhohn who contributed so many theoretical insights to cultural anthropology; but when I last called on him in 1960 during a survey of ethnological research in museums he showed me the notes he was preparing for a work on Navaho material culture (Kluckhohn, Hill, and Kluckhohn 1971), which has now appeared posthumously. This gorgeous book sets a standard and provides hope for a renaissance of studies by ethnologists of man's arts and industries. The material culture is set over and against its environment; how it varies and relates regionally; how it is learned; how it sustains the value system, the roles of kinship, the fit between ecology and economy; how it affects political structure, and its vital place in religion and ceremonialism. Its authors have achieved a definition adapted from Osgood and others: "Our descriptive criteria include actions and technical knowledge associated with the manufacture and use of the product, and ideas, both secular and religious, that promote or inhibit the manufacture and use of the product as well as place it in the Navaho cosmos." The fieldwork, which was begun by W. W. Hill in the thirties while still a student of Buck and Spier at Yale, has been carried on and greatly extended by his students and those of Kluckhohn.

Anticipating the new ethnography, Gene Weltfish, a student of Boas, studied the distribution of basketry techniques both in the museum and in the field and sought through linguistic methods to learn the conceptual categories of material culture which serve as tribal and temporal indicators (1958, 1960).

Of general works on material culture, three deserve mention. For the old-fashioned quality of the thought and its rhetoric, I admire Sayce's *Primitive Arts and Crafts* (1933, 1963), which takes off from Dixon and draws its main examples from European and classical prehistory, from Africa, as well as the Americas, and the areas that are strongly represented in the ethnographic collections of the British Museum. Sayce makes numerous suggestions of problems awaiting research, and his book affords a vista of British cultural anthropology before social anthropology broke away (see also Forde 1937).

The content of technologies has been best handled by European workers—the Danes and Germans. A notable statement of the relation of material cultures to culture history is Birket-Smith's *The Paths of Culture* (1965), which I reviewed in the *American Anthropologist* (Fenton 1966*b*); but my second example is the comprehensive treatment of technology in relation to the cultural ecology of native peoples by a team of Austrian museum ethnologists (Hirschberg *et al.* 1966), a handbook that is both systematic and well documented by museum specimens and bibliography. Until an English edition is available, the work contains an English-German glossary.

The third example is the works of Robert F. G. Spier in which he restates the relation of technology to material culture (1968, 1970). His analysis leads to a series of mathematical functions for which the following rules may be written:

I. $M.C. < T.$: "Material culture is a product of man's technology."

II. T/m or $T/a >$ genre t/a: "The technology of a medium or activity produces a genre of techniques and artifacts." Here t is a specific mode of T, where $t =$ technique, and $T =$ technology.

III. A is a sequence of coordinated t's. Here $A =$ an activity.

In terms of the operation of these rules a whole series of problems become researchable through material culture: problems of time and space, of learning, retention and recall, of utilization, and of the relation of the objects and techniques for using them to other major activities of culture. One recalls Malinowski's famous canoe-building episode, the wampum records and mnemonic systems of the Iroquois confederacy, and the symbolism and use of masks in various cultures, the cases in point where the object is the key to a whole cultural realm.

ETHNOLOGICAL RESEARCH AND MUSEUM COLLECTIONS

In a recent paper on the interrelatedness of fieldwork, museum studies, and ethnohistorical research, I indicated how dated specimens could be made to serve the interests of culture history (1966a). Using examples from my own fieldwork, I further suggested that concepts derived from living culture supplement other techniques of historical interpretation, and when applied to historical documents, may yield insights which in turn exert a feedback effect on further fieldwork and on our understanding of the objects. The model then is circular.

We can see the creative results of this interplay between ethnology and museum study in the work carried out by the recipients of the museum research fellowships awarded by the Committee on Anthropological Research in Museums. Museum Research Fellow Sandra Dickey Harner, in "Knotless Netting Structures from South America," has demonstrated what can be done by working solely with collections to classify and improve typology. Furthermore, Harner's work has implications for archaeologists, provides a guide for the study of this ancient and widespread technique, and finally underscores the importance of proper training. This study "has demonstrated that anthropological research can yield results available through no other source. Certain of this research, in aspects of technology, can be done by people other than anthropologists. But anthropology is not training its students to do such work, and in the main existing faculties of anthropology are not interested if they are aware of the possibilities awaiting the student in such research" (Wenner-Gren Foundation 1968, pp. 18–19).

In neglecting the material basis that underlies, limits, and to a degree determines social life, anthropology is not fulfilling its mandate to study whole cultures. Unless anthropologists study technological advances and problems, as Phillip Dark and John C. Ewers warn us, the gap will be filled by others untrained in cultural interpretation. With all the studies we have of Pueblo ceremonialism and politics, we are still in the dark about the material culture of the Keresan pueblos, which Martin Murphy, a student of Leslie White, is undertaking in the museum and in the field.

The ability to relate artifacts to other aspects of culture comes from the inevitable emphasis on functionalism that derives from ethnographic training. Adrienne Kaepler's "Reconstruction Ethnography of Society Islands Material Culture," undertaken at the Bishop Museum with CARM support, presupposes such training.

Dated artifacts in museums afford good evidence of culture history. Given the poor state of catalogs of most early museum collections here and abroad, to be able to relate an object to a particular dated expedition or voyage such as Captain Cook's or the voyage of the *Beagle* is often the best evidence available as to period and provenience. The logic of having such collections studied, cataloged, and related to documentary sources seems compelling. CARM has supported the preparation of a catalog of Polynesian artifacts from the Wilkes expedition (1838–1842) by Martha Cooper.

In nonliterate societies artifacts provide models of the past. Frequently memory systems depend on spatial arrangement of objects or designs for recalling long streams of verbal information (Fenton 1950, 1971). Two studies undertaken by museum research fellows are to the point: the first is an examination of Santa Clara Pueblo pottery in the museum and in the field by Betty Le Free; and the second involves scrutiny of Bella Coola ceremonial art in collections and discussing them in the field with informants by Margaret Stott. Perhaps these examples of research undertaken on specific problems will attract more students than general preachments.

Of greater importance to the development of anthropology are the indications of new directions of research that flow from the discovery of improved methods of research on museum collections. Some of these derive from the "new archaeology"; others derive from ethnoscience. The application of attribute analysis to ethnographic specimens is illustrated by Carol Kauffman's research into Haida carving, which utilized museum collections and extended to the observation and interview of carvers on the Northwest Coast. A parallel study in another medium is Margaret H. Friedrich's application of structural models and methods to the analysis of design and style, the effects of social interaction among artists, and the implications of ethnographic analysis for archaeological interpretation. Working on San Jose painted pottery in Mexico and at the Field Museum, Mrs. Friedrich has put her archaeologist colleagues on notice as to the limitation of inferences that can be made from lesser-known materials (Friedrich 1970).

CURRENT PROBLEMS IN MUSEUM WORK

In recent years American students have not clamored for access to the ethnographic collections in museums. This is not true in Europe. There, material culture studies show some vigor and enjoy modest status. Two beautifully illustrated catalogs of ethnographic collections in Germany and Austria greeted the Americanist Congress meeting in Stuttgart in 1968 (Feest 1968; Benndorf and Speyer 1968). And I am told by George Henri Rivière (former director general of International Council of Museums, UNESCO) that, during the student demonstrations in Paris in 1968, one of the demands was for access to the museum collections and some instruction in their study (see also Sturtevant 1969, p. 639). This demand is partly due to the decline in opportunities for fieldwork abroad and partly reflects suggestions emanating from French structuralism as to how the collections can be rearranged for viewing and study at various levels of competence. Indeed, Rivière used many of Lévi-Strauss' ideas in the plan for the new Musée National des Arts et Traditions Populaires. The latter sees the anthropological museum as an opportunity for the extension of the field of research; he advocates that every teaching department of anthropology should have a museum attached to it; and its purpose should be not so much to preserve objects as to help men to understand other men (Lévi-Strauss 1963, pp. 375–76). The plan calls for synchronized exhibits of objects, sound, and light together with pertinent manuscripts illustrating a major cultural activity, backed up by study collections of varying degrees of complexity as the student penetrates his specialty.

The whole problem of access to collections and improving their usefulness for research is a complex question that can be touched on only briefly here by sketching the principal findings of CARM. The first problem is one of inventory. What is there, how much of it, and where is it? The baffled student needs answers to these questions before he can plan and undertake research. In North America alone collections are concentrated in large museums and scattered widely in small repositories, many of them private. There are no true duplicates of ethnographic specimens and they are not interchangeable, for "museum specimens are unique cultural and historical documents" (Sturtevant 1969, p. 640). By a careful estimate, there are a million and a half such specimens in the United States alone; of these, half are in five large museums (there are two hundred thousand specimens in the U.S. National Museum alone). There are perhaps four and a half million specimens in the museums of the world. It would require 140 man years to prepare an "Index Ethnographicum," such as I proposed more than a decade ago (Fenton 1960), at a cost of fifty cents per specimen. Time and inflation run on while the specimens deteriorate at an alarming rate. (Ricciardelli 1967a, 1967b).

Several things can and are being done about it. Under the direction of the late Stephan de Borhegyi of CARM, John Hunter prepared an inventory of ethnological collections in museums of the United States and Canada (1967), which has gone through two editions. Second, the pilot study for inventorying ethnological collections, which Ricciardelli and his students carried out from the Stovall Museum in the museums of Oklahoma, with National Science Foundation support and the guidance of CARM, has since been extended to Missouri, New Mexico, and Arizona. Mary Jane Schneider, one of Ricciardelli's student supervisors, has overseen the expansion, which has been greatly facilitated by the preparation of *A Guide to Inventorying Ethnological Collections* (Schneider 1970), an essential dictionary for data processing.

There is no longer any excuse for not making documented collections in the field. Sturtevant has provided students with an excellent *Guide to Field Collecting* (1967), and in recent years CARM has made some modest grants to students going into the field to enable them to collect systematically specimens for their host museum.

The future of material culture studies is linked to the future of museums of man, which are going to have to be liberated from the sleeping giants, the offspring of the Victorian era, called natural history museums, with which anthropology has an unnatural affinity. Most thoughtful museum anthropologists feel that our natural affinity is with history and art, and they point to the success of the Musée de l'Homme and the National Museum of Anthropology in Mexico City. Access to study collections at all levels is essential. Exhibits will be concept oriented and worthy of modern anthropology. As research institutions they will be communities of scholars, staffed by scientists, curators, aids, interns, and students. Responsibilities for the collections will be defined clearly, and curating must be given equal rank with teaching.

A serious problem facing museums today is the integrity of collections. Keeping large blocks of material intact is essential for research purposes. It must not be allowed to deteriorate, it should be restored, and it should be kept for posterity. Museum conservation is no longer in its infancy, it is well developed in art museums, and it has now spread to the Field Museum which has established a laboratory of considerable importance for anthropology.

A more serious question is how to maintain the collections in the face of demands for their return to the descendants of original owners. This is partly a matter of local pride that state and national museums have continually to face and compensate for and partly a misunderstanding of the nature of museums. From civil rights activists we now hear the bogus principle enunciated that no museum should keep objects relating to a living culture. By Red Power advocates it is stated in genocidal terms: "No museum should harbor the artifacts of an ongoing culture when the act of harboring inhibits the very life of that culture." It does not matter if the facts run contrary; the mere fact that the principle is stated is tantamount to truth. It usually has religious overtones as in the recent controversy over the New York wampum collection: to keep it for all of the people including the Indians or return it to the heirs of its original keepers at Onondaga. In these confrontations history is no longer relevant. Objects which formerly were primarily political in character are now endowed with religious significance, and the mere assertion of religious symbolism is sufficient to weigh the balance of equity without having to show cause why they have become religious lately. We anthropologists are equally at fault and we should not complain too loudly because we find ourselves caught up in the feedback from our own field studies. Our published reports have made evident what was not previously plain to a generation that largely ignored the old people with whom we worked.

Another area of museology on which material culture studies

bear is the testing of museum exhibits as teaching tools. The museum public is a community of a kind that should attract the social anthropologist. There has been surprisingly little research of visitor behavior in museums. The best such study of *Anthropology and the Public: The Role of Museums* (1960) is by a Dutch ethnomuseologist, Dr. H. H. Frese, which might well be emulated in another cultural setting: it tells us a great deal about anthropology in museums but even more about museums and Dutch society. Marvin Harris' experiment with filming the behavior of museum visitors at the Metropolitan Museum of Art offers intriguing possibilities. Borhegyi's surveys at the Milwaukee Public Museum should not be overlooked.

Ethnographic collections become of increasing importance as cultures vanish from the world. Since many of these contain specimens that are undocumented, we can learn much from the archaeologists about how to study them. Museums of Europe are full of what I call "Ethnological Chippendale": the specimens are what someone says they are; but where the documentation exists to prove their authenticity, we can extrapolate from them to similar pieces, in the manner of the art historians who can teach us much. The other source of information is from ethnologists working in the field with descendants of the original makers.

So let us get it all together—the ethnographic field study, the museum study collection, and the archaeological excavation. In the field of material culture studies there is much work to be done. With stimulation and training provided by groups such as the Committee on Anthropological Research in Museums, with an ethnology sensitized to the material side of life, and with a revived, vibrant museology of man, this work will go forward.

REFERENCES CITED

Benndorf, Helga, and Arthur Speyer
    1968   *Indianer Nordamerikas, 1760–1860.* Offenbach a. M., Deutschen Leder-
            museum.

Birket-Smith, Kaj
    1965   *The Paths of Culture.* Madison: University of Wisconsin Press.

Boas, F.
    1888   *The Central Eskimo.* Sixth Annual Report, Bureau of American Eth-
            nology. Washington, D.C.: Smithsonian Institution.

Boas, F., *et al.*
1938   *General Anthropology*. New York: Heath.

Buck, Peter H. (Te Rangi Hiroa)
1930   *Samoan Material Culture*. Bernice P. Bishop Museum, Bulletin 75. Honolulu.
1950   *Material Culture of Kapinga-Marangi*. Bernice P. Bishop Museum, Bulletin 200. Honolulu.

de Laguna, F., ed.
1960   *Selected Papers from the American Anthropologist, 1888–1920*. Evanston, Ill., and Elmsford, N.Y.: Row, Peterson.

Dixon, Roland B.
1902   Basketry Designs of the Indians of Northern California. *Bulletin*, Vol. 17, No. 1. New York: American Museum of Natural History.
1928   *The Building of Cultures*. New York: Scribner's.

Feest, C. F.
1968   *Indianer Nordamerikas*. Wien: Museum für Völkerkunde.

Fenton, William N.
1950   The Roll Call of the Iroquois Chiefs: A Study of a Mnemonic Cane from the Six Nations Reserve. *Smithsonian Miscellaneous Collections* 111 (15) :1–75.
1960   The Museum and Anthropological Research. *Curator* 3:327–55.
1966a   Field Work, Museum Studies, and Ethnohistorical Research. *Ethnohistory* 13 (1–2) :71–85.
1966b   Review of Birket-Smith, 1965. *American Anthropologist* 68:530.
1968   Report of the Committee on Anthropological Research in Museums. In Ch. Frantz, ed., *Annual Report, 1967*. American Anthropological Association. April, 1968. Pp. 47–49.
1971   The New York State Wampum Collection: The Case for the Preservation of Cultural Treasures. *Proceedings of the American Philosophical Society* 115:437–61.

Forde, C. Daryll
1937   *Habitat, Economy and Society*. New York: Harcourt, Brace.

Foster, George M.
1948   Some Implications of Modern Mexican Mold-Made Pottery. *Southwestern Journal of Anthropology* 4:356–70.

Frantz, Ch., ed.
1968   *Annual Report, 1967*. American Anthropological Association. April, 1968. (Subsequent reports are available for 1969 and 1970.)

Frese, H. H.
1960   *Anthropology and the Public: The Role of Museums*. Medelingen van Het Rijksmuseum voor Volkenkunde, No. 14. Leiden.

Friedrich, Margaret H.
1970 Design, Structure, and Social Interaction: Archaeological Implications of an Ethnographic Analysis. *American Antiquity* 35:332–43.

Gould, Harold A.
1957 The Implications of Technological Change for Folk and Scientific Medicine. *American Anthropologist* 59:507–16.

Greenman, Emerson F.
1945 Material Culture and the Organism. *American Anthropologist* 47:211–29.

Harrison, H. S.
1930 Material Culture. *Encyclopaedia Britannica*.

Hirschberg, Walter, Alfred Janata, W. B. Bauer, and C. Feest
1966 *Technologie und Ergologie in der Völkerkunde*. Mannheim: Bibliographisches Institut.

Hunter, John E.
1967 *Inventory of Ethnological Collections in Museums of the United States and Canada*. 2nd ed. Milwaukee: Committee on Anthropological Research in Museums, American Anthropological Association.

Kluckhohn, Clyde, W. W. Hill, and Lucy Wales Kluckhohn
1971 *Navaho Material Culture*. Cambridge: Belknap Press of Harvard University Press.

Kroeber, A. L.
1900 Symbolism of the Arapaho. *Bulletin*, Vol. 12. New York: American Museum of Natural History. Pp. 265–327.

1902 The Arapaho. *Bulletin*, Vol. 18, Pts. 1–2. New York: American Museum of Natural History.

Lévi-Strauss, Claude
1963 *Structural Anthropology*. New York and London: Basic Books.

Linton, Ralph
1923 *Material Culture of the Marquesas Islands*. Memoirs, Bernice P. Bishop Museum, Vol. 8, No. 5. Honolulu.

1955 *The Tree of Culture*. New York: Knopf.

Lowie, R. H.
1916 Plains Indian Age-Societies. *Anthropological Papers*, Vol. 11, Pt. 13. New York: American Museum of Natural History.

1920 *Primitive Society*. New York: Horace Liveright.

1929 *Culture and Ethnology*. New York: Peter Smith.

Mason, Otis T.
1894 North American Bows, Arrows, and Quivers. *Annual Report, 1893*. Washington, D.C.: Smithsonian Institution. Pp. 631–79.

1902 Aboriginal American Basketry. *Report, 1902*. Washington, D.C.: U.S. National Museum. Pp. 171–548.

1966   *The Origins of Invention.* Cambridge, Mass.: M.I.T. Press. (First published in 1895.)

Morgan, L. H.
1881   *Houses and House-Life of the American Aborigines.* Contributions to North American Ethnology, Vol. 4. U.S. Geographical and Geological Survey of the Rocky Mountain Region. Washington, D.C.: Government Printing Office.

Osgood, Cornelius
1940   *Ingalik Material Culture.* Yale University Publications in Anthropology, No. 22. New Haven.

Parker, Arthur C.
1910   *Iroquois Uses of Maize and Other Food Plants.* New York State Museum, Bulletin 144. Albany: University of the State of New York. (Reprinted in W. N. Fenton, ed., *Parker on the Iroquois.* Syracuse University Press, 1968.)

Quimby, George I.
1968   Material Culture. *Encyclopaedia Britannica.*

Ricciardelli, Alex F.
1967a A Census of Ethnological Collections in United States Museums. *Museum News* 46 (1):11–14.
1967b A Model for Inventorying Ethnological Collections. *Curator* 10 (4): 330–36.
1967c *A Pilot Study for Inventorying Ethnological Collections.* Norman: Stovall Museum of Science and History, University of Oklahoma.

Robbins, Michael
1966   Material Culture and Cognition. *American Anthropologist* 68:745–48.

Sapir, Edward
1916   *Time Perspective in Aboriginal American Culture: A Study in Method.* Memoir 90, Geological Survey of Canada, Anthropological Series, No. 13. Ottawa.
1921   *Language.* New York: Harcourt, Brace.

Sayce, R. U.
1963   *Primitive Arts and Crafts.* New York: Biblo and Tannen. (First published, Cambridge, 1933.)

Schneider, Mary Jane
1970   *A Guide to Inventorying Ethnological Collections.* Columbia: Museum of Anthropology, University of Missouri.

Shepard, Odell, ed.
1927   *The Heart of Thoreau's Journals.* Boston: Houghton Mifflin.

Speck, Frank G.
1914   *The Double-Curve Motif in Northeastern Algonkian Art.* Memoir 42, Geological Survey of Canada, Anthropological Series, No. 1. Ottawa.

Spier, Leslie
    1921   The Sun Dance of the Plains Indians: Its Development and Diffusion. *Anthropological Papers*, Vol. 16, Pt. 7. New York: American Museum of Natural History.

    1928   Havasupai Ethnography. *Anthropological Papers*, Vol. 29, Pt. 2. New York: American Museum of Natural History.

    1930   *Klamath Ethnography*. University of California Publications in American Archaeology and Ethnology, Vol. 30. Berkeley.

    1933   *Yuman Tribes of the Gila River*. Chicago: University of Chicago Press.

Spier, Robert F. G.
    1968   Technology and Material Culture. In James A. Clifton, ed., *Introduction to Cultural Anthropology*. Boston: Houghton Mifflin. Pp. 130–59.

    1970   *From the Hand of Man: Primitive and Preindustrial Technologies*. Boston: Houghton Mifflin.

Sturtevant, William C.
    1964   Studies in Ethnoscience. In A. K. Romney and R. W. d'Andrade, eds., *Transcultural Studies in Cognition*. *American Anthropologist*, Special Publication 66 (3):99–131.

    1967   *Guide to Field Collecting of Ethnographic Specimens*. Information Leaflet 503, Museum of Natural History. Washington, D.C.: Smithsonian Institution. 41 pp.

    1969   Does Anthropology Need Museums? *Proceedings of the Biological Society of Washington* 82:619–50. Washington, D.C.

    1973   Museums as Anthropological Data Banks. In Alden Redfield, ed., *Anthropology Beyond the University*. Southern Anthropological Society Proceedings, No. 7. Athens: University of Georgia Press.

Waugh, F. W.
    1916   *Iroquois Foods and Food Preparation*. Memoir 86, Geological Survey of Canada, Anthropological Series, No. 12. Ottawa.

Weltfish, Gene
    1958   The Linguistic Study of Material Culture. *International Journal of American Linguistics* 44 (3): 301–11.

    1960   The Anthropologist and the Question of the Fifth Dimension. In Stanley Diamond, ed., *Culture in History*. New York: Columbia University Press. Pp. 160–77.

Wenner-Gren Foundation for Anthropological Research
    1968   *Report for the Fiscal Year, February 1, 1967–January 31, 1968*. New York: Wenner-Gren Foundation. Pp. 18–19.

    1969   *Report for the Fiscal Year, February 1, 1969–January 31, 1970*. New York: Wenner-Gren Foundation.

    1971   *Report for the Fiscal Year, February 1, 1970–January 31, 1971*. New York: Wenner-Gren Foundation.

Wissler, Clark

1904   Decorative Art of the Sioux Indians. *Bulletin*, Vol. 18, Pt. 3. New York: American Museum of Natural History.

1910   Material Culture of the Blackfoot Indians. *Anthropological Papers*, Vol. 5, Pt. 1. New York: American Museum of Natural History.

1914   Material Cultures of the North American Indians. *American Anthropologist*, n.s. 16: 447–505. Reprinted in 1915 in *Anthropology in North America*. New York: G. E. Stechert. Pp. 76–134. Also in de Laguna 1960, pp. 801–61.

1923   *Man and Culture*. New York: Thomas Y. Crowell.

1934   *North American Indians of the Plains*. Handbook Series, No. 1. Rev. ed. New York: American Museum of Natural History.

Part Two

The Material
Configuration

Miles Richardson

The artifact—the cultural object, the material expression of man's internal imagination—is the subject of the five chapters in this section. The science of old artifacts is another way of saying archaeology, and appropriately, the first article of the five is in that field. Prodded by the writing of people like Lewis Binford, archaeologists have recently added to their traditional concern with chronology a refreshing interest in the social patterns of ancient societies. The pattern of child-care practices of the Neanderthals is reconstructed by archaeologists Ralph Rowlett and Mary Jane Schneider. Once the prototype of a shambling half-wit who could only utter "ugh" when he saw his first true man, the Neanderthal is emerging in the recent literature as a brilliant innovator who successfully exploited the arcticlike environment of the Upper Pleistocene in Eurasia. The data that Rowlett and Schneider present further support the image of Neanderthal as fully sapient: a wise man who showed compassion for his aged and crippled fellows and a mounting concern for the protection, education, and care of his children.

Ordinarily, we think of material culture as being composed of utilitarian baskets, pottery, and projectile points; yet in a literal sense material culture also includes works of art. Indeed, the distance be-

37

tween a utilitarian object and an esthetic one and between their respective creators is not as great as it may seem. The craftsman, carefully crouched over his work stock and pulling a finely honed tool down its length, is a near relative—a first cousin at least—to the more dashing, temperamental artist. Constituting an integral part of a volume on material culture, then, are the next two articles on the esthetic aspects of artifacts. The two articles neatly complement each other. Bill Holm writes about the work of a single, individual artist, a Kwakiutl Indian of the Northwest Coast. As he points to the stylistic devices that marked the products of the artist's hand, such as formal relationships between positive-negative design elements, the use of flat planes, and the avoidance of unnecessary curves, Holm builds a strong case for the importance of the individual artist in "primitive" art. His article is a corrective to the view that sees the art of primitive society as a uniform product of an anonymous mass. The chapter by Arthur Miller looks at the magnificent murals of the ancient city of Teotihuacan, located near Mexico City. A flourishing metropolis prior to 1000 A.D., Teotihuacan was one of the first monuments to civilized man in the New World. Yet, as Miller's detailed analysis of mural art demonstrates, the older jaguar-man symbolism continued to permeate the imagination of the civilized Mesoamerican and served to locate certain of his activities within the city.

The remaining two articles in this section also complement each other. The first is a reconstruction of a single traditional object, the beam press, on the island of Corfu, off the west coast of Greece. The author, Augustus Sordinas, uses archaeology, ethnohistory, and ethnography to reconstruct not only the beam press and its operation but also the sociocultural system of which it was a part. In a particularly vivid manner, the slow, laborious turnings of the press reflect the harsh life of the peasantry, who had to hurl themselves against the machine in order to make it move. The other chapter, by Michael Robbins and Richard Pollnac, surveys a number of both modern and traditional objects used in a region of the contemporary East African state of Uganda. Like Sordinas, Robbins and Pollnac examine the sociocultural matrix surrounding these objects. They use statistical devices to investigate the relationship between ideational modernity and object modernity. Their unexpected conclusion that the connection between modern ideas and modern objects is at best tenuous

cautions us to proceed carefully in our theorizing about the congruence between material and nonmaterial culture.

This section begins with a study of how man, 100,000 years ago, raised his children. It ends with an examination of how man today adjusts to the increasing tempo of modernization. The section opens with an argument for the use of objects as a device to infer past forms of behavior and closes with a plea for caution in our speculative leaps from objects to ideas and back again. Such a temporal and conceptual range characterizes the study of material culture.

Chapter 3

The Material Expression of Neanderthal Child Care

Ralph M. Rowlett and Mary Jane Schneider

ABSTRACT   Archaeologists may use material culture to make inferences about the nonmaterial aspects of a society's life. Intentional burials and, in particular, burials with grave goods provide fairly specific and relatively reliable inferences about past cultures. In the case of the Neanderthals of Mousterian culture, graves and grave goods not only demonstrate the compassion that Neanderthal society had for its aged and crippled members, but also indicate a growing concern for the protection, education, and care of children. The increasing attention given to children's burials is particularly true of the West European Neanderthals. Among the twenty-one intentional burials in that region, twelve were of children, and ten of those twelve burials had grave goods. The greater attention that Neanderthal displayed toward his children may be related to the increase in the size of the Neanderthal brain, an increase, which because of a large and slow-closing fontanelle, may have necessitated a more delicate and more prolonged infancy.

The archaeologist recovers the nonperishable remains and attempts to reconstruct the way of life of past peoples and to detect the processes molding these lifeways. There is little direct opportunity to know how these people spoke or thought, so their lives must be reconstructed through interpretations and inferences based primarily on their material culture. The intellectual posture of all archaeologists, regardless of the problems which they are trying to solve or the discipline which they follow, is of necessity that of cultural materialism, because the material aspects of culture and the relative positions of these things in and upon the earth compose their basic data. Thus, when archaeologists attempt to discern the less concrete aspects of a cultural inventory—the trading network, the kinship, the political unit, the religion and lore—they necessarily must reach these realms by means of the intersection of such aspects of culture with material culture. Therefore, any advance in the understanding of the relationship of material culture to its makers and surrounding conceptual milieu is an advance in archaeological theory.

Archaeologists in practice tend to regard material culture as concretized, fossilized remnants of past human behavior. A great number of artifacts in any assemblage, when excavated by modern techniques, may be assigned with a high degree of reliability to such categories as the ecological, economic, social, or ideological fields of any particular culture.

In most cases much finer discrimination may be made, and indeed, the same material items may reflect many different human activities. The raw material itself suggests something of the extractive activities and territorial range occupied and the trading contacts, if exotic in nature, of the people. Traces of manufacturing techniques reveal information on habitual motor habits as well as fabricating processes and technology. In chipped stone tools, for instance, certain aspects of flaking may well be the same regardless of the ultimate purpose for which the tools were being made. These generalizations do not necessarily represent the attitudes or ideas of the manufacturers. Bricks can be classified by color, or size, or shape, but this does not tell us anything about the person who made the brick or how it was used. Attempts have been made to reach the ideas of the makers through the application of statistics and the development of concepts concerning the relationship among technological, social, and ideological processes, but most archaeologists have been concerned with the technological aspect of material culture because the attributes are present in the artifact and provide information when there is nothing else to study.

While technique of manufacture may influence the form, the latter is largely determined by the purposes for which it was made and the alterations coming from use. This functional aspect of material culture concerns the context of use of the artifact, that is, who used it and how it was used, and comes closer to reaching the social and ideological concepts of the producer of the object, but this type of information is usually not available from archaeological material. The archaeologist may infer function for an item on the basis of its attributes and assign a functional name such as knife, scraper, ax or hoe, but there is usually little direct evidence of who used them or that these items were actually used for those purposes. Except for the most simple or highly critical items, there are often relatively arbitrary attributes which can usually be termed *stylistic* in that they are particularly derived from the social and ideological interests of their owners and makers and not from the configuration necessary to achieve the more utilitarian task at hand. Even a quite utilitarian tool may be found in such a context as to indicate a symbolism beyond its apparent purpose, for example, the ceremonial whetstone in the Sutton Hoo royal ship burial of eastern England.

There is, however, a type of artifact which does have a known function and other important properties yielding information concerning the social and ideological life of early people. The graves of the dead and grave goods provide information for the archaeologist because their functions are known. While the grave and its contents represent material items of the culture, the overlap of this data set with the nonmaterial aspects of culture is very great, as the main purpose of the grave is to give expression to some of the most desperately clung-to beliefs, aspirations, and emotions of individuals within a society. Thus, graves are an important source of data about a people and their behavior since a grave is one of the most securely known functional classes of material culture and at the same time concerns some of the less concrete aspects of culture. A grave holds a body and implies a certain regard for the dead. The way in which the body is placed in the grave may give some information concerning the attitude toward the dead. If objects are placed in the grave with the body, then these can give even more information. The amount and type of grave goods can give evidence about the social position of the person and, if in a cemetery, may lead to conclusions about the social organization of the group. The very presence of grave goods implies a belief in life after death. The following discussion concerning the attitudes toward children held by Neanderthals of Mousterian culture is based on inferences drawn from the presence or absence of grave goods and the relative ages of the individuals with whom the goods are associated.

NEANDERTHAL BURIALS

Neanderthal man lived in Europe, the Near East, and western Asia in the period from about 100,000 to 35,000 B.C. During those years he adapted himself to a drastically changing climate, from an interglacial to early Wurm. He evinced signs of advanced cultural elaboration by burying his dead and showed considerable sympathy by maintaining disabled and crippled individuals until they died from other causes. Because of the numerous burials, a large number of skeletal remains of Neanderthal man have been found. The presence and type of burials and the circumstances under which they have been found continue to provide evidence concerning the physical aspects of Neanderthal and his cultural activities.

Before reviewing these data there are several problems and cautions which should be noted. Anthropologists generally treat the long span of time in which Neanderthal man lived on a single temporal plane, but, in reality, the remains of some 130-plus individuals range over a period of 65,000 years. The sample, in this respect, is too small to be used as the basis for any strong claims, particularly since we do not have exact dates for these remains so that we cannot group elements which might be appearing at the same time in an era. However, the material culture of the Neanderthals, the Mousterian industry, remains fairly stable over this period of time (Bordes 1961, pp. 803–10), so that we might suppose that the social culture also remained relatively constant. In any case, it is common practice to treat the remains as if they were from a single temporal plane, and that will be the procedure in this paper.

Certain judgments also have to be made as to what constitutes a burial. Intentional burial here is understood as the deposition of the body in a prepared grave or in other deliberate mortuary placements (such as a fissure or cave chamber) which precludes covering solely by natural agency or by incidental cultural activity—such as the way skeletal parts of cannibal victims may become covered over by routine cultural activities. There have been disagreements about most of the skeletons and the circumstances of their uncovering. Many of the disagreements seem to center around the presence or absence of a grave and of grave goods. What is considered by one to be a grave is not so interpreted by another. Grave goods to one author are scattered animal remains to another. The exact interpretations which have been made are presented in the accompanying tables with indications of the questionable cases.

A third problem concerns the availability of extant evidence. Scandalously, a number of the sites have never been reported in detail. A few skeletal finds have held the most interest, and some of these have been described in great detail with a wide variety of opinions, while others have gone unnoticed. Information concerning age, sex, and presence of grave or grave goods and exact industrial affinity is particularly difficult to obtain. An example of this difficulty is the twenty-two skeletal remains from La Quina, only two of which have been described in detail.

In this study, the La Quina adult woman has been accepted as a burial. The nearly complete female skeleton found in Level 3 at La Quina (Henri-Martin 1912, 1921) has sometimes been described as the body of a woman who had drowned in the Voultron River which runs in front of the rock shelter. While the geological content of Level 3 is indeed composed of fluviatile materials transported there by the river, there is nonetheless a cultural component that is full of industry. What is more, this deposit is described by the excavator himself, Dr. Henri-Martin, as being composed of extremely thin lenses of alluvial material which would have been deposited by occasional incursions of shallow water at that level, while in the intervening times the river would have been running much slower. The current would have been slow here, so it would seem unlikely that a woman would have drowned in such a languid, shallow pool. On the other hand, any burial inserted in front of the rock shelter at this time would, of necessity, have been put down into these fluviatile gravels and river pebbles. In such a situation, with the techniques utilized in 1912, the margins of any grave pit would have been difficult to see. Perhaps the burial was simply laid down, as is sometimes the case, and such loose, easily transported material as was available was piled over the body. Even if the woman's body had been thrown into the river, which was suggested as an alternative hypothesis by Dr. Henri-Martin, this would still count as a burial because it would be a distinct mode of disposal of an entire body. Neil Tappen (personal communication) says that the physical condition of the bones suggests immediate coverage rather than any prolonged exposure to the elements.

One should also keep in mind that the reluctance to admit burial of the La Quina woman would be consistent with Dr. Henri-Martin's opinion that the Neanderthals were extremely primitive creatures. He called them "para-human." Since this view is no longer consistent with what is known about Neanderthal man in the light of the other indications, such as those mentioned here and the now known, extremely primitive fossil men such as *Australopithecus* and *Homo erectus*, one has reason to believe that the reluctance to admit that the dead body was ritually disposed of was tied in with the then current concept of the intelligence and primitiveness of the Neanderthals. It would have been a remarkable coincidence in many regards if the woman had fallen into the river right in front of a Mousterian habitation and drowned and then was just left to lie in the shallow water instead of being retrieved or washed farther downstream.

We follow S. R. Binford (1968) in excluding the intentionally inhumed Le Moustier young man, because the circumstances of his excavation by a sales-minded antiquities dealer make it difficult to determine the nature of grave goods, if any.

One-armed Shanidar I is counted as a burial. Even though he was killed by a rockfall, the parts of his body which extended beyond the fatal boulders had been carefully covered with stones by his fellows, according to the excavator (Solecki 1971, pp. 105–15).

WESTERN EUROPEAN AND
NEAR EASTERN DIFFERENCES

Neanderthal man, when accompanied by cultural remains, has invariably been associated with some facies of the Mousterian industrial complex, widespread in time and space in Europe, the Near East, North Africa, and western Asia. Burials are most frequent in western Europe and the Near East, with a few reported from eastern Europe and central Asia (Map 3.1). Although geographically segregated facies of the industry have not so far been distinguished, in a recent

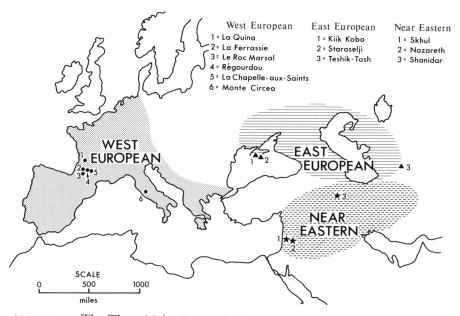

West European   East European   Near Eastern
1 = La Quina   1 = Kiik Koba   1 = Skhul
2 = La Ferrassie   2 = Staroselji   2 = Nazareth
3 = Le Roc Marsal   3 = Teshik-Tash   3 = Shanidar
4 = Régourdou
5 = La Chapelle-aux-Saints
6 = Monte Circeo

MAP 3.1   The Three Major Zones of Mousterian Burials and the Location of Selected Sites

study of Paleolithic burial practices, S. R. Binford (1968) has demonstrated consistent differences in the burial practices of western European and Near Eastern Neanderthals. The western European burials tend to occur marginally to habitation places, with some instances of family groups, while Near Eastern burials are much more likely to occur in the habitation areas themselves, seemingly reflecting a funeral rite involving the entire band. The occurrence of the burials of infants and children in both geographic areas is interesting inasmuch as later cultures of fully sapient man, many with agriculture or metallurgy, were much more casual about the disposal of those who died very young.

In this study children are regarded as being no older than twelve years, which is not only a reasonable figure, but an operationally convenient one, as hardly any burials are known of those that died between the estimated ages of twelve and eighteen. In western Europe, of a total of twenty-one burials, there are twelve children and nine adults, including one aged individual. Over 57 percent of the burials are those of immature individuals. In the Near East the proportions

TABLE 3.1   Summary of Neanderthal Child Burials

Site	Remains	Age	Sex	Burial	Grave Goods
West European					
Spy, Namur, Belgium	Teeth, tibia	10?		X	
Combe Grenal, Dordogne,	Mandible	10–12		X	Stone block cist
France	Trace	4–6		X	Stone block cist
La Ferrassie, Dordogne	Complete skeleton	5		X	3 pieces of flint
	Complete skeleton	4		X	3 pieces of flint
	Complete skeleton	0		X	3 pieces of flint
	Complete skeleton	4		X	3 pieces of flint
Le Moustier, Dordogne	?	2½		X	Fine lithic pieces; rocks covering head
Pech de L'Aze, Dordogne	Skull fragments	8		X	Food offerings
La Quina, Charente, France	Skull fragments	8		X	
Roc Marsal, Le Bugue, France	Complete skeleton	5–6		X	Surrounded with stones; lower jaw of horse; flint tools
Gibralter	Skull fragments	5		X	Flint tools
East European					
Staroselie, Crimea, USSR	Complete skeleton	1½		X	Flint tools
Kik-Koba	Complete skeleton	0–1		X	
Teshik-Tash, Uzbekistan, USSR	Complete skeleton	8–10		X	Surrounded with goat horns
Near Eastern					
Skhul, Mount Carmel,	Complete skeleton	8–10	M	X	
Palestine	Complete skeleton	4–4½	M	X	
	Complete skeleton	5–5½	M	X	
Shukba, Wadi Natuf	Complete skeleton			X	
	Complete skeleton			X	
	Complete skeleton			X	
	Complete skeleton			X	
	Complete skeleton			X	
	Complete skeleton			X	
Amud Cave, Lake Tiberias, Palestine	Complete skeleton			X	
Nazareth, Israel	Complete skeleton			X	Grave goods cited, no details given
Shanidar, Kurdistan, Iraq	Fragmentary skeleton			X	

are twelve children and twelve adults including two aged ones, or 50 percent immature persons (Table 3.1). Since among ethnographically known peoples of primitive culture the numbers of children who die before attaining maturity compose about one third to one half of the deaths that occur (Howells 1960, pp. 158–74), it appears that the total sample of Neanderthal children is not biased toward adults as is often the case wih archaeologically known peoples. The slightly higher percentage of children in western Europe seems perhaps explicable by early Wurmian Europe's periglacial climate being more rigorous than that of the Near East. In addition, the burial of children in the Near East in the margins of sites (Binford 1968), which are much less likely to be dug by professional excavators, may bias that population toward adults. Finally, certain mortuary practices among western European Neanderthals would help to enhance the detection and perception of burials. The very presence of grave goods makes it easier to note burials when the bones have mostly disappeared (Peyrony 1934).

Burials with grave goods occur with a much greater frequency in western Europe than in the Near East. Fifteen of twenty-one burials in Europe have grave goods and only five of twenty-four in the Near East have grave objects. Grave goods in Europe tend to consist of flake tools (Fig. 3.1), bone flakes and segments, pebbles of distinctive form and color, stone blocks on or around the remains, and animal bones, which perhaps are the remains of food offerings. With one exception, mentioned below, the last two kinds of grave goods—stone blocks and animal bones—are the only ones detected thus far in the Near East.

Careful inspection of the details shows that the western European proportions of grave good inclusions are due to the frequency of grave goods with burials of children.[1]

	West European		Near Eastern	
	Children	Adults	Children	Adults
Grave Goods	10	5	1	4
No Grave Goods	2	4	11	8

Not only are most of the grave goods buried with children in western Europe, but all five examples of adults with grave goods seem to be special cases compared to the four other burials. For example, the La Chapelle-Aux-Saints man with grave goods is the stooped, arthritic,

---

1   The East European sample, which includes the west-central Asiatic Teshik-Tash boy, appears to resemble the practices in western Europe. However, the sample is too small to justify any definite statement.

East Europeans

	Children	Adults
Grave Goods	2	0
No Grave Goods	1	1

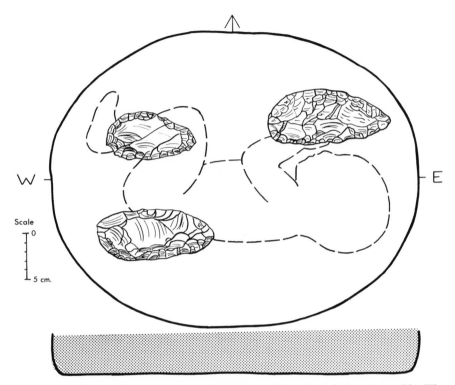

FIG. 3.1   Plan of Burial 5 at La Ferrassie and Section of the Grave Pit. The position of the body of the baby, less than one year old, is schematized, as decay of bones makes an exact, detailed plan impossible. Sidescrapers are in their exact positions. (Redrawn from Capitan and Peyrony 1921, Peyrony 1934, and Bergounioux 1958.)

virtually toothless old-timer who had perhaps the greatest longevity of any Neanderthal yet found. Certainly any man who lived to be fifty-five or sixty in a group where only 5 percent reached fifty or more (Vallois 1937, p. 512) would likely be assigned special status beyond that of ordinary folk, and in any case his ailments and age so crippled him that obviously he had to be maintained until his death.

The Near Eastern Neanderthals also displayed a compassion toward their crippled members. One of the burials at Shanidar was an arthritic one-armed cripple, who had lived to be around forty. His right arm and shoulder had never fully developed, and, indeed, his arm had been amputated below the elbow sometime during his youth. That such an individual could live to maturity is ample evidence of the care that Neanderthal society provided for its members (Clark and Piggott 1965, p. 63).

Another remarkable adult Near Eastern burial is also at Shanidar (Leroi-Gourhan 1968). Shanidar IV, a young adult male skeleton, flexed on the right side with a stone cist surrounding the body, had received mammal remains as an offering, but the most noteworthy of the grave goods are the flowers which were put into the grave. A number of pollen samples were taken from this particular burial by the excavator, Ralph Solecki, because the curious dark brown loamy soil overlying a dark organic discolored layer was contrasted with the rather loose and light-colored cave detritus. Upon examination of this pollen, Dr. Willem van Zeist of Groningen found that it was composed almost exclusively of the pollen of the small, but very brightly colored flowers of the Near East. These include primarily milfoil (*Achillea*); a ragwort (*Senecio* type *Desfontainea*) with yellow flowers (not to be confused with ragweed); a kind of cornflower (*Centaurea*); a small lilac *(Muscari)* with blue flowers; as well as a lesser number of mallow *(Althea)*. It is supposed that the body was laid to rest on a litter composed of numerous supple branches of these herbs. This Neanderthal burial lay below the level dated by carbon 14 back to 48,000 B.C. at least. The flowers cited bloom here at this present time in the Zagros Mountains in May and June. Since this was at an altitude of 822 meters during the Pleistocene, it would be more realistic to suppose that the burial took place between the end of May and early June in those days.

The most outstanding example of grave goods in the Near East occurred with Skhul V who was about fifty years old (Fig. 3.2, see also Table 3.2). The presence of grave goods with the adult man and woman at La Ferrassie in western Europe may be due to their having been inhumed along with children, presumably their own, in an ostensible family cemetery. The remains at Régourdou (Dordogne) and a cranium from Monte Circeo, both with grave furnishings, seem to have been placed at cult shrines.

Regardless of the frequency with which perishable grave goods, such as flowers, may have been put in graves, the fact still remains that European children were the ones most likely to have received tools and other decay-resistant offerings. These circumstances, of course, also make the graves more detectable, particularly when the skeleton

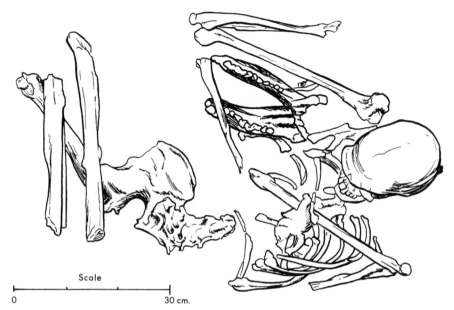

FIG. 3.2   Skhul V Burial Showing Skeleton with Wild Boar (*Sus scrofa*) Mandibles. (Redrawn from Garrod and Bate 1937.)

has badly deteriorated. An added peculiarity of the western European situation is that the children with grave goods are all seemingly less than five to six years of age. The two children without grave goods are Spy and La Quina, whose ages range from eight to ten years.

CHILD CARE

This treatment of children among Neanderthals in western Europe reveals clearly, across a minimum of 370 centuries of unlettered time, how much they loved and cherished their children and how they attempted to express their affections by concrete symbols. Like the care of the disabled at La Chapelle and Shanidar, like the ingenious Levallois flint-chipping technique which preserved the pristine sharpness of unretouched flint, these practices show that Neanderthal man is far from being the brutish lout of all-too-familiar characterization. These cultural data are also consistent with a growing independent trend among physical anthropologists to recognize large-brained Neander-

TABLE 3.2   Summary of Neanderthal Adult Burials

Site	Remains	Age	Sex	Burial	Grave Goods
West European					
Neandertal, Germany	Complete skeleton	45	M	?	
Spy, Namur, Belgium	Skull fragments, post cranial	35		X	
	Skull fragments, post cranial	25	M	X	
La Chapelle-aux-Saints, Corrèze, France	Complete skeleton	50	M	X	Food offerings; grave protected by bones, tools
La Ferrassie, Dordogne, France	Complete skeleton		M	X	Flint tools; bone splinters
	Complete skeleton		F	X	Flint tools; fibers
Le Moustier, Dordogne	Complete skeleton	18	M	?	?
La Quina, Gardes-les-Pontaroux, Charente, France	Complete skeleton	25	F	X	
Régourdou, Dordogne	Mandible, post cranial		M	X	Stone blocks; next to grave of cave bear
Gibralter	Skull		F	X	
Monte Circeo, Italy	Skull		M	X	Skull in circle of rocks
East European					
Kiik-Koba	Teeth, hand, and foot fragments		M	X	
Near Eastern					
Shanidar, Kurdistan, Iraq	Complete skeleton	25	M	X	Encircling stone; mammal bones; flowers
	Complete skeleton	40	M	X	Stone blocks on lower body
	Partial skeleton		F	X	
	Partial skeleton		F	X	
Tabun, Mount Carmel, Palestine	Complete skeleton	30	F	X	
Skhul, Mount Carmel	Complete skeleton	35	F	X	
	Complete skeleton		M	X	
	Complete skeleton	40	M	X	Flint tool between hands
	Complete skeleton	35	M	X	
	Complete skeleton	35	M	X	
	Complete skeleton	35	F	X	
	Complete skeleton	50	M	X	Wild boar mandible in arms

thal man as, after all, not being very different physically from modern, contemporary man, designated *sapiens* (Brace 1967, pp. 84–96).

Indeed, the loving care reflected in Neanderthal treatment of their children strongly implies that by Mousterian times there had come a greater emphasis on child rearing, with perhaps more attention paid to caring for the immature, especially the infant and toddler. The utter helplessness of the infant and the slow maturation rate are among the most outstanding biological characteristics of man. While there is no denying that most mammalian mothers, above all primate ones, lavish a great deal of concern on the young, it is unarguable that the *sapiens* infant requires more care to raise than do the offspring of other primates and mammals.

Since the postcranial physique of man had nearly acquired its present form by the time of the Mindel glaciation and, as often noted, the Mindel-Riss Swanscombe and Steinheim females look like *sapiens* and Neanderthal except for their small brains of about 1275–1325 cubic centimeters (Coon 1963, p. 496), it would appear that the increased cranial capacity—approximately 1500 cubic centimeters among Neanderthals, slightly less among contemporary man (Brace 1967, pp. 83–87)—appears coincidentally with greater concern for small children. Could it be that advances in child care realized by Neanderthalers of Mousterian culture helped make it possible for the survival of children with large, growing brains and slow-closing fontanelles, children who might otherwise have been liable to injury under more rudimentary practices of child rearing? The emphasis on supplying the children with tools in burials perhaps hints at a greater emphasis on education, thereby taking advantage of the long learning period available for immature humans.

Undoubtedly there were many other factors involved in the evolution of man affecting brain size and intelligence, so the matter of child care could have been only one of them. Nor is it meant to imply that only the western European Neanderthals so loved their children that they precipitated this advance. If there is any validity to our inferences about child-rearing practices, the equally advanced Near Eastern Neanderthals would have shared these practices, too. The Near Eastern customs in this regard are obscured by their different emphasis in burial rites, which stressed the entire social group, thereby the active adults, and not the family, the generative unit, as in Europe. The Shanidar remains show that the Near Eastern Neanderthals were as compassionate as those in Europe, and of course the western Asiatic boy of Teshik-Tash was not so very far away from southwestern Asia.

Therefore, it seems likely that the greater emphasis on child care would have been a widespread cultural phenomenon by Mousterian times.

REFERENCES CITED

Bergounioux, F. M.
  1958 "Spiritualité" de l'Homme de Néandertal. In G. H. R. von Koenigswald, ed., *Hundert Jahre Neanderthaler*. Köln: Bohlau Verlag. Pp. 151–66.

Binford, S. R.
  1968 A Structural Comparison of Disposal of the Dead in the Mousterian and the Upper Paleolithic. *Southwestern Journal of Anthropology* 24:139–54.

Blanc, A. C.
  1939 L'Homme Fossile du Monte Circeo. *L'Anthropologie* 44:253–64.

Bonifay, E.
  1964 La Grotte du Régourdou: Stratigraphie et Industrie Lithique Moustérienne. *L'Anthropologie* 68:49–64.

Bordes, F.
  1961 Mousterian Cultures in France. *Science* 154:803–10.
  1968 *The Old Stone Age*. New York: McGraw-Hill.

Boule, M.
  1908 L'Homme Fossile de la Chapelle-aux-Saints. *Compte Rendu de l'Académie des Sciences* 147:1349–52.
  1908–1909 L'Homme Fossile de la Chapelle-aux Saints (Corrèze). *L'Anthropologie* 19:519–29, 20:257–71.
  1909 Découverte d'un Squelette Néanderthaloide. *L'Anthropologie* 20:603–604.
  1911 L'Homme Fossile de la Chapelle-aux-Saints. *Annales de Paléontologie* 6:111–72.
  1925 L'Homme de Néanderthal en Galilée. *L'Anthropologie* 35:602–604.

Boule, M., and H. Vallois
  1957 *Fossil Men*. New York: Dryden Press.

Bouyssonie, A., J. Bouyssonie, and L. Bardon
  1908 Découverte d'un Squelette Humain Moustérien à la Chapelle-aux-Saints (Corrèze). *Compte Rendu de l'Académie des Sciences* 147:1411–14.
  1913 La Station Moustérienne de la "Bouffia" Bonneval, à la Chapelle-aux-Saints. *L'Anthropologie* 24:609–34.

Bouyssonie, J.
  1954 Les Sépultures Moustériennes. *Quaternaria* 24:609–34.

Brace, C. L.
  1967 *The Stages of Human Evolution*. Englewood Cliffs, N.J.: Prentice-Hall.

Breuil, H.
  1921 Sur les Sépultures Moustériennes. *L'Anthropologie* 31:342–45.

Brueil, H., and A. Blanc
  1936 Le Nouveau Crane Néanderthalien de Saccopastore (Rome). *L'Anthropologie* 46:1–16.

Capitan, L., and D. Peyrony
  1909 Deux Squelettes Humains au Milieu des Foyers de l'Époque Moustérienne. *Revue de l'Ecole d'Anthropologie* 19:402–409.
  1912 Station Préhistorique de la Ferrassie. *Revue Anthropologique* 22:29–50.

Clark, Graham, and Stuart Piggott
  1965 *Prehistoric Societies.* New York: Knopf.

Coon, Carleton
  1963 *Origin of Races.* New York: Knopf.

David, P., and F. H. Bordes
  1950 Découverte d'une Calotte Cranienne Fragmentaire et des Dents Humaines dan un Niveau Moustérien Ancien de la Chaise, Charente. *Compte Rendu de l'Académie des Sciences* 230:779–80.

Fraipont, C.
  1936 *Les Hommes Fossiles d'Engis.* Archives de l'Institut de Paléontologie Humaine, Memoire 16. Paris.

Fraipont, J., and M. Lomest
  1887 Recherches Ethnographiques sur les Ossements Humains Découverts dans les Dépots d'une Grotte Quaternaire à Spy. *Archives de Biologie* 7:387–733.

Garrod, D. A. E., and D. Bate
  1937 *The Stone Age of Mount Carmel.* Vol. 1. Oxford: Clarendon Press.
  1942 Excavations at the Cave of Shukbah, Palestine, 1928. *Proceedings of the Prehistoric Society* (Ser. 2) 8:1–20.

Garrod, D. A. E., L. H. D. Buston, E. G. Smith, and D. Bate
  1928 Excavation of a Mousterian Rock-Shelter at Devil's Tower, Gibralter. *Journal of the Royal Anthropological Institute* 58:33–113.

Henri-Martin, H.
  1911 Sur un Squelette Humain de l'Époque Moustérienne Trouvé en Charente. *Compte Rendu de l'Académie des Sciences* 153:728–30.
  1912 État des Travaux dans le Gisement de la Quina en 1912. *Congrès Préhistorique de France* 8. Angouleme: La Société Préhistorique Française. Pp. 282–96.
  1921 *L'Homme Fossile de la Quina.* Paris.
  1936 Comment Vivait l'Homme de la Quina à l'Époque Mousterienne. *Préhistoire* 5:1–23.

Howells, F. C.
  1958 Upper Pleistocene Men of the Southwest Asian Mousterian. In G. H. R.

von Koenigswald, ed., *Hundert Jahre Neanderthaler*. Köln: Bohlau Verlag. Pp. 185–98.

Howells, W.
  1960   Estimating Population Numbers through Archaeological and Skeletal Remains. In Robert F. Heizer and Sherburne F. Cook, eds., *Application of Quantitative Methods in Archaeology*. Viking Fund Publications in Anthropology, No. 28. New York: Wenner-Gren Foundation. Pp. 158–85.

Jullien, R.
  1965   *Les Hommes Fossiles de la Pierre Taillée*. Editions N. Paris: Boubée et Cie.

Klaatsch, H., and O. Hauser
  1910   Homo Aurignaciensis Hauseris. *Praehistorische Zeitschrift* 1:173–338.

Klein, R.
  1965   Middle Paleolithic of the Crimea. *Arctic Anthropology* 3:14–67.

Lafille, M.
  1962   Gisement dit "Roc de Marsal," Com. de Campagne-du-Bugue (Dordogne). *Bulletin de la Société préhistorique française* 58 (11–12) :712–13.

Leroi-Gourhan, A.
  1968   Le Néanderthalien IV de Shanidar. Comptes Rendus des Séances Mensuelles. *Bulletin de la Société préhistorique française* 65 (3):79–83.

McCown, T., and A. Keith
  1939   The Stone Age of Mount Carmel. Vol. 2. Oxford: Clarendon Press.

Manishi, Suzuki, Watanabe, and Takai
  1963   Preliminary Report on Amud Cave. Tokyo: University of Tokyo.

Movius, H. L.
  1953   The Mousterian Cave of Teshik-Tash, Southeastern Uzbekistan, Central Asia. Trans. by C. C. Chard. *Bulletin*, No. 7. American School of Prehistoric Research. Pp. 11–71.

Nemeskeri, J., and L. Harsanyi
  1962   Das Lebensalter des Skelettes aus dem Neandertal (1856). *Anthropologisher Anzieger* 25 (4) :292–97.

Peyrony, D.
  1921   Les Mousteriéns Inhumaient-ils leurs Morts? *Bulletin de la Société Historique et Archeologique du Perigord*.
  1934   La Ferrassie. *Préhistoire* 3:1–92.

Piveteau, J.
  1959   Les Restes Humains de la Grotte du Régourdou (Dordogne). *Compte Rendu de l'Académie des Sciences* 248:40–44.

Solecki, R.
  1957   The 1956–57 Season at Shanidar, Iraq. *Quaternaria* 4: 1–8.
  1960   Three Adult Neanderthal Skeletons from Shanidar Cave, Northern Iraq. *Annual Report, 1959*. Washington, D.C.: Smithsonian Institution. Pp. 603–35.

1961   New Archaeological Discoveries at Shanidar, Northern Iraq. *New York Academy of Sciences* 23:690–99.

1971   *Shanidar: The First Flower People.* New York: Knopf.

Suzuki
1962   Ein Neues Neandertaler-Skelett in Galiläa entdeckt. *Anthropologisher Anzieger* 25 (4) :305.

Turville-Petre, F.
1929   *Researches in Prehistoric Galilee, 1925–26.* London: British School of Archaeology in Jerusalem.

Vallois, H.
1937   La Durée de la Vie Chez l'Homme Fossile. *L'Anthropologie* 47: 499–532.

1950a   Découverte d'une Nouvelle Mandible Néanderthalienne en Italie. *L'Anthropologie* 54:542.

1950b   Review of "Il cranio del Secondo Paleantropo di Saccopastore" by S. Sergi. *L'Anthropologie* 54:95–98.

1955   Nouveaux Restes Néanderthaliens en Europe. *L'Anthropologie* 59: 167–68.

Vandermeersch, B.
1966   Nouvelles Découvertes de Restes Humains dans les Couches Levalloiso-Moustériennes du Gisement de Qafzeh (Israel). *Compte Rendu de l'Académie des Sciences* 262:1434–36.

Vertes, L.
1959   Das Mousterien im Ungarn. *Eiszeitalter und Gegenwart* 10:22–40.

ESTHETICS

Chapter 4

The Art of Willie Seaweed: A Kwakiutl Master

Bill Holm

ABSTRACT   Modern man usually thinks of the art of the so-called primitive people as being a collective, anonymous product. He rarely considers the individual artist in primitive society as having a career that begins, expands, and ends as the individual's talent develops and changes under the influence of other individual artists. Yet primitive art in a real sense is the product of unique, creative individuals. While each artist shares in the same artistic language, each has his own idiomatic expressions which mark his work and set it apart from others.

Willie Seaweed, chief of the Nákwaktokw Kwakiutl, was such an individual. His artistic career began before the turn of the century and continued into the 1960s. During his long career, he traveled throughout Kwakiutl country filling commissions of village chiefs to make masks, totem poles, and other ceremonial objects. A consideration of the twenty-four *hámatsa* masks known to be Seaweed's work reveals a careful use of the compass, straightedge, and template to produce masks characterized by a concern with the formal relationship of positive-negative design elements, the use of flat planes, and the avoidance of unnecessary meandering of lines. The eye of the mask, eccentric with three compass centers in a row, is particularly distinctive. In contrast to the perfunctory handling by other artists, even the interior of a Seaweed mask was carefully finished. These characteristics reflect the self-conscious actions of a creative individual working within the context of his society's art forms.

59

Northwest Coast Indian artists, like "primitive artists" of other cultures, have been largely anonymous in our time. Moreover, when modern man, a product of a society which puts great emphasis on names, fame, and individual accomplishment, looks at a collection of masks or other works of art from such exotic cultures, he is unlikely to visualize an individual human creator behind each piece. Seldom will he be helped toward personalizing the faceless "primitive artist" by the labels he might read. Work might be identified as "Northwest Coast," "Alaska," or "British Columbia Coast." At best a tribal identification might be made, although the likelihood of its being inaccurate is considerable. The idea that each object represents the creative activity of a specific human personality who lived and worked at a particular time and place, whose artistic career had a beginning, a development, and an end, and whose work influenced and was influenced by the work of other artists is not at all likely to come to mind.

Yet this is the case, and being so, it is possible to identify (with the usual pitfalls associated with attribution) the work of a particular artist, recognize the stages of his artistic development, and assess the place of his work in its milieu. Analysis of individual artists' styles has become a significant part of the increasing scholarly attention to Northwest Coast Indian art. It is hoped that from the various studies in progress will come techniques and systematization to replace the guesswork so common in the past (Holm 1972b, pp. 77–83).

Indian artists of the northern part of the Northwest Coast, from Bella Coola through southeastern Alaska, adhered to a very highly developed system of art conventions in their two-dimensional work, at least in the historic and protohistoric period (Holm 1965, pp. 20–21). Each artist was using the same artistic language. The accent and idiom he brought to that language personalized his work and distinguished it from that of others.

The work of Kwakiutl artists from the middle of the general Northwest Coast area can be differentiated in the same way, but with somewhat less facility, because the conventions there were less rigid and there is no easily definable norm to which the variants may be compared. By examining groups of similar articles, the characteristics by which they either differ from or resemble one another can be seen. Groups of like objects, which share stylistic details, can be tentatively assigned to individual, though perhaps still anonymous, makers. If one—or better still, several—of these pieces is known to come from the hand of a particular artist, the group might reasonably be attributed to that artist. Such attributions are not without the potential of error. A number of known Kwakiutl artists produced during their apprenticeships pieces which cannot be distinguished from the work of their masters. In every known case, however, once the junior artist started to produce on his own, the distinctive character of his style began to develop. A creative person is not long satisfied copying the every stylistic idiosyncrasy of another. He will keep to that which satisfies him and fill it out from his imagination and from what strikes his fancy in the work of other artists. The whole development of Northwest Coast Indian art, or any body of art which is a recognizable entity, depended upon this sort of borrowing and mutual inspiration. As artists work, their styles develop and change, new ideas come along, old ones are discarded, and although this progression can be a confusing factor in attribution, it can also be related to the larger picture of changing trends within the areal style.

WILLIE SEAWEED'S ARTISTIC CAREER

Willie Seaweed, a chief of the Nákwaktokw Kwakiutl from Blunden Harbour (Map 4.1), was an artist whose work invites this kind of examination. His long artistic career extended from before this century, when the native culture still dominated Kwakiutl life, until the 1960 decade of television and space exploration (Fig. 4.1). His credentials as a Kwakiutl were impeccable. Born about 1873 to the Eagle (the first to receive in a potlatch) of the *Gyíkhsum numaym* and the daughter of the head chief of the *Dzídzumeylakula numaym*, he was of noble line in both the Nákwaktokw and Gwásila tribes. George Hunt's version of Seaweed's rather complex genealogy was published by Boas as an example of endogamy (1921, pp. 781–82). The Gwásila and the Nákwaktokw are regularly mentioned by Kwakiutl informants from other villages as sources of many of their most respected mask and dance prerogatives.

As Heýhlamas, ranking chief of the Nákwaktokw, Willie Seaweed was always in the forefront of fostering the traditional ways of his people. The Canadian government gave him an unintentional sort of stamp of approval and official recognition for his involvement in tribal

MAP 4.1
Kwakiutl Country
and the Home of
Willie Seaweed

affairs when he was among those arrested in 1922 for potlatching and forced to relinquish their paraphernalia!

When Willie Seaweed was born, the Kwakiutl tribes were living in big communal houses which were not to give way entirely to the white man's frame house for another fifty years. All transportation was by canoe, and blankets were everyday wear. The days of intertribal war and revenge raids were hardly over. Seaweed told Dr. C. F. Newcombe in 1914 that his own father had been taken when a boy in a raid by Kitkatla Tsimshian, only to be rescued when the raiders reached Bella Bella on their journey homeward (Newcombe 1914). Newcombe engaged him as a guide to old Nákwaktokw sites in 1914 and referred to him at that time as "the Blunden Harbour chief" (Fig. 4.2).

The similarity of the name Seaweed to that of the marine plant is entirely coincidental. It is in fact a respected chief's name in several of the Kwakiutl tribes. Literally translated "paddling recipient," it refers to the paddling which brings far-flung tribes to his great potlatches. Exactly how this name was settled upon as the official Canadian family name is unknown to me, but anglicized versions of native names are not uncommon among the Kwakiutl. However, few Kwakiutl referred to him by that name. He was generally known by his chief name, Heýhlamas (Right Maker) or more often and more familiarly as Kwághitola (Smoky Top, "like a volcano," as one person explained it).

FIG. 4.1
Willie Seaweed,
Heýhlamas, Chief of the
Nákwaktokw, 1873–1967.
(Photograph by Richard
Pattinson.)

FIG. 4.2
Willie Seaweed, 1914.
(Photograph by C. F. Newcombe,
courtesy of the Provincial
Museum of British Columbia.)

According to several of my most knowledgeable Kwakiutl informants there was (theoretically at least) only one official mask carver
for each village group, and Willie Seaweed had that place among the
Nákwaktokw. It was considered a prestigious position, and the occu-
pant was always a *nákhsola*, a nobleman. If the exclusive character
of the position ever applied, it has not been so in fact for many years,
and the number of accepted carvers in a given village varied according
to the talent available. Blunden Harbour, the principal village of the
Nákwaktokw in historic times, and the Gwásila village of Takush
Harbour in Smith Inlet, at once isolated bastions of tradition and
loci of fabled privileges, produced an inordinate number of recognized artists. Some of those who preceded Seaweed and certainly
influenced the character of his work are known, as are some of his contemporaries whose styles affected and were affected by his. Many masks
collected before the turn of the century in the northern Vancouver
Island area exhibit characteristics which could well be precursors of

later Seaweed usages. Some of these may be in fact early Seaweed productions, but they have not been so identified. He must have been
carving by the early 1890s when most of the first great Kwakiutl collections were made (excepting the Jacobsen material of a decade
earlier in Germany and, through Karl Hagenbeck, in the Field
Museum).

Most Kwakiutl carvers began their careers in their adolescent
years, usually apprenticed to a master artist, in many cases the novice's
own father. Seaweed's father was a recognized carver, but he died before his son was born, so the future master received no direct training
from him. His older half brother Johnny Davis (Lulákhunhid) certainly had an influence on the development of Seaweed's style. Davis
was a well-recognized carver, one of the most frequently mentioned by
informants discussing artists of earlier days. His picture appears twice
in Curtis' volume on the Kwakiutl, wigged and dressed in archaic costume, as a chief holding his copper and as a warrior (Curtis 1915, pp.
98,196). Johnny Davis, according to identifications made by Seaweed
and others, did make many of the masks now seen in the great museum
collections. Three *hámatsa* masks, for example, in the Smithsonian's
collections (Boas 1897, Plate 31, Figs. 78, 82) have been identified as
coming from his hand. February 21, 1895, when they were collected, is
admittedly a long time ago and memories fray in seventy years, but the
identifications were made forcefully and deserve consideration. In any
event, they came from Seaweed's village during the early formative
years of his career and probably influenced his style. Later masks by
Johnny Davis (some of which have been incorrectly attributed to
Willie Seaweed) resemble Seaweed's masks of like date in ways which
suggest the two carvers derived ideas from one another.

Willie Seaweed and his Blunden Harbour contemporaries, the
brothers, Chief George (Poódlidakumi) and Charley George, Sr.
(Hyílhyidi), and George Walkus of Smith Inlet, produced work which
perhaps could be characterized as a Blunden Harbour-Smith Inlet
school. These four and others from the area, in mutually borrowing
ideas and innovations, carried the somewhat austere classic late nineteenth-century art of the area into a baroque period, which reached its
culmination in the cannibal masks of the 1940s and 1950s. The sons of
some of these, Charley George, Jr., Charley G. Walkus, and Joe Sea-

weed, continue the tradition, although in their own directions and in some ways returning to a less flamboyant style. They also must be classed as later contemporaries of Willie Seaweed since their careers overlapped his by many years.

All of the above-mentioned carvers' work was in demand, and they were often commissioned to make masks, totem poles, and other ceremonial objects by chiefs from other Kwakiutl villages, so that nothing is gained from knowledge of the location of its ultimate Indian owner. Carvers often traveled long distances to their patrons' villages to work, and Willie Seaweed was no exception. For example, about 1918 he went to Campbell River, a 250-mile, round-trip journey from Blunden Harbour, to make masks for Kwatell, a chief there. In other cases the commissioned work was finished at home and delivered to the customer. Even large pieces were sometimes done this way. The beautiful memorial pole of *dzónokwa*, *hókhokw*, wolf, and *kólus*, once towering over the graves at Fort Rupert but now moved to the neighboring park and badly repainted, was carved at Blunden Harbour with the help of Joe and towed across Queen Charlotte Strait to its place of erection (Fig. 4.3). The widely illustrated *dzónokwa* and thunderbird pole in the cemetery at Alert Bay was likewise carved in Blunden Harbour. It too was repainted during the restoration of the Alert Bay poles in 1958. The work was well done, but it more nearly reflects the style of the supervisor of the restorative painting, Henry Speck (Ódzistalis), than it does that of the original artist whose distinctive elements can be seen dimly through the now-weathered overpainting.

Since these artists were professionals in the sense that they regularly produced pieces for which they were paid (although none of them derived his entire livelihood from his art), it is of interest to know what constituted acceptable return for the work. The patron, or the informant speaking from the patron's point of view, is likely to paint a rosy picture of the artist's take, while the carver puts forth the opposite view. One informant declared that $150 in cash and $150 worth of clothes and other goods (a rather respectable sum for the period, 1930) had been paid to Willie Seaweed for two *hámatsa* masks, while Seaweed himself said that carvers got little return for their efforts. Even with today's very favorable market for fine Indian work, newly made masks bring only little more than the 1930 price men-

FIG. 4.3 *Dzónokwa* Figure on Memorial Pole, Fort Rupert, British Columbia, 1954. (Photograph by Sidney Gerber.)

tioned. On the other hand, the two 1930 Seaweed *hámatsa* masks have appreciated (in the collectors' market) in the neighborhood of 2,000 percent in the intervening forty years.

Willie Seaweed made or decorated examples of almost every kind of object produced by the artists of his tribe. Masks of all kinds, totem poles both monumental and model, rattles, headdresses, whistles, ceremonial screens, coppers, drums, house fronts, cradles, settees, painted plaques, and even walking sticks come to mind. I have seen and in most cases photographed eighty-five examples of his work, the identity of which I am reasonably certain, and I am never surprised by the amount that keeps turning up. Not all those described as "Willie Seaweed" pieces are that in fact, however. It is a name that is becoming known and might enhance a piece offered for sale or add prestige to a mask in a collection.

THE HÁMATSA MASK

The *húmsumhl,* or *hámatsa* mask, is particularly well suited to expository treatment. These masks, of limited and somewhat standardized iconography, were produced over a considerable period by the southern Kwakiutl, allowing observation of changes in form over time and area. The masks and the dance in which they figure are the subject of a larger study which I have in progress. Seaweed made numbers of the masks, many of which have been positively identified by the artist and others. Many of these have been illustrated (Hawthorn 1967). I know of twenty-six masks of this type by Seaweed, most of which I have examined carefully, measured, weighed, diagramed and photographed. There are certainly more, but even this number far exceeds that firmly attributable to any other Kwakiutl carver. Each was made for Indian use.

The earliest documented object known to be a Seaweed piece is a beautifully designed and finished *galókwiwe,* or crooked-beak-forehead mask, of a special type known as *háhyilasto,* or "raising-top" (Fig. 4.4). Somewhat contrary to traditional practice, Seaweed made it for himself. Ideally a carver is commissioned to make needed masks even though the mask owner can carve. However, exceptions to the rule are common enough. More accurately the mask was made for

FIG. 4.4   Raising-Top Crooked-Beak Mask, Circa 1910. Actual size thirty-four inches; Provincial Museum of British Columbia.

Willie's son, Joe Seaweed, who was being initiated as *hámatsa*. Interestingly, this took place when Joe was a tiny baby, perhaps shortly after his birth in 1910, and Willie danced as proxy for his son. A broad band of copper is attached to the inner edge of the forehead. At a certain point in the dance the beak is opened and shut rapidly, while at the same time the forehead raises, exposing the polished copper in a series of flashes.

The Seaweed characteristics of meticulous craftsmanship, conscious concern with formal relationships of positive-negative design elements, use of simple flat planes as in the surface of the nostril, and avoidance of unnecessary meandering in planes and lines were already established. The nostril form is to be seen, with variations, on many of his later crooked-beak masks and is related to the nostril of a Johnny Davis raven mask in the United States National Museum (Boas 1897, Plate 31). The eye, with its flat compass-drawn iris and precise, slightly constricted eyelid line in black with red lining, is the forerunner of a form standardized in his masks thereafter. This mask does differ from later Seaweed *hámatsa* masks in several ways. There is no pulley wheel for the jaw-control string, which merely passes over a wooden rod inserted through the mask, and the jaw is hinged with a separate strip of leather nailed along each side. Later Seaweed masks usually show another form of hinge (Fig. 4.5). The other characteristic

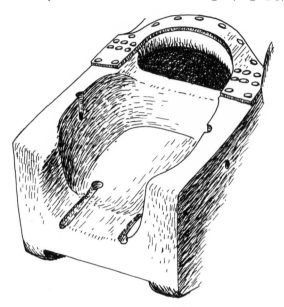

FIG. 4.5
Inside a Typical Seaweed
Hámatsa Mask. The mask
shows the unique
characteristics of grooves for
harness attachment and a
one-piece, leather jaw hinge.

which differentiates this mask from the artist's later productions is the use of native paint, or at least native paint medium. The red pigment appears to be vermilion and the black, graphite, all applied rather thinly in a matte medium. Later Seaweed used commercial paint almost exclusively.

In 1914 Seaweed sold this mask to Dr. C. F. Newcombe, who was in the area collecting for the Provincial Museum of British Columbia and gathering data on the Kwakiutl. Seaweed sold a number of other articles to Dr. Newcombe, among them another *hámatsa* mask made for him by Mungo Martin apparently for Joe's initiation as *hámatsa* (Fig. 4.6, top). Called *wákhsqumi húmsiwe* (both-sides-face cannibal-forehead mask), it comes from a story obtained through marriage with the Awíkenokw of Rivers Inlet. Mungo Martin, some years younger than Willie Seaweed, was already an established carver by 1910, having apprenticed to his stepfather, the famous carver Charley James. His

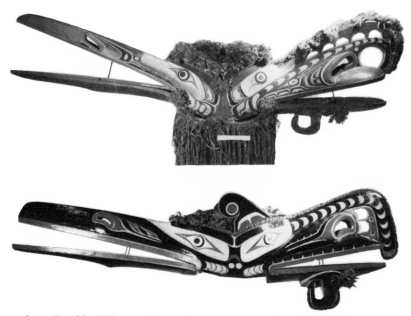

FIG. 4.6   Double *Hámatsa* Masks. Top was carved by Mungo Martin around 1910; actual size seventy-three inches; Provincial Museum of British Columbia. The bottom mask was done by Willie Seaweed before 1920. It is a "copy" of the Martin one; actual size seventy-two inches; University of British Columbia Museum, A 7992.

early style is seen in this mask in contrast to Seaweed's. It changed less over the years as illustrated by the three eyesocket diagrams in the Mungo Martin column of the chart comparing styles of Kwakiutl artists (Fig. 4.7).

To replace the masks sold to Newcombe in 1914, Willie Seaweed made a series of masks which he called "copies" but which were not strictly copies in the sense in which we use the term. The *wákhsqumi húmsiwe* (Fig. 4.6, bottom) is a copy primarily by its being a combined *gwákhumhl* (raven mask) and *galókhwumhl* (crooked-beak mask). Considering the fact that it was made after its predecessor was long gone to Victoria, it is remarkably similar in size and concept. However, it is very much a Seaweed mask and exhibits characteristics which we now can point to as typical of nearly all later *hámatsa* masks by this carver. The spiral ears or horns on this and another mask of the same series were added after 1950. The mask was used in a film made

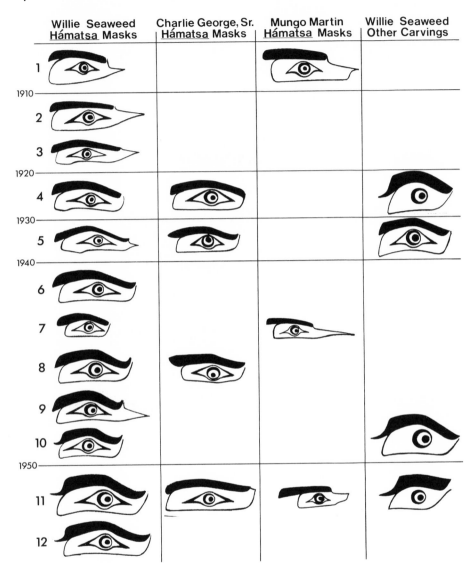

FIG. 4.7   Comparison of Eyes, Eyebrows, and Eye Sockets in a Temporal Series of Kwakiutl Masks Carved by Different Artists

at that time in Blunden Harbour, and the ears were not in evidence (Orbit Films 1951*a*). Stylistically, they are from a much later period than the mask.

In construction, this and the others of the series are like later Seaweed *hámatsa* masks. They all use pulley wheels for the jaw-control string (complete metal pulleys in the double mask, wooden spoollike wheels in the other two), the leather hinges run completely across the lower jaw, and the inside form, harness details, and attachment of cedar bark decoration are like those details of subsequent Seaweed pieces. The *háhyilasto* (Fig. 4.8) and the *hókhokw* (Fig. 4.9) both

FIG. 4.8   Raising-Top Crooked-Beak Mask, Pre-1920. Actual size thirty-three inches; Private Indian Collection, Port Hardy, British Columbia.

show early forms of the recurved eyebrow and drooping eyesocket, and in all three the fully developed Seaweed eye form is present. The long tapering lid line closely paralleling the iris top and bottom and the compass-drawn eccentric circles of iris and pupil are characteristic (Fig. 4.10).

On the jaw of the two-face mask is carved a large face with a massive hooked beak, the prototype of many more such on Seaweed *há-matsa* masks. This one clearly derives from its counterpart on the

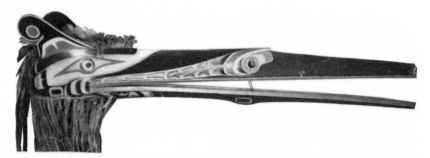

FIG. 4.9   *Hókhokw* Mask, Pre-1920. Actual size sixty-four inches; Private Indian Collection, Port Hardy, British Columbia.

FIG. 4.10
Typical Seaweed Eye as
Standardized by 1920. The
three compass centers are
shown in white.

Mungo Martin original. Similar faces without the protruding beak appear on the *hókhokw* of the series and on another *háhyilasto* of the same general period. Some, including Seaweed himself, told me it is merely an ornament, while others insisted it comes from a story. In any case, it is not a Seaweed invention, but an adaptation of a feature of earlier masks (Boas 1897, Plate 30).

A raven mask illustrates the slightly recurved eyebrow and deeply curved eyesocket seen in some Seaweed masks of the 1920 era (Fig. 4.11, top). Compass-drawn nostril and eye are characteristic. The precision apparent here was achieved by careful workmanship and the sensitive use of compass, straightedge, and templates. His masks are remarkably symmetrical. Every flat plane is really flat, no curved lines meander without purpose, no negative areas in painting happen unplanned. A telling comparison can be made with a striking mask made at the same time as a companion piece to the raven but by another carver (Fig. 4.11, bottom). This crooked-beak mask has been mistakenly attributed to Seaweed, but is almost certainly the work of his associate, Charley George, Sr. It was not unusual for a man to commission more than one artist to make a set of masks. The time available was perhaps too short for one man to do the whole job. I know of

three other sets on which two men worked together. In each case there
was an attempt to match the appearance of the masks insofar as each
artist's personal style would allow. Seaweed and George probably
worked in close association in Blunden Harbour on these two masks.
They may have used the same paint cans! But the differences in each
man's conception are clear. Less precision in shaping decorative elements, meandering lip and nostril lines, irregular nostril, and less
controlled treatment of elements at the corner of the mouth mark the
crooked-beak as another's work. The eye looks remarkably like a Seaweed eye, but close comparison shows differences, most noticeable in
the comparatively narrow red rims and the very unusual carving of
the detail of the iris-pupil area.

The attachment of cedar bark trim differs in the two masks. The
raven exhibits Seaweed's completely standardized technique: edge
bark folded and cleated under wooden battens against the inner faces

FIG. 4.11   Companion Pieces. At top is a raven mask carved by Willie Seaweed
in the 1920s, actual size thirty-four inches. At bottom is a crooked-beak mask by
Charlie George, Sr. Also done in the 1920s, this is a companion piece for the
raven mask. Its actual size is thirty inches. Both are in the University of British
Columbia Museum; top cataloged A 4249, bottom, A 4250.

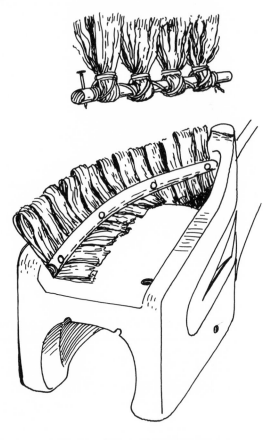

FIG. 4.12.
The Attachment of
Cedar-Bark Trim in a
Seaweed Mask. The top sketch
shows bundles of cedar ready
to be nailed to the center area
of the mask. The bottom
sketch shows how folded bark
strips are cleated to the inside
rim of the mask.

of the eyebrow ridges and the center bark tied in bundles on one or
several sticks nailed to the top (Fig. 4.12). The bark on the other mask
is not folded and is cleated under a tin strip, while the center bark is
nailed into individual bundles. Both arrangements and combinations
of them were used by others, but Seaweed almost invariably followed
the one he used here. Interestingly, he did forego the use of the one-
piece leather hinge and the pulley on the controls, and in these re-
spects the two masks are very similar. Of a total of 262 *hámatsa* masks
examined, 31 used pulleys, and of those, 21 were by Willie Seaweed
(Fig. 4.13). Other artists used the compass in their work, but none
with the consistency of Seaweed. The typical eccentric eye with its
three compass centers in a row approaches the status of a signature, as
well as something of a microcosm of Seaweed's work (Fig. 4.10). A
Willie Seaweed mask is as easily recognized from the inside as it is from

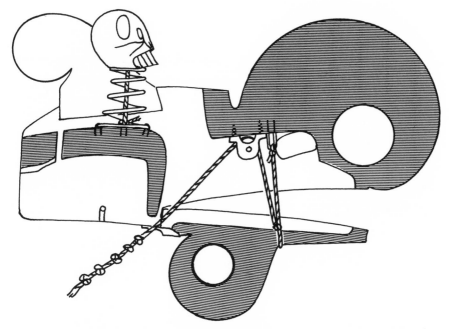

FIG. 4.13   Diagram of a Typical Seaweed *Hámatsa* Mask. (Holm Collection.)

the outside. His passion for precision led him to finish the interior with nearly the same perfection of work as he used on the details of the carving. This is in marked contrast to many masks which are roughed out in the most perfunctory manner.

The peculiar nostril of a 1920 *hókhokw* (Fig. 4.14) was said to have been suggested by his son Joe, then ten years old and already on the way to becoming an artist in his own right. Seaweed accomplished

FIG. 4.14   *Hókhokw* Mask, 1920s. Actual size sixty-four inches; University of British Columbia Museum, A 6346.

FIG. 4.15   *Hókhokw* Mask Worn in a Dance at Alert Bay, British Columbia, 1968. Actual size seventy inches; James Sewid Collection.

an interesting synthesis of his two prevailing eyesocket forms in this mask. Apparently well documented as being made in 1930, the form of another *hókhokw* (Fig. 4.15) suggests an earlier date. A feature not seen heretofore on Seaweed masks is the carved wooden skull (*khuwikw*) mounted on a bedspring on top of the mask. Sometime since 1962 another artist has added ears to the mask. Seaweed himself attached ears in later years to some of his earlier masks.

Sometime around 1943 Willie delivered a beautiful pair of masks to Kingcome Inlet (Fig. 4.16). Joe Seaweed identified the raven mask of the pair as his own work. He was then over thirty years old and had been carving with his father for years. Working together, using the same templates, the work is understandably indistinguishable, and yet Joe's masks are not copies of his father's. The two masks are probably unsurpassed for cleanness of line and form. Joe worked on many commissions jointly with his father. The two were hired in 1951 to carve four large eagle figures (Fig. 4.17), now in the Provincial Museum in Victoria, as a memorial to three brothers who were lost at sea near

FIG. 4.16   Willie Seaweed with Unfinished Masks, Early 1940s. The mask supported by Willie's left hand is a raven mask and the work of his son Joe. The masks are now in the University of British Columbia Museum, A 6121 and A 6120. (Photograph courtesy of Mrs. Lucy Brown.)

FIG. 4.17   Eagle Memorial Figures Made by Willie and Joe, 1951. (Provincial Museum of British Columbia.)

Alert Bay in December, 1951. They collaborated on several sets of face masks for the *atlákim* and *gitakhanís* dances. Four of the latter are now in the Burke Museum, University of Washington (Holm 1972*b*, p. 37). Two of these are by Willie (Fig. 4.18) and two by Joe. When not working directly with his father, Joe Seaweed produced more individualized work. He is still engaged in carving both for Indian use and the collector market (Holm 1972*b*, p. 9). It will be interesting to watch the continuing development of his style.

In 1943 Mungo Martin and Willie Seaweed collaborated on a set of *hámatsa* masks for Peter Smith, a chief of the Tláwitsis band at Turnour Island. The two by Seaweed are stylistically distinguishable from the mask by Martin. They were made in a hurry and show some lack of finish.

A particularly fine *hámatsa* mask from 1943 illustrates the first use by Seaweed of curled ears (Fig. 4.19). Seaweed told the owner that while working on the mask he dreamed that he should add the ears. Some very early *hámatsa* masks had similar appendages, which he may have seen in his youth (Boas 1897, Plate 30, Fig. 1).

FIG. 4.18
Gitakhanís Mask, 1930s.
Actual size eleven inches;
Burke Memorial Museum of
the University of Washington,
25.0–316.

FIG. 4.19   A *Hókhokw* Mask Illustrating the Use of Curled Ears, 1943. Actual size sixty-four inches; Private Indian Collection, Kingcome Inlet, British Columbia.

FIG. 4.20   Crooked-Beak Mask, 1940s. Actual size thirty-three inches; Holm Collection.

A mask of the mid-1940s from my own collection shows the same strongly curved eyebrows and sockets, compass- and template-drawn circles, a completely typical Seaweed construction (Fig. 4.20). The ears of the crooked-beak mask have been enlarged and modified in proportion to bring them into scale with the mask, typical of the constant search for perfection which Seaweed brought to his work. This mask also mounts a skull, again on a bedspring, which refers to the man-eating character of the *hámatsa*. Many very early *hámatsa* masks were hung with wooden skulls, but the spring idea seems to have been Seaweed's. It gives dramatic movement to the skull in the firelight of the dance house, but the difficulty of managing the fifteen-pound mask is compounded for the dancer by the sudden shifts of balance. The pronounced flair of the cheeks in many late Seaweed crooked-beak masks recalls a similar feature on an old mask made for Seaweed's father-in-law by a carver named Hayógwis and now in the Burke Museum (Holm 1972a, p. 16).

Copper teeth mark a mask of the late 1940s which returns to an earlier feature, the thin plywood crest over the eyebrows (Fig. 4.21). When asked about its meaning, Willie Seaweed laughingly replied, *"Tlákukw boóhla"* (imitation of red cedar bark)! Since there is plenty of genuine cedar bark on this and other masks with the same feature, I'm inclined to view the comment as facetious, although it does resemble the folded and cleated edge bark which it replaces.

Around 1950 Seaweed made a flamboyant mask that dramatically emphasizes the comments made by Mungo Martin, Tom Hunt, and others, that masks were plain in the old days but became progressively more elaborate in later times (Fig. 4.22). The hooks above and below the jaws have been greatly exaggerated, but the basic structure of the mask remains typical. This mask is still used by its Indian owner.

Perhaps the last *hámatsa* mask to be made by Willie Seaweed is now in the Museum of Anthropology of the University of British Columbia (Fig. 4.23). It was made for Tom Hunt and is uniquely documented by a photograph taken August 7, 1954, of the mask under construction and its maker (Fig. 4.24). The great control and precise organization of planes characteristic of Seaweed's work are evident in the unpainted mask. Two compass centers are clearly visible in the original slide from which the print was made, showing that the eccentricity of the hole in the curving beak was organized in typical Seaweed

FIG. 4.21   Crooked-Beak Mask, 1940s. Actual size twenty-seven inches; University of British Columbia Museum, A 3537.

FIG. 4.22   Crooked-Beak Mask, Circa 1950. Actual size thirty-six inches; Private Indian Collection, Kingcome Inlet, British Columbia.

FIG. 4.23   Crooked-Beak Mask, 1954. Actual size forty-one inches; University of British Columbia Museum, A 8377.

fashion. In this mask with its late-style curling ears and massive beaks are over eighty circles or arcs of circles.

CHARACTERISTICS OF SEAWEED'S ART

An examination of other kinds of work from Seaweed's hand shows the same characteristics seen in the *hámatsa* masks. A great sense of mass, emphasized by skillful control of planes, is a feature of all his sculpture (Fig. 4.25). The *hámatsa* masks exemplify this as well as any other of his works, but the effect is often lost by their being almost invariably illustrated in flat-lighted profile. The same precise, careful organization of planes is reflected in his painting (Fig. 4.26; Orbit Films 1951b). In all his works one can see the emphasis given straight lines, arcs of circles, and the clear-cut angularity of ovoids and U forms (Figs. 4.27, 4.28). Seaweed seemed always to be aware of the total area or volume he dealt with and worked for the complete integration of every part with the whole. A conscious striving to make every design

FIG. 4.24   Willie Seaweed Working on the Crooked-Beak Mask of 1954. (Photograph by Sidney Gerber.)

element take its proper place in the total scheme is suggested in almost every piece. The designs were intellectualized, evidenced as much by their precise visual balance, careful juxtaposition of smooth curve and angle, and the byplay of intricate detail and broad unbroken mass as by his ingenious use of compass and template (Fig. 4.29). The structure of a mask or painting impresses the observer who takes a Seaweed piece in hand.

The wonder is how the results of this drive for perfection avoid the stiffness and sterility usually associated with such an approach. Perhaps such perfection of design *is* detrimental to the dramatic impact of some masks. But a mask mounted on the museum wall, no matter how skillfully lighted and displayed, is a very different thing from the same mask in the firelight of the big house, reflecting, then jerking into deep shadow, cedar bark swinging heavily around the nearly hid-

FIG. 4.25
Killer-Whale-in-Sun Mask, Pre-1920. Actual size thirty inches; Burke Memorial Museum of the University of Washington, 25.0–227.

FIG. 4.26   Detail of *Sisiuhl* on Small Painted Plaque. (Private Indian Collection, Alert Bay, British Columbia.)

1943   Late 1940's   1954

FIG. 4.27   Ears from *Hámatsa* Masks

FIG. 4.28   Angular Ovoids and ∪ Forms

FIG. 4.29   Wolf Mask, 1930s. Actual size twenty inches; James Sewid Collection.

den dancer, then shuddering and the long beak snapping in response to the song and the time beating of the singers (Fig. 4.15). The evocative powers of Kwakiutl masks have been denigrated because of their fantastic form by writers who have never seen them in their own setting. They seem unrelated to "real" monsters, I suppose. Willie Seaweed fully understood what the atmosphere, physical and psychological, of the winter ceremonial did for a mask on a skillful dancer.

What sort of man produced these many marvels of craftsmanship? He was a small man physically. In company with other artists of his tribe he was an accomplished dancer, a song leader, composer, actor, comedian. His humor and skill at comedy were well known and appreciated. I remember the near hysterics of the Indian audience at his portrayal of the *noóhlmahl*, the fool dancer, sensitive about his nose, or his officious Indian doctor demanding (in his native language) a knife from a visiting anthropologist so he could operate on a *toógwid* dancer who was making strange noises! The bumble bee masks (Fig. 4.30), although paraphernalia of a prized family prerogative, reflect this humor as do many other of his masks (Hawthorn 1967, Fig. 117). He was a very warm and friendly person (Fig. 4.31). I was privileged to know him, if only intermittently and during the last few years of his life. Willie Seaweed died in the spring of 1967, at the age of ninety-four. His work spanned a time of great change, changing itself but never losing its essential character or its meaningful relationship to Kwakiutl culture.[1]

FIG. 4.30   Bumble Bee Masks for Children. Actual size between eight and nine inches; Private Indian Collection, Alert Bay, British Columbia.

FIG. 4.31   Willie Seaweed Among Singers at a Winter Dance, Fort Rupert, British Columbia, 1963

1 In addition to the many other Kwakiutl who have freely given information on the subject of this paper I would like to especially acknowledge the help of the late Willie Seaweed, the late Mungo Martin, Joe Seaweed, Charlie George, Jr., James Sewid, Charles G. Walkus, William Scow, the late Henry Speck, Peter Smith, Philip

REFERENCES CITED

Boas, F.

1897   *Social Organization and Secret Societies of Kwakiutl Indians.* Report, 1895. Washington, D.C.: U.S. National Museum. Pp. 313–738.

1921   *Ethnology of the Kwakiutl.* Bureau of American Ethnology Annual Report, 1913–1914. Vol. 35. Washington, D.C.: Smithsonian Institution. Pt. 1, pp. 41–794, Pt. 2, pp. 795–1481.

Curtis, E. S.

1915   *The North American Indian.* Vol. 10. Norwood: Plimpton Press.

Hawthorn, A.

1967   *Art of the Kwakiutl Indians.* Seattle: University of Washington Press.

Holm, B.

1965   *Northwest Coast Indian Art: An Analysis of Form.* Seattle: University of Washington Press.

1972a   *Crooked Beak of Heaven.* Seattle: University of Washington Press.

1972b   Heraldic Carving Styles of the Northwest Coast. In *American Indian Art: Form and Tradition.* Minneapolis: Walker Art Center and Minneapolis Institute of Art.

Newcombe, C. F.

1914   Unpublished Field Notes. Provincial Archives, Victoria.

Orbit Films

1951a   *Dances of the Kwakiutl.* Seattle: Orbit Films.

1951b   *Blunden Harbour.* Seattle: Orbit Films.

Paul, Tom Hunt, and James Dawson. Audrey Hawthorn has made the magnificent collection of Kwakiutl material at the University of British Columbia Museum of Anthropology available for study and Peter Macnair of the British Columbia Provincial Museum has done likewise. The Sidney Gerber Collection in the Thomas Burke Memorial Washington State Museum of the University of Washington contains a number of Seaweed pieces and has been very useful.

Chapter 5

Form and Meaning in Some Teotihuacan Mural Paintings: Architectural Contexts

Arthur G. Miller

ABSTRACT   An evaluation of the function of Teotihuacan buildings is one of the most problematical aspects of urban study at that immense classic-period metropolis. Significant progress has been made toward understanding the architectural functions at Teotihuacan largely through the use of conventional archaeological data and of ethnographical analogies.

The argument here is that a contextual study of mural painting at Teotihuacan may help clarify the ancient uses of Teotihuacan buildings and can serve to complement interpretations made by conventional archaeological data. Unlike large sculpture at Teotihuacan and elsewhere in Mesoamerica during the classic period, mural painting could not be moved from its original location by ancient peoples. The murals are, therefore, closely related to the original function of the buildings and rooms at Teotihuacan with which they are associated.

A comparison of the motifs and forms of the murals in certain building complexes at Teotihuacan reveals a rich visual language employing a human-animal symbolism, in which the human-jaguar component predominates. The orientation of the man-animal motifs with respect to entrances, patios, and inner rooms probably locates areas in which patterns of human activities occurred. The form of the murals suggests the quality of the activity: sharp, angular forms perhaps relate to aggressive action; curvilinear ones may connote pacific patterns of behavior. The human-animal motifs, and in particular the man-jaguar ones, consistently appear on the east side of Teotihuacan patios. The location suggests that activities ideologically tied to the jaguar symbolism occurred in these surroundings.

One of the most important problems in dealing with the architecture of ancient Teotihuacan is that of discovering the original purposes of the buildings and building complexes found there. It is an obviously fundamental question which is greatly complicated by the fact that ancient Teotihuacan was one of the largest preindustrial cities in the Western Hemisphere with a history of more than five hundred years. Teotihuacan was a city of enormous size and complexity. It was more extensive than imperial Rome and had a population that was one fifth of Rome's. At its apogee during the Xolalpan phase, the city had 75,000 to 200,000 inhabitants (Millon 1967a, 1970a).

Certain broad understandings about urban Teotihuacan architecture have been common for some time, and other valuable ones have been surfacing as a result of the important work of the Teotihuacan mapping project under the direction of René Millon. Most investigators seem to agree that the structures forming the center of the city were largely given over to official urban functions, at least for part of the city's history. This urban center has long been called the ceremonial zone of Teotihuacan (Map 5.1). It begins at the north-central sector of the city and extends from the Pyramid and Plaza of the Moon along the Street of the Dead. It includes the major structures on the east and west sides of that great north-south axis of the city, most notable of which are the well-known Pyramid of the Sun and its contiguous structures and the Street of the Dead macrocomplex (as defined by Wallrath 1967, pp. 113–22). The southern limit of the ceremonial zone is at two immense open areas on either side of the Street of the Dead called the Ciudadela on the east and the Great Compound on the west. It is surely too simplistic to refer to this ceremonial zone of Teotihuacan as a section of the city reserved exclusively for religious activity. In fact, Millon has suggested other functions as well for the buildings in this area, and his observations are supported by archaeological data he has collected during the past decade of work at the site (1970a). Among the most interesting information to come out of detailed investigations of this central area is the definition of obsidian workshop areas within it by Michael Spence (1967). The location of these workshops corroborates Millon's hypothesis that economic activities in conjunction with religious and administrative ones occurred in this central zone (1967b).

Since the well-known excavations of Sigvald Linné at Tlamimi-

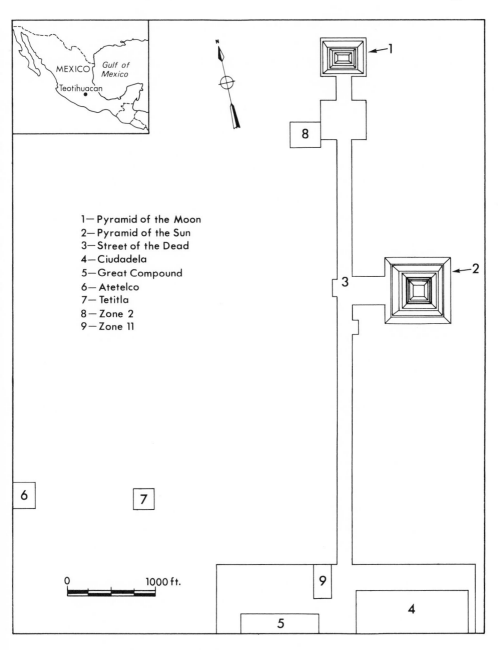

1—Pyramid of the Moon
2—Pyramid of the Sun
3—Street of the Dead
4—Ciudadela
5—Great Compound
6—Atetelco
7—Tetitla
8—Zone 2
9—Zone 11

MAP 5.1   Teotihuacan and the Location of the Mural Complexes

lolpa (1934) and Xolalpan (1942), a type of architectural complex
called the outlying-elite-residential complex has been known. Architectural complexes similar to that of Xolalpan have been excavated
from other outlying sectors of the city. I am referring to the sites of
Tetitla, Atetelco, Zacuala, and Yayahuala in the western sector of the
city. Some of these "one story apartment buildings" (Millon 1970a)
have been clearly associated with domestic activities, such as cooking
and food storage.

An understanding of the functions of the architecture at Teotihuacan has been based upon primarily archaeological data. Obvious
suggestions of function come from architectural forms, such as temple
platforms and large room complexes. The artifactual and ceramic associations of a structure or group of structures can suggest the period
of construction and the domestic or ritual activity, as well as the kind
of people living in an area of buildings or the inhabitants' ethnic
background. An example of the latter use of technological data is the
recent isolation of the so-called Oaxaca Barrio in the western sector of
the city by members of the Teotihuacan mapping project. In a delim-
ited area Monte Albán ceramic types were found in surface collections
and in structural fill; a Monte Albán IIIA urn and a Zapotec stele were
also found associated with structures in the Oaxaca Barrio, all suggesting that the inhabitants of this area were Oaxacaños living together in a neighborhood which was a distinct part of the immense
metropolis of Teotihuacan (Millon 1970a).

An understanding of the functions of the architecture at Teotihuacan has been based also on ethnohistorical analogy. William
Sanders (1967) has compared his Teotihuacan Valley Maquixco excavation TC8 with the documented Aztec calpulli and has suggested that
the social organization of Teotihuacan times may also have been
similar to that of the Aztec calpulli. Sanders notes that TC8 is similar,
although smaller and simpler, to Yayahuala, located within the borders of the city proper (1967, p. 130).

Given the magnitude of the problems of interpreting the function of Teotihuacan architecture, it seems that various methods for
extracting information from the archaeological data should be employed. The archaeological data I would like to examine briefly here
are among the best known from the city: the mural paintings. In fact,
when one thinks of Teotihuacan, it is difficult not to call to mind the

splendid mural painting that is known to come from the site. And, of course, Teotihuacan mural painting is most intimately associated with that distinctive material form under investigation: architecture.

THE MURALS AND THEIR IMPLICATIONS

A distinctive characteristic of mural painting is that the information it contains is not primarily technological. Wall painting is, of course, made by technological processes, but its most valuable historical information lies in two spheres: chronology and iconography. The chronological implications of the body of mural painting from Teotihuacan are an important part of understanding the architectural sequence of the city. The murals are inextricably associated with the architectural forms they adorn and are extremely valuable as a means of dating the structures. Whereas free-standing monumental sculpture of Teotihuacan may have been moved any number of times by successive populations during the city's history of more than half a millennium, the wall painting of Teotihuacan was never moved from its original position during pre-Columbian times. If one can date by archaeological association the building upon which a mural is found, then it is possible to date the mural painting. And, conversely, if one can date the mural painting by a kind of stylistic seriation, then the mural serves as a means to fix or corroborate the date of the building upon which it is found.[1] Such chronological interrelating of architecture and mural painting is yet to be done, primarily because of the incompleteness of the archaeological record of Teotihuacan architecture and also because of the difficulties of chronologically ordering a mural corpus consisting of paintings of such varied style and subject matter.[2]

While an index of time is one use of the complex mural compositions of Teotihuacan, there exists the other historical use of these

1   There is always the possibility of the repainting of an old painted wall. But even a later repainted mural reflects the time when a structure was in use.

The ideas of the present chapter were first presented by Dr. Miller at the 1969 meeting of the American Anthropological Association. The chapter was essentially completed in 1970 (editor's note).

2   For an attempt at chronological ordering of Teotihuacan murals on the basis of stylistic seriation and archaeological associations, see Clara S. H. Millon's unpublished work of 1966. A published resumé of Teotihuacan mural chronology can be found in R. Millon, 1967b.

paintings: Teotihuacan mural paintings can be studied as iconography, as objects which carry meaning. Because they are usually more complex in form than architecture, sculpture, and artifacts, these paintings can bear more information about the period in which they were painted. Although it is probable that some of the Teotihuacan wall painting was simply decorative, most of it was surely expressive of certain specific ideas and beliefs.

Like other aspects of the investigation of Teotihuacan prehistory (and unlike the study of Old World iconography, which is based wholly or in part upon information in written sources), the study of meaning in Teotihuacan mural painting must look to nontextual evidence to attempt to reconstruct the web of ideas that gave impetus to the extensive mural designs at Teotihuacan. For example, it would seem logical that mural designs in what have been interpreted as large, elite residence complexes might have lineage signs as their subject matter; paintings on the walls of possible administrative centers might contain information about official function and status; and paintings on the walls of religious structures might refer to ancient Teotihuacan ritual practices and beliefs. As one would expect, it does not seem to work out so neatly and so simply because urban Teotihuacan is a site of enormous size and complexity. Much of both the mural record and the archaeological record is incomplete or so recent that it has not yet been published. Nevertheless, I think that some hypothetical observations about some Teotihuacan murals and their architectural functions can now be made.

The observations that I will make, in which mural iconography is an indication of architectural function, are tentative and suffer from inadequate association with all-important archaeological data. Nevertheless, I suggest the following cases as illustrative of an approach to understanding the iconography of the murals and, subsequently, the functions implicit in the architecture associated with the murals. First I shall discuss the iconography of the White Patio of Atetelco in careful detail because it is the most complete architectural complex bearing painting at Teotihuacan. Subsequently, I shall discuss the iconography and architectural function of the Principal Patio at Tetitla, a South Complex of Zone 2 mural fragment, followed by the Patio of the Jaguars, Room 5 of Zone 11, and finally Room 10 of Zone 2.

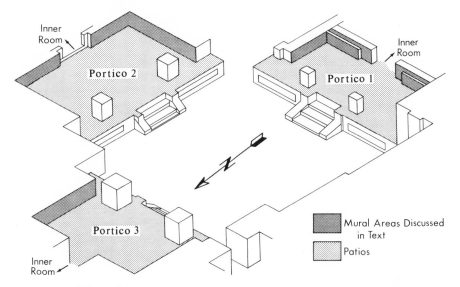

FIG. 5.1   The White Patio at Atetelco with Porticoes 1, 2, and 3

THE WHITE PATIO OF ATETELCO

The White Patio of Atetelco (Fig. 5.1) is part of an early building level of the room complex at Atetelco, located about 1.5 kilometers southwest of the Pyramid of the Sun; it is the westernmost architectural complex with mural painting yet discovered at Teotihuacan. It is located in an area of at least three one-story apartment blocks, each fifty-seven square meters in size, all of which bear mural paintings: Tetitla, Zacuala, and Yayahuala. Three one-room structures, each with a front portico, face an open patio on the patio's north, south, and east sides. The reconstruction of the mural designs of the porticoes, begun in the 1950s and continuing to the present day, is largely the result of careful work by Agustín Villagra. Most of the upper walls of the three porticoes are reconstructed on the basis of mural fragments found lying on the floors of the porticoes and patio. Although there are some aspects of these mural reconstructions which are questionable, in general the lower-wall paintings are genuine, and the reliability of the reconstruction of the upper walls is good (Villagra 1951a, 1951b, 1952).

No previous interpretation of the White Patio murals has attempted to examine the paintings as they relate to their architectural setting and to each other. Typical of previous interpretations is the explanation that the paintings of Portico 2 showing a netted jaguar and conch-bearing figures refer to the Aztec cult of Tlaloc (Villagra 1951a, pp. 161–62; Von Winning 1968, pp. 31–33); Burland, on the other hand, relates the paintings to the Aztec god Tepeyolloti (1954, p. 8).

In the following analysis Portico 1 refers to the portico of the south structure of the White Patio, Portico 2 refers to the portico of the east structure, and Portico 3 refers to the portico of the north structure.[3] The descriptions of the paintings of Porticoes 1, 2, and 3 will fall into two categories: motifs and form. By motifs I mean the recognizable things represented, such as coyote, man, hair, and atlatl darts, as well as things which are elements of paraphernalia and design but which are not yet recognizable to the writer, such as details of costume decoration and border decorations. By form I mean something less easily defined yet nevertheless patently obvious to the observer, *i.e.*, the general visual quality of the composition as being angular and hard or curvilinear and soft. The dominant motif of Portico 1 is seen as coyote and coyote parts. Portico 2 is more complex, being composed of jaguar, coyote, conch, and serpent motifs. Portico 3 consists primarily of bird motifs.

I hope to demonstrate that Porticoes 1 and 3 are similar in that they are composed of rigid and harsh motifs which reinforce the aggressive content of the compositions. Thus, the coyote and its impersonator in Portico 1 are related to hunting or warrior imagery in Portico 3; both the motifs and the forms contribute to a general meaning of violence and aggression. Portico 2 is distinct in being composed of curvilinear and soft forms which contribute to the nonaggressive, indeed harmonious, groupings of such naturally opposite animals as coyote and jaguar (representing highlands and lowlands?).

---

3   The paintings of the two club-footed figures located in the northwest corner of the White Patio are not included in the analysis. The chronological relationship of the figures to the paintings of the porticoes is not clear to me, and I have been unable to gain access to the archaeological report of that excavation. The mural decorations of the inner room of each portico will also not be discussed since they are simple and appear to be decorative; they are composed of a single band of spiked scrolls around the base of the walls. Villagra (1956–57, p. 13) suggests that these spiked scrolls represent waves of water and compares them to similar motifs falling from the hands of the Tlaloc of Tepantitla.

PORTICO 1 OF THE WHITE PATIO

The largely restored wall paintings of the south portico off the White Patio at Atetelco (Figs. 5.2–5.4) have a lower dado of motifs which appear to be coyotelike creatures. These coyotes, one following the other, are depicted revealing their bared teeth and very large claws. From their open mouths with protruding tongues emerge speech scrolls. The animals' backs, tails, and legs are edged with representations of spaced-out spalls of bone or flint or obsidian—hard, cutting substances—the opposite of feathers. Above these animals, walking in the same direction (surrounded by small objects shaped like question marks) and dressed in the skins of the animals painted below them, are small figures enframed in diamond-shaped net designs which create a wallpaper effect. These ornately attired small figures wearing coyote skins (Fig. 5.4) carry in one of their hands, held close to their bodies at waist level, bunches of what appear to be pointed obsidian atlatl darts. In their other hands, extended out in front of their coyote masks, the figures hold feathered atlatls which serve to propel the darts. Speech scrolls issuing from the mouths (again with protruding tongues) of these upper-wall coyote-men are similar to those emerging from the animals below, except that here each figure is shown with two scrolls, and the second scroll is reversed, as it issues downward and then curls upward. The south-wall animals and figures face the doorway; the east- and west-wall animals and figures face out toward the patio (Figs. 5.2, 5.3).

The borders of the Portico 1 paintings are most interesting, and their form is suggestive of meaning. The lower wall of Portico 1 is enframed on top and on either side of the south dadoes and on the top and on one side of the east and west dadoes (Figs. 5.2, 5.3). These dado borders consist of two parallel bands separated by a row of small bullet-shaped objects, which may represent the top of a basket weave pattern, and three thin horizontal lines. Below these lines is a scallop-edged band of herringbonelike lines similar to and presumably representing the lines which indicate the hair of the coyotes below. Superimposed on top of the coyote hair are what appear to be bordered, multipointed spearheads. Above the central row of bulletlike objects is a band of imbricated rectangles which reappear in circular arrangement as the

FIG. 5.2   East Wall of Portico 1 of the White Patio

FIG. 5.3   Southwest Corner of Portico 1

nodes of the net in the upper register. Three large, rectangular medallions, rounded on the corners, appear evenly and symmetrically spaced on the border. These medallions enclose diagonal bands similar to those inserted in the midsections of the two coyotes.[4] Surrounding the medallions are two bands of coyote fur, scalloped on the outside edges.

The upper wall, about three times the height of the dado below it, is also enframed on the top and on either side of the south wall and on the top and on one side of the east and west walls (Figs. 5.2, 5.3).

4 See Villagra (1956–57, pp. 9–10) for a discussion of the religious meaning of these medallions based on comparisons of similar forms in the codices.

These upper-wall borders are decorated on the outermost edge with a row of the base parts of the spearlike objects found in the dado borders below. The next band is a row of small bullet-shaped objects like those in the dado borders. Inside there is a narrow band edged on both sides by two parallel lines and a stitch design. Superimposed upon this band is a spaced-out row of shells or possibly seeds. The innermost band is slightly wider than the total width of the three narrow ones just described. It is composed of long, rounded, imbricated scale or feather forms, each decorated by a double center line and a row of inward pointing saw-toothed lines. Interrupting those four bands which form the upper-wall borders are undulating lines marking off areas for the evenly spaced medallions formed of concentric, saw-toothed, rounded-diamond shapes. On one or both sides of each circle is a hand clutching what looks like a plant stalk. Around the outside edge of the medallions are fan-shaped tassels.

The larger area of the upper wall is crisscrossed by frames separating each of the upper-wall figures (Fig. 5.4). These thick, netlike, diamond-shaped frames are formed by what appear to be herringbone lines similar to and presumably representing the herringbone lines forming the hair of the coyotes below and part of its border as de-

FIG. 5.4   Detail of an Upper South-Wall Figure from Portico 1

scribed above. Superimposed on these coyote-skin borders are the forms shaped like question marks, which also appear surrounding the upper-wall figures within the net. Also on this diamond border is the fan-shaped tassel which recurs on the upper borders. These hook and fan motifs probably represent the leading wing edges and tail of a bird. The most notable visual characteristic of these net borders is the motif at each node of the net: a coyote head hangs downward from a circular medallion formed by an imbrication of the rigid, bordered rectangles which appear in a linear arrangement in the lower register borders.

Although the netlike, diamond-shaped frames of the upper wall and the upper and lower borders differ from each other in detail, all are similarly formed by angular, hard-edged shapes which are rigid and sharp in appearance. Even the scallop-edged coyote skins of the borders do not suggest pleasant tactile sensations. This visual characterization is not unlike the rigid and sharp quality of the claws and obsidian edges of the lower-register animals and the darts and atlatls carried by the figures of the upper register. The entire painting, then, is largely composed of sharp, rigid forms. The weapons of hunting or warfare carried by the upper-register figures may show part of the figures' function, *i.e.*, as hunters or warriors. The hunter or warrior status of the figures above may have been symbolized by those prowling coyotes with bared teeth and extended claws in the lower register who are also edged on their backs, tails, and limbs with representations of hard spalls of bone, flint, or obsidian. The configuration of weapon-carrying figures associated with prowling coyotes is outlined by borders whose form is as sharp and angular as the motifs they enframe and whose details refer to the coyotes and the costumes of both the somewhat anthropomorphic coyotes and the animalistic men shown above.

PORTICO 2 OF THE WHITE PATIO

The walls of the portico associated with the eastern building of the White Patio (Figs. 5.5–5.7) have a far more rounded formal appearance than do the murals belonging to Portico 1 discussed above. This soft, round quality is accentuated by the sweeping interlace nets of the upper register and the intertwined serpent forms and animal legs of the lower- and upper-wall borders. The animals depicted on the da-

FIG. 5.5   Reconstruction Drawing of the East Wall of Portico 2 of the White Patio. (After Villagra 1951a, Fig. 12.)

FIG. 5.6   Southeast Corner of Portico 2

does of the portico are in pairs, the north and south dadoes showing a netted jaguar followed by a coyote facing the patio (Fig. 5.6). In each of the two east dadoes flanking the door leading into the inner room, the order and direction of the animals are reversed; here a coyote is followed by a netted jaguar facing the door (Fig. 5.5). As in Portico 1, these lower-wall animals walk in the same direction as the small repeated figures on the wall above them.

FIG. 5.7 Detail of an Upper East-Wall Figure from Portico 2

The netted jaguars wear feather headdresses and are edged with representations of spaced-out spalls of bone, flint, or obsidian as in the coyotes of Portico 1. The coyotes are very much like those of Portico 1, except that underneath the coyote's curling speech scroll there is a trilobe motif from which drops emerge. The netted jaguars have this speech scroll and trilobe as well. Besides the differences of netting and herringbone hair, the most distinctive physical characteristics which distinguish these two animals from one another are the shapes of their mouths and their teeth. The netted jaguar is shown with the blunt mouth and large, curving fangs of a feline, whereas the coyote is shown with the long mouth and characteristic straight tooth of the canine. Emerging directly from the mouth of each netted jaguar is a bifurcated serpent's tongue. On the east walls (Fig. 5.5) the neck of the netted jaguar is longer and his body shorter than that of the coyote. While the netted jaguar's tail is edged on its upper side, it is the lower side of the coyote's tail which is edged. The coyote is further distinguished from the jaguar in having finlike forms projecting back from the joints of its legs and its jaw.

Above these complicated animals and walking in the same direction are small figures enframed in the interlace net design giving a wallpaper effect as in Portico 1. Each figure (Fig. 5.7) has superimposed upon it, or possibly held in one hand, a conch shell which issues speech scrolls and droplets from either end. These richly adorned figures with bird headdresses also have speech scrolls, and they hold in the other hand an ornate staff similar to one held by a figure in a mural from Zone 11 of the Instituto Nacional de Antropología e Historia (INAH) Proyecto Teotihuacán excavations. Each small profile figure wears directly beneath his nose a horizontal bar with curled ends from which are suspended three jaguar fangs.

The lower-wall dado (Figs. 5.5, 5.6) is bordered on the top and sides by an interlace of two serpentine forms; one is netted; the other is decorated with an inner scalloped edge and herringbone hair or coyote skin, similar to that of the upper-wall diamond frames in Portico 1. Upon the coyote skin are evenly spaced maguey spines. The serpent interlace begins on one side with a downward-pointing coyote head with protruding tongue and ends on the other with a coyote tail. Directly beneath the coyote head is a circle connected to an upside-down trilobe. Six drops emerge from this form. There are evenly spaced, netted jaguar legs superimposed on this interlace of netted and coyote-skin serpentine motifs.

The upper-wall borders also are formed of two distinct serpentine motifs, one of which (the scalloped coyote skin with superimposed maguey spines) is similar to the lower dado border. The other of the two serpentine elements is decorated with sections of obsidian knife blades which appear in Portico 3. Instead of the evenly spaced, netted jaguar legs, coyote legs are superimposed on this upper-register serpentine interlace. Alternating with these coyote legs are goggle-eyed faces wearing the curled horizontal bar and fangs of the conch-bearing profile figures. Arranged on either side of each goggle-eyed figure are two small coyote tails. The most distinctive features of these frontal images are their bifurcated serpent tongues, which are similar to those of the netted jaguars of the lower wall. Directly outside the serpentine border is a row of seedlike motifs which emit drops in the lowest section of the vertical border. The next outer border is a row of bullet-shaped motifs and the familiar spalls of bone, flint, or obsidian, which are visible in Portico 1 and which here edge sections of the lower-wall animals and the upper-wall figures and their interlace frames.

In general, the upper-wall borders are predominantly curvilinear in form, as is evident in the sinuous, serpentine, dog-headed creatures forming the border surrounding the door. The hard, angular forms, such as the spalls of obsidian or bone or flint, serve to accentuate the predominantly curvilinear quality of the borders by the artistic device of visual juxtaposition.

The Portico 2 mural is a splendid complication of design which closely interrelates the form of the animals, conch-bearing figures, and their borders. As in Portico 1, human figures appear above animals, but not dressed in the skins of the animals. It is not clear what the upper-wall figures have to do with the alternating coyotes and jaguars depicted below them. Perhaps the ornate staff each holds in out-stretched hands is a symbol for whatever the coyote signifies. There are, however, two costume elements which closely relate the upper-wall figures to at least one of the prowling animals below: the jaguar fangs and the conch shell. In the Patio of the Jaguars in Zone 2 of Teotihuacan, the conch shell is also associated with the jaguar. Furst (1968, p. 166) discusses the conch and jaguar association.

PORTICO 3 OF THE WHITE PATIO

The Portico 3 walls (Figs. 5.8–5.10) differ most distinctly from those of the other two porticoes in that the upper east and west walls are different from the north wall and in that animal motifs are not figured prominently. In form, Portico 3 shares, particularly in the upper-wall netting, the hard angular design of Portico 1 directly across from it.

The dadoes of Portico 3 depict enframed masked and goggle-eyed profile figures, one on each dado of the north wall facing the door and two on the east and west dadoes facing the patio. These figures are similar to the Portico 1 coyote-men in that they hold bunches of atlatl darts in one hand. In the other hand in front of their mouths, instead of the atlatl of Portico 1, each holds an obsidian knife blade piercing an object similar to the one found at the base of the lower dadoes of Portico 2. As in the Portico 1 figures, but differing in that they curve in the same direction, two speech scrolls curl from each figure's open

FIG. 5.8   Northeast Corner of Portico 3 of the White Patio

mouth. The figures are dressed in a complex of sharp and clawlike forms and obsidian knife blades, especially in the headdress. Surrounding the figures are wild arrays of "the Arthur Murray diagram" dance steps.

Above these profile figures of the lower-wall dado on the east and west walls and enframed in diamond-shaped net designs, there are similar goggle-eyed figures, each clutching atlatl darts in one hand and a bludgeon in the other (Fig. 5.10). Each figure confronts an eagle which appears to be stunned or dead and dripping blood, possibly as the result of a blow from the bludgeon. The small figures occupying the diamond-shaped net designs of the upper north wall (Fig. 5.8)

FIG. 5.9   East Wall of Portico 3

wear eagle costumes and hold atlatl darts in one hand and an atlatl in
the other in the manner of the coyote-men of the upper walls of Portico
1. Are the men of the north wall who wear the costume of the eagle
being bludgeoned on the east and west walls? As in Portico 1, the nodes
of the upper-wall nets are cartouches formed by circular imbrications
of bordered, rounded rectangles. Inside each of these cartouches is the
frontal view of an upside-down bird head. Frequently in Mesoamerican iconography, upside-downness signifies conquest or death.

    The lower-wall dadoes are enframed by a narrow border of circles

FIG. 5.10   Detail of an Upper West-Wall Figure from Portico 3

and groups of parallel lines. Inside the wider outer border there is a band of intertwining serpentine forms similar to those of Portico 2 with spearpoints and what appear to be maguey spines superimposed upon them. Evenly spaced in the dado borders are frontal, masked, goggle-eyed figures in the upper borders of Portico 2. The familiar row-of-bullets motif and a row of obsidian knife blades form the remainder of the dado border.

The upper-wall borders are enframed by a feather motif edged first by a row of circles, then by a row of triangles capped by the familiar spalls of bone, flint, or obsidian. Superimposed upon this border are evenly spaced, rounded rectangular medallions formed by a narrow border of a scaly or feathered motif and shells. Enclosed within these medallions are feathered or scaly felines. The medallions alternate with large shell motifs similar to the large painted shells at Tetitla.

In general, the upper-wall borders of Portico 3 are predominantly angular in form, as is particularly evident in the row of cartouches, each formed by a circular imbrication of rigid, overlapping, bordered rectangles and obsidian knife blades, in the border surrounding the door (Fig. 5.8) and in the linear imbrication of the rigid edges of the feathered diamond-shaped net of the upper walls. The overall formal quality of Portico 3 is angular and harsh, as in Portico 1.

ANIMAL-MAN INTERRELATIONSHIPS
IN THE WHITE PATIO MURALS

The animal motifs of Portico 1 are primarily associated with the coyote, whereas the animal motifs of Portico 3 are primarily associated with birds. What may be bird motifs are represented on the coyote hair of the Portico 1 upper-wall netting. These are the leading wing edges and tail forms prominently visible in the birds of the Portico 3 end walls and in the bird costumes of the human impersonators of the upper register of the Portico 3 inner wall. The upper-wall coyote impersonators of Portico 1 are surrounded by hook motifs which may also refer to the leading wing edges of the birds and bird-men represented in Portico 3, directly across the patio.

Some of the animal motifs of Portico 2 are similar to those in the other two porticoes, for example, the coyote motif of Portico 1 and the bird motif in Portico 3. In Portico 2, however, the coyote bears fins at the joints of the legs as well as at the jaws and is associated with trilobe motifs and netted jaguars. A profile bird head along with wing scroll and tail feathers appears as part of the headdress of the upper-wall figures of Portico 2. Thus there are coyote, jaguar, and bird motifs represented in Portico 2.

However, Portico 2 is distinct by being replete with conch-shell imagery which is not evident in the other two porticoes. Serpent, jaguar, and coyote appear together in Portico 2, whereas in the other two they do not. The goggle-eyed faces of the upper border are a distinct condensation of jaguar, coyote, and serpentine motifs in the Portico 2 paintings; they have jaguar fangs, coyote tails, and serpents' bifurcated tongues. Except for the serpentine borders of the dadoes of Portico 3, the serpentine motifs of this east portico are not part of the north and south portico designs. The structure associated with the distinct Portico 2 murals is on the east side of the court and clearly has the dominant position in the three-structure complex.

As described above, the forms of the murals of the White Patio of Atetelco convey the visual impressions of hardness and softness. The hardness of the predominantly angular lines of Porticoes 1 and 3 and the softness of the predominantly curvilinear lines of Portico 2 imply juxtaposition. This richly expressive visual language of forms may suggest that the Portico 1 and 3 murals are concerned with some kind of aggression and the Portico 2 murals are concerned with its opposite. Exactly what these opposites are may never be known. It is clear, however, that the murals of Porticoes 1 and 3 are similar in form and that the Portico 2 murals are different in form and therefore set apart from the others.

The directional movement of the upper- and lower-wall figures of the three patios at Atetelco is suggestive of the function of the White Patio. The end-wall figures of Portico 1 face toward the patio, whereas the inner-wall figures face toward the doorway leading to the inner room. This directional arrangement of the portico walls is repeated in Porticoes 2 and 3, but is complicated by different designs on the end walls which face the patio. In Portico 1, the end-wall designs, both the upper and lower, are the same as those of the inner wall. In Portico 2, however, the order of the animals depicted on the dado is reversed from that of the inner-wall dadoes. In Portico 3, it is the upper end walls which differ from the inner walls, not in arrangement, but in kind; instead of the eagle-men of the inner walls, figures confront eagles, apparently clubbing them. This distinctness of direction in all three porticoes between the end walls relating to the patio and the inner walls relating to the inner room, plus the differences of motifs on the walls, probably indicates the activities performed in each of those areas. If this interpretation of the meaning of direction and motif is true, the Portico 1 depiction of activity for the inner room is the same as for the patio.

The Portico 2 depiction of activity for the inner room is indicated by a coyote leading a netted jaguar and by a coyote-headed serpent border enframing the door; the activity in the patio is indicated by a netted jaguar associated with a bifurcated serpent's tongue followed by a coyote. Thus, the inner-room directional indicators emphasize coyote in association with serpent, whereas the patio is indicated by jaguar in association with serpent. It may be that the coyote-serpent and its concomitant meaning signify the function of the inner room, while it is the netted jaguar-serpent and its associations which signify the function of the patio with relation to Portico 2.

The Portico 3 upper walls on the east and west sides, which show repeated confrontations between atlatl-bearing personages and birds, directionally relate to the patio. It is possible that this represents bird sacrifice which may have taken place on the patio. These paintings of Portico 3 may also have to do with the recording of conquest over some group of people symbolized by birds. The Portico 3 upper wall on the north side, repeatedly showing men dressed in bird costume, directionally relates to the inner room. It is possible that the donning of bird costume inside the chamber was part of the ritual of sacrifice which had been performed outside on the patio; or, the donning of bird costume represented a ritual act symbolizing one group seizing power over another.

While the above is largely guesswork, it is nevertheless very clear that there is a coherent interrelationship among the paintings of Porticoes 1, 2, and 3 and that the murals of the Atetelco White Patio porticoes depict rich and complex animal-man interrelationships in and between upper and lower registers. The complicated borders refer to the animal and human interrelationships by being composed of animal and man-made forms. In Portico 1 there is a coyote-bird-man re-

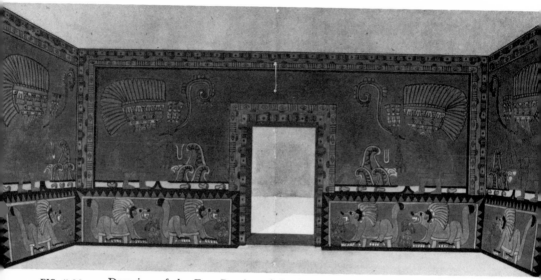

FIG. 5.11   Drawing of the East Portico of the Principal Patio at Tetitla. (After Séjourné 1966, Fig. 15.)

lationship. In Portico 2 the coyote-jaguar-bird-serpent complex is featured. Portico 3 depicts bird-man associations. Also, it is clear that these Atetelco portico paintings facing the patio and those facing the inner room probably refer to activities which were once performed in those areas.

THE PRINCIPAL PATIO AT TETITLA

The murals shown in Figure 5.11 were first discovered and published in 1963 by Laurette Séjourné as part of the decoration of Level 4 of the Principal Patio at Tetitla, a block of rooms, porticoes, corridors, and patios, measuring fifty-seven square meters, which has recently been described as one of several one-story apartment blocks in a western sector of the ancient city of Teotihuacan (Millon 1970a). Tetitla is located about one and a half kilometers southwest of the Pyramid of the Sun. Decorating the portico of the structure on the east side of the patio, the murals were described as depicting powerful yellow *"tigres"* with traits and colors of a violence unknown in Teotihuacan (Séjourné 1963, p. 47, Foto 39).

In a later work, Séjourné published a photograph of one of the animals being excavated (1966, Lam. XLII) and a poor colorplate of the head of one of the animals (1966, Lam. XLIX). She also published a line drawing of one of the animals with its dado border (1966, Fig. 152). In addition, she reproduced a colored reconstruction drawing of the entire painted portico on the east side of an open patio (1966, Fig. 15) showing "yellow jaguars" above which are depicted some individuals with arrows (1966, p. 263). There is no statement in her book on how the murals of the upper register were reconstructed. Direct examination of the murals at the site verifies the lower dado and its border as well as part of the border and footprints and profile feet of the upper wall.

Séjourné suggests that the *"tigre"* is kneeling in front of the temple door it flanks (1966, p. 262, Fig. 100). She sees the red and black triangles which enframe the *"tigres"* as signifying *"el rayo solar,"* which, she states, indicates the land of wisdom where differences are reconciled. She describes the animals as being inflamed and suspended on a seat of precious material, and she ascribes the trilobe forms emerging from the mouths of the animals as being cross sections of hearts which are incrusted with jade. This heart ejection scene symbolizes, she explains, the end of the nocturnal course of this *"sol de tierra"* (*i.e.*, *"el tigre"*) which signifies the conquest of gravity. The sources for Séjourné's interpretations of the Figure 5.11 murals are not given in the text of her book (1966), although her explanations are vaguely reminiscent of Aztec mythology.

The portico of the important east structure of the main patio at Tetitla is painted with designs depicting specific animal-man interrelationships, as are the portico murals of the White Patio at Atetelco. These paintings show a lower register of orange felines resting on what appear to be green metates, or low seats. In front of each of their open mouths two red trilobe motifs with green incrustations and dripping red drops arch toward the ground. Each of the inner dadoes of this portico flanking the door leading into the inner room bears two of these seated jaguars. The end-wall dadoes depict only one jaguar. Both dadoes are complemented by an upper register of large, partly destroyed figures whose costume elements suggest that they wear animal skins (Fig. 5.11). Unlike Portico 1 at Atetelco (Figs. 5.2–5.4), this Tetitla wall painting represents a single large figure above the lower dadoes. The large upper-wall figures each extend a handful of atlatl darts, much larger in size than could be actually used; the felines below possess exaggerated fangs and claws. The band of red and black triangles of the lower-register border and those of the felines' feather headdresses are repeated in the curious triple arrangement of what may be a convention for obsidian knife blades, a convention found at Atetelco (Figs. 5.8, 5.9) and in the South Complex mural painting discussed in this paper (Figs. 5.12, 5.13).

The upper-wall borders are all of the same red and orange design, which enframes the end walls' upper and outside borders and continues to the floor level, enclosing the dado as well. The disembodied half eyes shown alternating on two sides of the central orange band of the upper-wall borders are similar to the border and falling panel in Figures 5.16 and 5.17, discussed subsequently in this paper. If these alternating half eyes are a pictorial convention for water, as I have previously suggested (Miller 1969, pp. 110, 133), then Figure 5.11 exhibits a possible association of water and jaguar.

The restoration drawing shown in Figure 5.11 is unexplained and questionable and, therefore, does not merit the kind of careful description which suggests meaning as was done with the relatively reliable Atetelco mural reconstruction. However, if one accepts the reconstruction as generally, if not specifically, valid, one sees that there is an animal configuration portrayed here: the upper figures, carrying enlarged atlatl darts, walking on bright yellow footpaths indicated by red footprints, and confronting what may be a stylization of a mound of obsidian knife blades, are depicted above felines with exaggerated teeth and claws.

The animals and figures on the end walls of this portico from the east structure of the Principal Patio at Tetitla point in the same direction as do those on the inner walls, *i.e.*, facing the doorway leading into the inner room. This east structure is clearly the most important in Level 4 of this patio at Tetitla; it is accentuated by its size and the directional indications of the animals and figures, while the other mural designs associated with this patio are static, with no directional indications (see Séjourné 1966, Fig. 100).

There is very little about the aspect of these jaguars at Tetitla which suggests animal ferocity, even though their mouths are open to expose huge teeth and fangs. The two dripping trilobe forms in front

FIG. 5.12   East Wall on the Left Side of Room 3, South Complex, Zone 2

of each feline's mouth may be an indication of the animal's roar. But they are not natural animals. The round bird eyes, the birdlike claws, and the feather headdresses suggest that they stand not for a natural species, but for a human concept: the jaguar-bird-man. The pieces of furniture upon which the animals rest may be depictions of Teoti-huacan thrones, suggesting that the animals may have been a sign for power. Instead of a powerful individual positioned on the throne (if it is a throne) whose tenure in office could have been no longer than his lifetime, here in the dado of Figure 5.11 the jaguar-bird-man is substi-tuted and may have symbolized a perpetual office. It is possible that the immortal office of power is repeatedly depicted on the dadoes below and that the mortal individual filling the office is depicted above.

A SOUTH COMPLEX MURAL

The mural fragment shown in Figures 5.12 and 5.13 is located on the east wall in a small room in the group called the South Complex, located near the plaza of the Pyramid of the Moon, Zone 2. This badly faded mural has never been published. Figures 5.12 and 5.13 resemble the Tetitla murals of the Principal Patio (Fig. 5.11) showing a familiar configuration of animals in a lower register and human figures above them. And like the Tetitla mural, this animal-man grouping faces a doorway, here leading to an open patio rather than to an inner room as at Tetitla. The animal and human figures are, however, significantly smaller in size in the South Complex murals. Like the Tetitla example, here the feline rests on a kind of seat, which has tassels. The lowest horizontal section of this South Complex mural consists of a row of what appear to be obsidian knife blades similar to those of the upper register of the Tetitla murals. Directly below the seated jaguar there is a new element in the animal-man configurations we have been examining: a zigzag motif forming rectangular blocks.

In this deteriorated example, the upper and lower registers both fall within the lower two meters of the wall, so that together they are

FIG. 5.13   Drawing of Mural Shown in Figure 5.12

only the size of the lower registers of the murals discussed previously. Unfortunately, the upper part of the wall is lost to us. Nevertheless, it is possible to see that the felines of the lower register are dressed in human costume. Here it is clear that the personage walking directly above the feline is dressed in a costume with a tail; it is certain that the figure is dressed in an animal skin; and it is possible that the figure wears the skin of the feline.

PATIO OF THE JAGUARS

Ignacio Bernal first published and briefly described the conch-blowing jaguar shown in Figure 5.14 (1963, pp. 33, 35, Fotos 29, 30). Since then this jaguar and others like it surrounding the restored Patio of the Jaguars of Zone 2 (Fig. 5.15) on the north, west, and south sides (the east side is occupied by a large temple platform) have become well-known examples of Teotihuacan mural painting and are frequented by hordes of tourists.

Peter Furst (1968, p. 166) has suggested that the anthropomorphic jaguars of the Patio of the Jaguars are metaphorical representations of priests: "One cannot help wondering whether the plumed and often anthropomorphic jaguars in the Teotihuacan murals, especially the conch-blowing jaguar procession below the Palacio del Quetzal-

FIG. 5.14   West Wall of Portico 1, Patio of the Jaguars, Zone 2

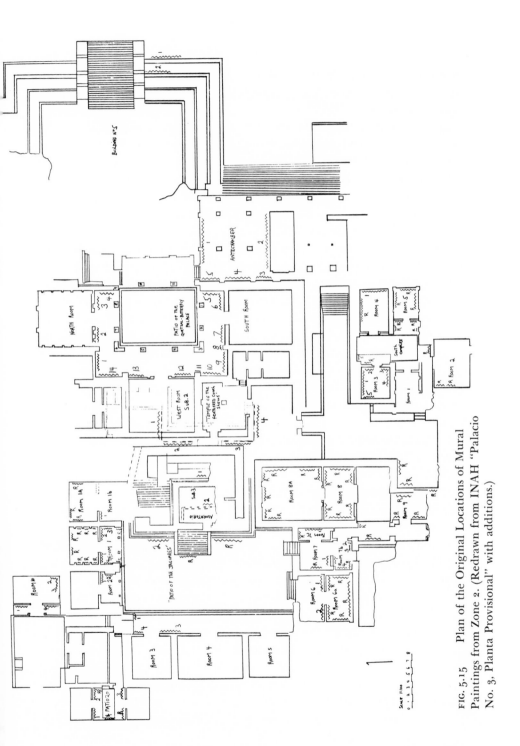

FIG. 5.15 Plan of the Original Locations of Mural Paintings from Zone 2. (Redrawn from INAH "Palacio No. 3, Planta Provisional" with additions.)

papalotl, are not metaphorical representations of priests, especially since, at least in Aztec times, the blowing of conches, even war conches, was the exclusive prerogative of the priesthood." Here is the passage from Sahagún which influenced Furst's thinking. It was written almost a millennium after the fall of Teotihuacan: "The blowing of shell trumpets: this was the charge of those who were young trumpet-blowing priests; and (they were) experienced and of various sorts" (Anderson and Dibble 1951, Bk. 2, Pt. 3, p. 205, "The Blowing of Shell Trumpets"). The Teotihuacanos may not have associated the act of conch blowing with the priesthood, but certainly they thought of it as a human action.

These recently discovered conch-blowing jaguars of the Patio of the Jaguars (Fig. 5.14) are markedly similar to, although much larger than, the animals of the jaguar-human configuration from the neighboring palace just discussed (Figs. 5.12, 5.13). Unfortunately the upper walls above these profile jaguars are lost to us. This jaguar on the lower-wall dado (Fig. 5.14), while exhibiting the huge fangs and claws of the Atetelco (Figs. 5.2–5.10) and Tetitla (Fig. 5.11) animals, is also decidedly anthropomorphic in appearance. This animal (Fig. 5.14) wears a headdress and is decorated along its spine with painted bivalve shells. These are human ornaments. The jaguar displays the round feathered eye of a bird and wears bird claws instead of cat claws. The jaguar holds in its left paw, as if blowing into or possibly drinking from, an elaborate feathered conch shell with two speech scrolls issuing downward from it and curving upward. Certainly this compounded animal's dress and behavior are those of men, not animals.

The jaguars decorating Porticoes 1 and 6 and the exterior of Room 3 all have borders at the top and on one side enclosing goggle-eyed, fanged faces set in five-pointed stars which may be representations of cross sections of conch shells; there is a bifurcated serpent's tongue suspended from the fangs. This goggle-eyed form is reminiscent of those of the upper border in Portico 2 at Atetelco which are associated with netted jaguars on the dado below (Fig. 5.5). This goggle-eyed cartouche also appears on its side in front of the feathered conch shell. The goggle-eyed cartouches of the border of Figure 5.14 alternate with feathered headdress forms including the familiar "stitched" trilobe form and concentric circles.

The borders of the smaller and possibly earlier conch-bearing jaguars of Portico 2 consist of serpentine interlaces reminiscent of the serpent interlace of Atetelco Portico 2 (Fig. 5.5), as one jaguar bears shells and the other, scales. Superimposed upon the interlace at regular intervals are rosettes of painted shells. The conch-bearing jaguars of the Patio of the Jaguars indicate, by the direction they face, the entrance to the inner rooms: they all point toward and flank on either side the door leading to the inner rooms. The Patio of the Jaguars is dedicated to jaguar imagery on the north, south, and west sides. The prominent east side is occupied by a large temple platform. If its now-destroyed structure bore paintings, I suspect that they would have pertained to jaguar imagery as well.

If directional orientation toward a room or toward a patio is indicative of activities performed in those areas, as I have stated previously, what was the function of the inner rooms off Porticoes 1, 2, and 6 and outside of Rooms 3, 4, and 5 as well (Fig. 5.15), all of which look onto the Patio of the Jaguars? The complete answer to this question may never be known, but an examination of the motifs in Figure 5.14 may help to suggest the purpose of the inner rooms. In Figure 5.14 the jaguar is clearly associated with the conch shell. We have also seen jaguar motifs associated with conch in the Portico 2 murals of the White Patio at Atetelco (Figs. 5.5–5.7). There, a man wearing jaguar fangs is bearing a conch shell, while one of the animals positioned below him is a netted jaguar.

The goggle-eyed form in the borders (Fig. 5.14) is combined with what I have suggested is the cross section of a conch shell. Also, this goggle-eyed motif with bifurcated serpent's tongue from the Figure 5.14 mural border is not unlike the goggle-eyed figures in the upper border of Portico 2 at Atetelco (Figs. 5.5, 5.6). Thus, at the Patio of the Jaguars and at Atetelco Portico 2, there are images of unmistakable jaguar-conch association, both in the main designs and in the borders.

But the partial configuration of the lower wall in Figure 5.14 of the Patio of the Jaguars describes a complex image that is, when considered as a whole, not only jaguar-conch but also jaguar-bird-conch-serpent. We have already seen that at Atetelco Portico 2 (Figs. 5.5–5.7), the complicated design is even more complex in its entirety, depicting coyote-jaguar-serpent-conch-bird-man. One reason that the Atetelco Portico 2 designs define more complex entities than those of the Patio of the Jaguars is simply that the Atetelco murals are complete, whereas the Patio of the Jaguars murals show only partial configurations. Another more obvious reason for greater complexity of the Atetelco Portico 2 is simply that it has more to say.

Obviously the Patio of the Jaguars animal (Fig. 5.14) and those discussed from Atetelco (Figs. 5.2–5.10), Tetitla (Fig. 5.11), and the South Complex (Figs. 5.12, 5.13) are not natural animals but complex compounds charged with the specific meaning that the ancient Teotihuacanos had in mind when they made such fantastic forms. It is clear that the meaning of these complex compounded images refers to human concepts which draw upon bits and pieces from natural species in order to give these concepts visual form. There is one important component missing in this Figure 5.14 animal compound which has been found in the examples already discussed: the human element. Man is, however, suggested in feathered headdresses worn by this very unusual animal, and he may have been represented in the upper wall.

A ZONE 11 MURAL

Another partial configuration can be seen in the lower right-hand wall (*talud*) of the portico in Room 5 of Zone 11 (Figs. 5.16, 5.17) depicting two profile felines, one following the other in the manner of the Atetelco, Tetitla, and South Complex animals mentioned previously. Room 5 and its portico are on the east side of an open patio. Known as Mural 24 of the unpublished Teotihuacan catalog, this *talud* painting has never, to my knowledge, been published. It is now in the Museo Nacional de Antropología in Mexico City. And like those animals at Atetelco, Tetitla, South Complex, and the Patio of the Jaguars, the felines of Figure 5.16 are wearing human costumes in the form of feather headdresses. In addition, these animals are further anthropomorphized by being clothed in a net costume. Falling panels enclosing two parallel bands of disembodied eyes similar to those in the borders are depicted instead of speech scrolls or conch shells issuing speech scrolls which we have previously seen.

The backs, tails, and legs of these profile felines are edged with spaced-out spalls of flint or obsidian or bone similar to those used to decorate the Atetelco coyotes (Figs. 5.2, 5.3, 5.5, 5.6). The bared teeth of these Zone 11 animals (Figs. 5.16, 5.17) and their enlarged bird

FIG. 5.16   East *Talud* on the Right Side of Portico 5, Zone 11

FIG. 5.17   Drawing of Mural Shown in Figure 5.16

claws emphasize the sharp and rigid quality of the animals, a quality which is accentuated by their placement above a visual foil: they appear to walk over very fragile objects, what I call "the broken-egg motif."

The jaguars in Figures 5.16 and 5.17 face an inner chamber, as surely did the jaguars of the left-hand *talud* now lost. The inner chamber bears very faded remains of the same design seen in Figures 5.16 and 5.17. Of these faded inner-room mural fragments, the west wall, left-hand side, has been removed from Room 5 and has been recently restored by the INAH restoration laboratory at Churubusco. It bears the same design as shown in Figures 5.16 and 5.17. Since the Figure 5.16 jaguar exhibits what has been tentatively identified as a water motif (Miller 1969, pp. 110, 133) substituted for the conch shell of the Figure 5.14 jaguar, it is possible that the meanings of water motif and conch are identical, one motif a simple substitution for the other.

The Figures 5.16 and 5.17 jaguars are also shown as having the round, feathered eye of a bird, similar to the eyes of the jaguars represented in Figures 5.5, 5.6, and 5.14. Thus, this Figure 5.16 jaguar painting represents the netted jaguar-water-bird compounded image. The anthropomorphic elements are net and feather headdress. As in the other compounded animal images discussed above, this animal is not a simple descriptive image of a species of animal in the natural world. It is instead a visual image for a complex human idea involving netted jaguar and water and bird and man. Is it possible that the now-lost upper wall bore a human figure wearing the costume elements indicated in the lower dado in the manner of the complete wall designs showing animal-man configurations previously discussed?

I would like to suggest here that the destroyed walls above the conch-blowing jaguars (Fig. 5.14) and the Zone 11 jaguars (Figs. 5.16, 5.17) possibly were decorated with profile figures dressed in jaguar skins in the manner described for the configurational relationships of the upper and lower walls of the Atetelco (Figs. 5.2–5.10), Tetitla (Fig. 5.11), and South Complex (Figs. 5.12, 5.13) paintings. Furthermore, it seems that the evidence presented above suggests the likelihood that, where profile animals are found in the lower register with the upper register missing, the upper parts of the walls were decorated originally with human figures dressed in the skins of the animals below them. According to this view, animal-man relationships form an important configuration in Teotihuacan mural painting. It is probable that this pictorial animal-man configuration recorded an important Teotihuacan belief or concept, important enough to be depicted on the walls of several structures.

OTHER ANIMAL-MAN RELATIONSHIPS IN TEOTIHUACAN MURAL PAINTING

Another way in which the Teotihuacanos may have expressed visually the metaphorical relationship between man and his animal counterparts can be seen in other examples of murals from near the Patio of the Jaguars in Zone 2. Figure 5.18 is one example. Instead of portraying the close relationship between a man and an animal by placing the man above the animal whose skin he wears, these murals present us with the animal held in the arms of the human figure.

The felines in this example decorate the lower walls (*talud*) of both the portico and the inner room of the east structure facing on a small open patio. It is interesting to note that here the portico and inner room of the east structure looking out on a patio are decorated with netted jaguars, whereas the patio itself is painted plain red or two values of red (Fig. 5.15, Room 10). Recalling the White Patio at Atetelco (Fig. 5.1) and the Principal Patio at Tetitla (Séjourné 1966,

FIG. 5.18   East *Talud* on the Right Side of the Portico of Room 10, Zone 2

Fig. 100), it will be remembered that it is also the structure on the east side of the patio which is most prominently decorated with jaguar images. Room 5 of Zone 11 is also on the east side of what was probably an open patio. This Zone 11, Room 5 mural has jaguar imagery as well. Thus, the east side of a patio may have been a place of particular importance reserved for functions pertaining to jaguar imagery. They are similar to each other; there are four on the east wall, one on the north wall, and one on the south wall.

The felines in the portico of Room 10 symmetrically face the door of Room 10 and are arranged on either side of the entrance to the inner room, indicated as Room 10 on the plan (Fig. 5.15). This directional arrangement pointing toward the inner room has been described for Atetelco, Tetitla, the Patio of the Jaguars, and Zone 11. As in those examples discussed previously, it is possible that the depiction of hand-held netted jaguars here pointing to the entrance of Room 10 suggests the function of that inner room.

Each feline wears blue netting similar in form to the Portico 2 jaguars at Atetelco and the Zone 11 jaguars. The feline in Figure 5.18

also wears blue and red bands of triangles and an anthropomorphic feather headdress similar to those adorning the animals from Tetitla (Fig. 5.11) and Zone 11 (Fig. 5.16). The spine of each animal (Fig. 5.18) and the underside of his tail are edged with red triangles similar to those at the base of the animal's feather headdress. Each feline holds one forepaw out in front of him as if to point the way to the inner room, or possibly as a dance step frozen in the image. Such a gesture is one that we would associate with human, rather than animal, movements. The triangles and feather headdress are ornaments associated with the adornment of important human personages at Teotihuacan (Kubler 1967, p. 6). Two green speech scrolls emerge from each feline's open mouth and include smaller scrolls along their upper edges; the first green scroll is horizontal, while the other curves downward and inward. What kind of animal is this that wears the adornments of men and whose speech is worthy of pictorial record?

The borders of these lower-wall paintings are distinctive, blue, chainlike nets which appear on one of the serpentine forms and on jaguar legs of the Atetelco Portico 2 lower border (Figs. 5.5, 5.6). Each netted feline has as a base a V-shaped geometric design which is possibly part of the figure's costume, giving the appearance that the feline is a substitution for the figure's head. Judging from the scale indicated by the human hands, the feline is a small one, perhaps a young jaguar or an ocelot.

What does the jaguar cub held in human hands signify? I am reminded of the Olmec sculptural scenes of a priestly man holding a jaguarlike infant, as if to present him to power. And also, in looking at Figure 5.18, the presentation of the child in Room 1, Structure 1, of the late classic Maya wall paintings at Bonampak comes to mind. These are examples from different regions and different times, but it is possible that they represent a theme similar to the one at Teotihuacan. If this is so, the Teotihuacan example is a characteristically more symbolic version of the presentation scene, showing a netted jaguar cub with round avian eye held in human hands.

If we consider the possibility that the jaguar cub held in human hands is indeed an animal counterpart of a young ruler or priest or heir, the painting may be part of jaguar power symbolism we have seen elsewhere at Teotihuacan. The theme of power being expressed

by an anthropomorphic jaguar-bird form also may be evident at Tetitla and at the South Complex (Figs. 5.11–5.13) where an anthropomorphic jaguar-bird is straddling a thronelike object, possibly
expressing a seat of power, an official position created by Teotihuacan
law, divine or temporal.

SUMMARY

What I hope to be incontrovertible is that the east side of certain
building complexes at Teotihuacan is stressed and is often decorated
with jaguar imagery. These are Teotihuacan murals depicting associations of men dressed in animal skins with animals dressed in human
garb: (1) as seen in Atetelco where in Portico 1, men dressed in coyote
skins are positioned above animals revealing fangs and claws as aggres-
sively as the figures above flaunt their atlatl weaponry (Figs. 5.2–5.4);
in Atetelco Portico 2 where men with jaguar attributes walk above
netted jaguars and coyotes (Figs. 5.5–5.7); in Atetelco Portico 3 where
the inner-wall figures wear bird costumes while those of the outer wall
seem to be bludgeoning similar birds (Figs. 5.8–5.10); (2) as seen at
Tetitla, Principal Patio, where men extend handfuls of enlarged atlatl
darts, while confronting symbolic mounds of sharp obsidian knife
blades, and are positioned above seated felines exhibiting their large
and sharp fangs and claws (Fig. 5.11); (3) as seen in the South Complex of Zone 2 where it appears that the figure walking directly above
a feline wears a costume of what is clearly an animal skin, possibly the
skin of that lower animal (Figs. 5.12, 5.13); (4) as seen in the partial
configurations of anthropomorphic felines at the Patio of the Jaguars
(Fig. 5.14) and Zone 11 (Figs. 5.16, 5.17) which were possibly complemented by human figures with animal attributes in the wall space
above; and (5) as seen in Room 10 of Zone 2 which shows human hands
holding small anthropomorphic felines (Fig. 5.18).

It is clear that the visual evidence suggests that these animal-man
associations on the east side of open patios are important in the extant
corpus of Teotihuacan mural paintings. It is probable that these
animal-man associations define, to some extent, the architectural functions of structures decorated with these murals. Not clear at this point
is what these animal-man groupings meant to the ancient Teotihuacanos. The interpretation of the images of animal-man groupings in

Teotihuacan wall paintings is open to debate and, surely, will be debated for some time to come. I think that it is now possible to assert with some confidence, however, that animal-man configurations in the Teotihuacan murals discussed in this paper were probably grounded in ideological systems with which the man-as-jaguar or nagual concept plays an important role.[5]

REFERENCES CITED

Anderson, A. J., and C. E. Dibble, trans.
    1951   *Florentine Codex: General History of the Things of New Spain.* By Fray Bernardino de Sahagún. Monographs of The School of American Research, Bk. 2, Pt. 3. Santa Fe: The School of American Research and the University of Utah.

Bernal, Ignacio, ed.
    1963   *Teotihuacán: Descubrimientos, Reconstrucciones.* Mexico: Instituto Nacional de Antropología e Historia.

Burland, C. A.
    1954   The Atelco (Atetelco) Frescoes. *New World Antiquity Newsletter* (10): 6–8.

Furst, Peter
    1968   The Olmec Were-Jaguar Motif in the Light of Ethnographic Reality. In Elizabeth P. Benson, ed., *Dumbarton Oaks Conference on the Olmec.* Washington, D.C.: Trustees for Harvard University. Pp. 143–78.

Kubler, George A.
    1967   *The Iconography of the Art of Teotihuacan.* Studies in Pre-Columbian Art and Archaeology, No. 4. Washington, D.C.: Dumbarton Oaks, Trustees for Harvard University.

Linné, Sigvald
    1934   *Archaeological Researches at Teotihuacan, Mexico.* Ethnographical Museum of Sweden, n.s. Publication No. 1. Stockholm.
    1942   *Mexican Highland Cultures: Archaeological Researches at Teotihuacan, Calpulalpan, and Chalchicomula in 1934–35.* Ethnographical Museum of Sweden, n.s. Publication No. 7. Stockholm.

Miller, Arthur G.
    1969   The Mural Painting of Teotihuacan, Mexico, and an Inquiry into the Nature of its Iconography. Ph. D. dissertation. Harvard University, Cambridge, Mass.

Millon, Clara S. H.
    1966   The History of Mural Art at Teotihuacan. Paper read at the Eleventh

5 The author thanks Dr. Edward Calnek of the Department of Anthropology, University of Rochester, for reading and criticizing a preliminary draft of this paper.

Mesa Redonda of the Sociedad Mexicana de Antropología on El Valle de Teotihuacán y su Contorno, August, 1966, at Museo Nacional de Antropología, Mexico.

Millon, René
  1967a Extensión y población de la ciudad de Teotihuacán en sus diferentes períodos: Un cálculo provisional. In *Teotihuacán Onceava Mesa Redonda*. Mexico: Sociedad Mexicana de Antropología. Pp. 57–78.
  1967b Chronología y periodificatión: datos estratigráficos sobre períod cerámicis y sus relaciones con la pintura mural. In *Teotihuacán Onceava Mesa Redonda*. Mexico: Sociedad Mexicana de Antropología. Pp. 1–18.
  1970a Occupational Specialization in Teotihuacan. Paper read at the Thirty-fifth Annual Meeting of the Society for American Archaeology, D.F. Saturday, May 2, 1970, at Museo de Antropología, Mexico.
  1970b Teotihuacán: Completion of Map of Giant Ancient City in the Valley of Mexico. *Science* 170:1077–82.

Sanders, William T.
  1967 Life in a Classic Village. In *Teotihuacán Onceava Mesa Redonda*. Mexico: Sociedad Mexicana de Antropología. Pp. 123–48.

Séjourné, Laurette
  1963 Exploration de Tetitla, Febrero-Octubre, 1963. In Bernal, Ignacio, ed., *Teotihuacán: Descubrimientos, Reconstrucciones*. Mexico: Instituto Nacional de Antropología e Historia.
  1966 *Arquitectura y Pintura en Teotihuacán*. S.A., Mexico: Siglo XXI Editores.

Seler, Eduard
  1915 Die Teotihuacan Kultur des Hochlands von Mexiko. *Gesammelte Abhandlungen zur Americanische Sprach-und Alterthumskunde* 5:403–585. Berlin.

Spence, Michael W.
  1967 Los talleres de Obsidiana de Teotihuacán. In *Teotihuacán Onceava Mesa Redonda*. Mexico: Sociedad Mexicana de Antropología. Pp. 213–18.

Villagra, Agustín
  1951a Las pinturas de Atetelco en Teotihuacán. *Cuadernos Americanos* (Año 10) 55 (1):153–62. Mexico.
  1951b Murales prehispánicos: copia, restauración y conservación. In *Homenaje al Doctor Alfonso Caso*. Pp. 421–26. Mexico.
  1952 Teotihuacán, sus pinturas murales. *Anales*, Vol. 5, No. 33. Mexico: Instituto Nacional de Antropología e Historia. Pp. 67–74.
  1956–57 Las pinturas murales de Atetelco, Teotihuacán. *Revista Mexicana de Estudios Antropológicos* 14:9–13.

Von Winning, Hasso
  1968 Der Netzjaguar in Teotihuacan, Mexico: Eine Ikonographische Untersuchung. *Baessler-Archiv*, Neue Folge, Band XVI. Berlin.

Wallrath, Matthew
    1967   The Calle de los Muertos Complex: A Possible Macro-Complex of Structures near the Center of Teotihuacan. In *Teotihuacán Onceava Mesa Redonda*. Mexico: Sociedad Mexicana de Antropología. Pp. 113–22.

TRADITIONAL TECHNOLOGY AND MODERN OBJECTS

Chapter 6

The *Ăi* or *Sfondéle:* A Beam Press from the Island of Corfu, Greece

Augustus Sordinas

ABSTRACT   The study of material objects, and of machines in particular, indicates not only the level of technological expertise that a society possesses, but also uncovers the socioeconomic context and organization surrounding the use of the objects. A comprehensive understanding of prehistoric and historic objects therefore necessitates a conjunctive study of archaeologic, ethnohistoric, and ethnographic data.

The *ăi* is an extinct beam press formerly used to produce olive oil on Corfu, Greece. Ethnographic work with elderly informants provided a description of the press; subsequent excavation uncovered nearly all of the essential parts of the *ăi*. The two sources of data give a picture of an inefficient machine that required long hours of extremely difficult labor to produce small amounts of oil.

Despite the press's inefficiency, Corfu peasants continued to use the machine long after richer landlords had imported the wooden screw press and, later, the metal screw press. As the ethnohistoric data substantiate, the continued use of the *ăi* reflected the peasant's marginal existence. The extreme deprivation in the peasant's environment—a deprivation produced in large measure by an exploitative landlord and merchant class—prevented him from accumulating sufficient capital to acquire the more efficient machines. Thus, the longevity of the *ăi* documents the longevity of peasantry on Corfu and illustrates the harsh quality of that existence.

FIG. 6.1   A Ruined Olive Oil Workshop Surrounded by Olive Trees at Kothoniki Near Kalafationes. This workshop was allowed to come to grief in the nineteenth century.

The visitor on Corfu walking amidst the vast olive groves or through the numerous villages of the island is liable to encounter large millstones or parts of gigantic wooden presses abandoned on the wayside. They are remnants of primitive mills and presses employed for centuries in the extraction of oil from the fruit of the olive tree (Fig. 6.1).

The island is geologically and climatically well suited for the culture of the olive tree as was shown long ago by my late father John B. Sordinas (1911, 1919). The olive tree belongs to the Oleaceae group which comprises thirty species, the most important of which are the *Olea sativa* (Linné) or *europea, typica,* or *communis,* and the "wild" variety, *Olea oleaster* or *sylvestris.* We do not know exactly where early domestication of the olive tree occurred, but it may very well have been in the low hills of coastal southern Anatolia including the Aegean region. Insofar as Corfu is concerned, we note that Homer mentions olive trees in the gardens of Alcinous (Wace and Stubbings 1962, pp. 528–30). But in spite of the obvious antiquity of the olive tree in Corfu, clear historical evidence shows that large-scale exploitation was instituted by the Venetians who occupied the island from the fourteenth through the end of the eighteenth centuries. By the sixteenth century, and thanks to a vigorous policy of directed change initiated a little earlier by the Venetians (Andreades 1914, vol. 2, p. 17), the olive tree became a distinct monoculture that dominates the entire economy of the island to this day.

At present Corfu (or Kérkyra; Map 6.1) is an olive-tree-covered island with three fifths of the land totally covered by large trees, some two hundred to three hundred years old. Most, because they had never been pruned until recent years, reached heights in excess of forty to fifty feet. According to the 1961 census, there were three million trees on the island. This seemingly endless forest with its dense silver-gray canopy has been the subject of many vivid descriptions. It goes without saying that the production of olive oil played a preponderent role in the economy of the island since the sixteenth century at least.

The machines employed for the extraction of olive oil reflect, and in many ways describe, the activities involved and tell us much about the various extraction techniques which slowly developed to meet the increasing production of olive oil. The location and distribution of these machines give further valuable information regarding the development of these techniques and of their relation to the settlement patterns. On the whole these aspects of the material culture of the island enable us to gain concrete insights into the behavior of a very large segment of the population for the past three hundred to four hundred years. This paper reconstructs one of these machines, a beam press, called by the peasants of Corfu the *ăi* or *sfondéle*. Through a conjunctive study of archaeology, ethnography, and ethnohistory, this chapter examines the interrelationships and mutual dependence between this particular representative of the material culture and the social organization of the island.[1]

1   The fieldwork for this research was carried out in the summer of 1968. A grant from the School of Arts and Sciences, Memphis State University, partly supported my research. I am grateful to Mr. E. Stamatopoulos for his unfailing help and patient study of the Corfu archives; to Mr. Th. Zissis, then Prefect of Corfu, for statistical information; to the Public Library of Corfu; to Mr. K. B. Nikolakis-Mouchas, President of the Société des Lettres de Corfou, and to Mr. V. Kollas, President of the Kerkyraikí Énosis, for giving me access to their rare publications. The editors of the Corfu newspapers, *Kerkyraiká Néa* and *Ephimeris tōn Eidísseon*, graciously published relevant reports. I am indebted to Mrs. A. Nikokavoura for

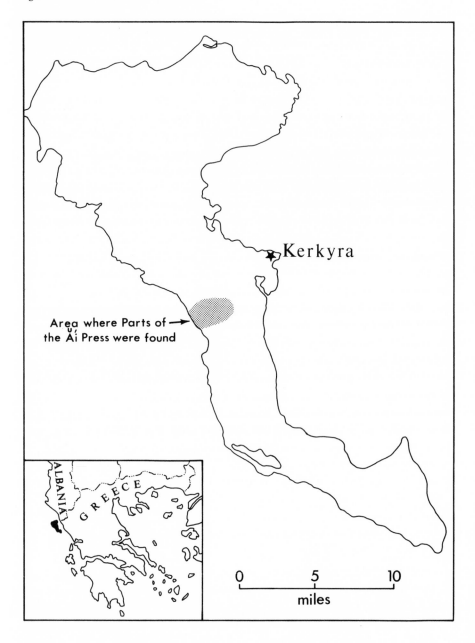

MAP 6.1   The Island of Corfu

GENERAL ASPECTS OF THE PROBLEM

The present study is a small part of a larger investigation, presently under way, aiming to examine the former social organization of the peasants of Corfu as it can be reconstructed from the remains of the material culture; changes in the inventories of tools, machines, and workshops; the peasant settlements; and the ethnohistoric documents of the preindustrial stage. Essentially, this study is an application of the technological and economic model as employed by Gordon Childe and Grahame Clark in their respective studies of prehistoric societies (Piggott 1965, p. 5, 1968, pp. 6, 9). But because of its peculiar nature, the present probe makes use of archaeological, ethnohistoric, and ethnographic data at the same time. These overlapping approaches furnish a dynamic understanding of the agents and mechanisms of social organization and change. Indeed, the position taken here is that in strictly controlled situations the utilization of all of these approaches is mandatory if a truly conjunctive interpretation of social history is sought. Thus, in view of the dominant role that the olive tree was made to play in the history of the island, we may ask, "What tools and machines were developed—and by whom—in order to meet with the production of more and more olives?" or "What was the material equipment which resulted from the changes instituted by Venice regarding olive oil production, and what were the subsequent orientations of the economy?" and "How does this equipment reflect the nature or perhaps levels of social organization?"

some of these reports and for her encouragement. My former schoolmate, Nicholas Pangratis, from the village of Kastellani, took an interest in my research and actively assisted me in the fieldwork.

Fifty villages were surveyed. Mr. Theodore Peristeris introduced me to many village dignitaries and informants. A total of 162 informants were interviewed. Only the names of key informants are indicated in the text, where necessary, together with their ages in 1968 and the names of their villages. The reader will note that most of the knowledgeable informants were in their eighties when interviewed. Thus, the information reported in this paper preserves the knowledge obtained from the last eyewitnesses to this type of material culture and social organization on the island of Corfu.

Preliminary reports of this survey were presented in a paper given at the Joint Meeting of the Southern Anthropological Society and the American Ethnological Society held in New Orleans, March 13–15, 1969, and another paper at the 68th Annual Meeting of the American Anthropological Association held in New Orleans, November 20–23, 1969. Also see Sordinas (1971, 1972).

I am indebted to Mr. R. Cockrell, Director of Art Services, Memphis State University, for suggesting the drawing for Figure 6.13.

This study attempts to answer some of the questions by probing the technology or, better still, the role and function of the machines (Rolt 1965, p. 112), for it is via the study of the machines that we can gauge the nature and level of social organization and, naturally, the amounts of goods and services that such a level of social organization can produce in time and space (Hultkranz 1968, pp. 289–310, and particularly Cohen's reply on p. 298; but see Usher 1954, p. 41).

For reasons of brevity and methodological rigidity only one machine is examined here, purposely isolated as a "single cultural phenomenon" (Leslie A. White 1945, p. 242). Unlike simple or primary tools, the definition of which perforce remains broad, vague, and rather unsatisfactory (Bock 1969, p. 221; Leslie A. White 1959, pp. 7, 53–57), machines are combinations "of resistant bodies so arranged that by their means the mechanical forces of nature can be compelled to do work accompanied by certain determinant motions (Releaux 1876, pp. 35, 503–504). This is the kinematic theory of the machine which clearly indicates that resistant bodies (artifacts if you wish) are arranged by culture to perform certain tasks, to produce work. As such, the life of any single type of machine is transitory, seldom outliving its usefulness and social function. The archaeologist is well aware of this, and his main concern is to identify and clearly define the purpose and function of artifacts—vibrant with life before, mute when discovered.

The machines examined here formed the equipment of traditional workshops or *ergasteria*, characteristic of a preindustrial economy (Weber 1947, p. 243). The term preindustrial, as used in this paper, reflects economies depending on animate sources of energy and having little specialization, strong personal and often kin relationships, lack of mobility, proximity of workshops and the production sources to the peasantry, much home handicraftsmanship, lack of centralization, little formal organization, few middlemen, small-scale production, very little rationality, lack of innovative stimuli and general lack of change, little standardization of parts, tools, weights or the quality of products, and no or irregular distribution (Bloch 1961, p. 73; Coleman 1956, pp. 27 ff.; Foster 1960–61, p. 175; Mintz 1961, pp. 54–57; Sjoberg 1955, pp. 439 ff.; Smelser in Dalton 1967, p. 30).

The old peasants of Corfu whom I interviewed in 1968 retained fuzzy memories of the form and function of some of these earlier ma-

chines. More precisely, they retained memories of certain "combinations of resistant bodies," and some of the peasants, but by no means
all, remembered the attendant motions of these bodies. Thus, in the
absence of the bodies themselves a precise reconstruction of the machines was well nigh impossible. Gradually, however, with the aid of
archaeological investigation, disconnected bits of information were
put together, and there emerged a more or less satisfactory picture of
the form, function, and role of some of these machines. Their study
indicates that the preindustrial rural economy of Corfu was characterized by a singular form of poverty and primitiveness in its material
culture from which a series of sociological generalizations can be de-
duced. Indeed, the proposition is offered here that the study of machines which are demonstrably vital to an economy will accurately
indicate not just the level of material culture per se but further, and
most importantly, the "technique," in other words, the social context
and organization that engendered them (Ellul 1964; Firth 1956, pp.
22, 35–36; Porak 1943).

That the level of social organization of the Corfu peasant was un-
enviable until the belated spread of industrialization is demonstrated
in various writings supported by considerable archival documentation. For instance, Grasset de Saint-Sauveur, for years a resident of
eighteenth-century Corfu, described the status of the peasantry as
follows: "Most of the land is in the hand of the smallest number of
people. It is impossible for the peasants to rise beyond a subsistence
level and develop the land" (1800, p. 160).[2] Abundant historical
evidence shows that this state of affairs continued throughout the nineteenth century. Although the union of the Ionian Islands with Greece
in 1864 triggered considerable social change, the status of the peasantry
changed but little until 1923, when by dictatorial decree the land
was turned over to the *coloni*.[3] Actually, Grasset de Saint-Sauveur's

2 Also see Scrofani (1797). Grasset de Saint-Sauveur was an astute observer who amassed
   many historical, statistical, and ethnographic details for a very fluid period. His
   work is little known but should be included in the books dealing with the rise of
   anthropological theory. The passage quoted is my own translation from the following: "Presque toutes les terres sont entre les mains du plus petit nombre de la
   population. La plupart des propriétaires sont privés de tout ce qui est nécessaire
   pour étendre la culture: ils en tirent leur substance personnelle, mais non un
   superflu qui les mettre en état de payer les travaux du paysan qui en développeroit
   la fécondité."
3 The social and economic history of Corfu remains to be written. Very interesting
   but disparate reports for the nineteenth century exist, however. See, for instance,

astute observations held true until just prior to World War II. At that time well-organized cooperative societies and reasonable loans advanced by the Agricultural Bank enabled the peasants to rise beyond a singularly low subsistence level for the first time.[4]

The general misery and poverty in the material culture and specifically the technoeconomic primitiveness of the olive oil workshops of preindustrial Corfu contrast sharply with the high level of technical development in the olive oil industry attained by the ancient workshops of Greece and southern Italy under the stimulus of the agrarian capitalism of advanced Hellenistic and Roman society (Beck 1900, pp. 66–87; Brehaut 1933, pp. 8–47; Drachmann 1932, *passim*; Forbes 1955, pp. 101–105, 131–38; Heichelheim 1938, p. 582; Rostovtzeff 1941, p. 100, 1957, p. 9565; Vickery 1936, p. 58). But before we make any further generalizations about the state of the preindustrial peasants of Corfu, let us examine some of the facts.

We know a good deal about the production of olive oil in antiquity and about the most important methods employed for the extraction of the oil from the olives. The operation consisted of two distinct and separate processes which in Corfu remained essentially unchanged until the end of World War II. The first of these two processes consisted of the crushing or "pulping" of the fruit as a preliminary step to the extraction of the oil. This was done with various forms of gigantic horse-drawn rotary mills (Fig. 6.2), the earliest of which, consisting of a single millstone, was replaced in the nineteenth century by a more efficient type employing two or three smaller millstones (Sordinas 1971, pp. 10 ff.).

Andreades (1914); Chiotes (1865); Damaskinos (1853, 1864); Davy (1842); Grimani (1856); Komiotes (1893); Partsch (1892); Pojago (1846–48); Santori (1852); Sathas (1880–90); Theotokes (1826); Typaldos (1864); and Yerakaris (1911). The bibliographies of Legrand and Pernot (1910) and of Pierris (1966) must be consulted. The rich and vastly unexplored archives of Corfu contain excellent ethnohistoric materials particularly regarding land tenure and the feudal system of Corfu known as *colonia*. For the comparable Latin American terms of *colon* and *colonato* see Schweng (1962). The Corfu system was a mixture of customary rights or privileges (*feudi diretti, censuali,* or *oblati,* and those deriving from the exercise of *jus patronatu*). Perhaps the term "patrimonial domain" proposed by Wolf (1966, p. 50) is more realistic.

4   This is shown in various ethnographic reports. See Blum and Blum (1965); Finlay (1856, pp. 193–94); Friedl (1962); Karavides (1931); Koty in Rose (1958); Lee in Mead (1955); Mavrogordato (1931); Sanders (1962); Sirakis (1925); Smothers, McNeill, and McNeill (1948); Stephanides (1948); Sweet-Escott (1954); and Whipple (1944).

FIG. 6.2   A Rotary Mill (*Monolithi*) Used to Crush Olives. Located at Kouramo near Kalafationes, the building, formerly an olive oil workshop, is now used as a stable.

The second process, which concerns us here, consisted of the pressing of the pulp for the extraction of the oil. Various presses or parts of presses are known to us from Hellenistic and Roman writers, classical pottery representations, and some classical and prehistoric sites. In spite of the impressive evidence, the reconstruction of these machines is not always complete or definitive (see Hörle 1929; Nix and Schmidt 1900; Drachmann 1932; Forbes 1955). Precisely for this reason the reconstruction of preindustrial presses on the basis of valid ethnohistoric documents and ethnographic reports can be so instructive.

THE UNCONFIRMED WEIGHTED BEAM PRESS

Many of the old peasants interviewed in Corfu in 1968 retained memories of crude means of exerting pressure on the pulp of the olives and

certain ideas about the "earliest" presses on the island. Purposely un-
aided during the interviews, the most articulate of these informants
made reference to types and gave descriptions which indicate with a
remarkable degree of consistency their awareness of variants of the
beam press of antiquity (Forbes 1958, p. 65). In the absence of tangible archaeological or ethnohistoric evidence (in 1968) on the island,
such reports, of course, are unconfirmed. The fact remains, however,
that the old informants were aware of the existence "in the old days"
of a simple and rather unsophisticated beam press which, although
fuzzy in their memories, was clearly distinguished from other types
with which they were more familiar by distinct terms. They referred
to this machine as the *lostós* or lever or simply, and very suggestively,
as the *város* or weight, terms making no sense whatever among the
young peasants in the context of modern olive oil presses.

According to these accounts, the *lostós* or *város* presses consisted
of two uprights (the Roman *arbores*) firmly fitted in the ground.
These uprights held in place a heavy horizontal beam or platen of
wood, called *blandrí* or *blándra,* equipped with two cylindrical holes
at either end for the insertion and mounting of the platen onto the
uprights. These holes were large enough to allow the platen to move
up or down the uprights freely (Fig. 6.3). According to the old informants, the platen was always lifted by four men and was temporarily held on their shoulders while other laborers stacked reed baskets
containing the olive pulp on a simple flat stone-bed called by the informants *grénda* (the Roman *ara*) lying immediately under the platen
between the two uprights. When this was accomplished, the platen
was lowered onto the bags. The weight of the platen caused some
of the oil to ooze out of the bags, not unlike the Pompeii fresco (Forbes

FIG. 6.3
A Simple Beam Press
Weighted Down by Stones.
(Oral Tradition.)

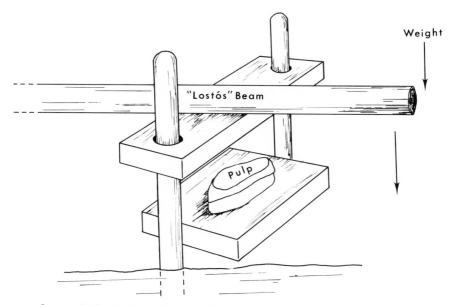

FIG. 6.4   A Simple Beam Press Weighted Down by a *Lostós*. (Oral Tradition.)

1955, p. 137, Fig. 32). But all the informants agreed that additional pressure was required. Two variants were described: (*a*) Pressure was exerted by simply placing stone weights (*város*) on top of the horizontal beam or platen (Fig. 6.3), or (*b*) considerable pressure was added by the operation of a long beam (the Roman *prelum*), called by the informants *lostós*, on the platen (Fig. 6.4). The *lostós* was drawn down either by attaching stone weights at its farthest end or by the operators themselves who—in the words of my informants— "jumped and climbed like cats" on the beam's end and held onto it until the pulp was pressed. No satisfactory explanation was given to me about where and how the fixed end of the beam was articulated (the *lingula* in Cato's press). Of course, it may have been in a hole in a wall.

An interesting variant called *geranió*, a term now employed only for Corfu's water sweeps, was described by Nick Kombolitis, age seventy-eight, from Varypatadhes, and George Cheimariós Tayaboúyas, age seventy-five, from Haghia Marina near Kalafationes. The beam of this variant is movable (Fig. 6.5), recalling the technology of manioc presses in the Amazon (Hoebel 1966, p. 247, Fig. 15–8).

FIG. 6.5   A *Geranió* Press. (Oral Tradition.)

Otherwise the application of the weight principle is retained. Sara-komenos (1930, p. 78) postulated even simpler presses, but there is no evidence of such a press in Corfu.

Generally, we note the crude means employed for the exertion of pressure and the effective lowering of the platen (that is, the harnessing of energy) when we compare these simple motions with the sophisticated *sucula* and *vectes* of Cato's press. At this stage of the investigation it is impossible to tell if the long *lostós* beam should be considered an evolutionary improvement over the stone-weighted platen insofar as Corfu is concerned. Neither can we hazard dates. However, the remembered details of the operation of the press are curious and rather surprising, particularly such details as the lifting of the platen with the shoulders or the climbing of the operators on the *lostós*. Perhaps these activities have not been entirely forgotten because they were practiced in the very recent past? All this, however, remains in the "suspense account" and can only serve as an introduction to the study of a better-documented machine.

THE ĂÍ OR SFONDÉLE BEAM PRESS

The unconfirmed reports mentioned in the preceding paragraphs lead us to the topic of this study: the beam press known to the old peasants by the interchangeable terms *ăí, sfondéle, ergáni*, or, rarely, *adráchti*[5] (terms presently making no sense whatsoever to the young villagers). The reconstruction of this press was achieved thanks to a combined form of ethnographic and archaeological inquiry plus luck.

Reliable statements[6] indicated that in the old days there had existed a heavy homemade beam press, made of wood, the platen of which was drawn down (to press) by the downward motion of two gigantic nuts made to screw on two uprights. According to these statements, the screwing of the nuts on the uprights was cumbersome and painful. Generally, the reports about the operation of this machine sounded fantastic and elicited the laughter of the younger peasants who happened to listen to their elders' accounts. In spite of the laughter and the general credibility gap on the part of the younger generation, there was no good reason why these reliable statements should be doubted. On the other hand, some documentation was necessary. Furthermore, in spite of the profusion in the terminology and the colorful reports about the operation of this "monster," details and exact measurements regarding the complete form and function of the press were sadly lacking. The picture was rendered even more garbled when some of the old informants understandably tended to confuse the term *lostós* with *ăí, sfondéle*, and *adráchti* and other more recent usages. I noted, however, that several among the oldest informants had been alluding to machines they had actually seen or worked with themselves fifty or sixty years ago. Therefore, I set out to find material traces of the machines. This was difficult. To begin with, these machines were made of wood which perished in most instances. Stone-beds survived better, but upon close inspection most of them proved to belong to early forms of wooden screw presses (Fig. 6.12).

5 I think that the term *ăí* is a reflex sound that could be identified with certain motions requiring cooperative effort very much like "heave-ho," the German "horuck," Russian "E-uch-nyem." If not onomatopoeic it could derive from the ancient Greek form meaning "go." *Sfondéle* is a derivation from the ancient forms meaning vertebra or wheeljoint or anything that turns on itself as, for instance, a whorl. The term *adráchti* derives from the ancient Greek word meaning mast or shaft.

6 This analysis is based solely on firsthand eyewitness reports. The most cogent information was obtained from Spyros Karydes, eighty-six, from St. George near Vȳrós; Aristides Anthis, eighty-two, from Kastellani, who drew Figure 6.5; Stefanos Pangratis, eighty-nine, from Kastellani; John Kardamis, ninety-four, from Kamara; Nicholas Kombolitis, seventy-eight, and Spyros Skiadopoulos, seventy-five, both from Varypatadhes. A complete list of the informants and distribution maps is published in Sordinas (1972).

On the whole, the workshop remains proved difficult to examine because they were either hopeless ruins or had been modified by successive generations of owners either to house later olive oil machines or simply to serve as stables or barnyards.[7] These successive changes obliterated all traces of the older machines. Moreover, to my knowledge, no records of these machines or any published descriptions for this area that could be consulted have been found (for summary reports see Sarakomenos 1930; Coon 1931; Nopcsa 1925). Thus, the oral tradition remembered by the older generation of peasants still living in 1968 was the only premise to work with. The search proved rewarding. Archaeological inquiry has shown that the oral traditions summarized in Figure 6.6 were essentially correct and were the accurate reflections by the octogenarian peasants of the *ăí* press and its role in peasant life and social organization half a century or more ago. Not only did archaeology corroborate the oral traditions, but it further provided tangible evidence for the reconstruction of the *ăí*. Furthermore, the evidence regarding the detailed measurements and the knowledge of the exact shape and function of the "constructive elements" (Releaux 1876, p. 437) of this machine have also corroborated the fantastic reports regarding the operation of the monster.

THE ARCHAEOLOGICAL FINDS

The pieces were put together as follows. A series of rather adventuresome, at times frustrating, explorations (often conducted in the immediate vicinity of enormous piles of manure) finally led me to a ruined workshop at the site of Sterní near the village of Varypatadhes

---

7 Matton (1960, p. 189) reports the existence of three thousand workshops on the island. Of course, some have been ruins for a very long time, others for less time, others were abandoned in the nineteenth century (*e.g.*, Fig. 6.1). Most of them ceased functioning after World War II. According to the official records of the Greek government, before World War II there were 1,202 functioning preindustrial workshops on the island. By 1967 only ten still functioned in remote areas on the island of Corfu, and seven more on some outlying islets (Memorandum No. 38333 of the Prefect of Corfu to the author, dated November 25, 1968).

  In 1970, with the cooperation of the government services of the island, I distributed to all the villages a questionnaire for the gathering of all the remembered information regarding still-functioning or ruined workshops in each village area. The returned questionnaires have enabled me to localize 1,252 workshops throughout the island (Sordinas 1972). The new information has further corroborated the findings described in this chapter.

in the center of the island. The former workshop consists of a large
fortified stone building typical of the isolated installations of earlier
latifundia. Presently it is owned by Vlassis Arvanitakis, age sixty-
eight, from Varypatadhes, who uses part of the ruined structure as a
barnyard. He graciously allowed me to excavate inside the building.
In the earth floor of this workshop we uncovered a large stone base
immediately recognized by the aged informants as the stone-bed of an
ăi press (Fig. 6.6, No. 1; Fig. 6.7). It is an asymmetrical and crudely
dressed monolith of conglomeratic limestone not found in the vicinity.
The same informants stated that in the old days such monoliths or
millstones were prepared by specialist stonecutters working in the
area of Haghii Dekka-Garouna, six to seven kilometers south of Varypatadhes, and were transported on wooden rollers by large groups of
laborers and volunteers. The top surface of the stone is fairly flat. At
its center a shallow and poorly executed circular gutter with a rough
opening on one side indicates the place where the pulp containers
were stacked for pressing. This gutter is called the navel, or dish, and
corresponds to the Roman *canalis rotunda*. Its diameter indicates the
shape and size of the pulp containers. On either side of the gutter and
at the two longitudinal ends of the stone-bed there are two rectangular
slots running through the stone-bed. They are important. The two uprights (Fig. 6.6, No. 2) were firmly positioned in these slots.

Of course, there was no trace of the actual uprights, but the size of
the slots indicates the thickness of the uprights at the base, and the position of the slots indicates exactly the distance between the two uprights. This leads to further calculations about the size of the platen
that was held by the two uprights. The measurements of the stone-bed
are as follows:

Maximum length measured at top surface	2.60 meters
Maximum width measured at top surface and center	1.20 meters
Thickness of stone-bed at center	0.70 meters
Diameter of circular gutter	0.85 meters
Depth of circular gutter	0.10 meters
Slots for the two uprights	0.20 $\times$ 0.15 meters
Distance between the two slots	1.25 meters

The overall size of this stone-bed agrees with average sizes given by the
informants, particularly in terms of its thickness and bulk. It was

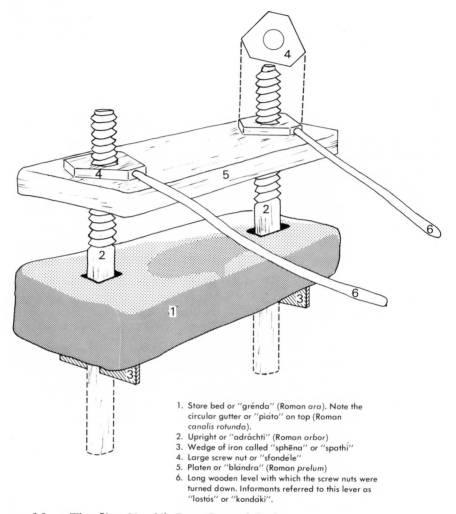

1. Store bed or "grénda" (Roman *ara*). Note the
   circular gutter or "piáto" on top (Roman
   canalis rotunda).
2. Upright or "adráchti" (Roman *arbor*)
3. Wedge of iron called "sphēna" or "spathí"
4. Large screw nut or "sfondéle"
5. Platen or "blándra" (Roman *prelum*)
6. Long wooden level with which the screw nuts were
   turned down. Informants referred to this lever as
   "lostós" or "kondáki".

FIG. 6.6   The *Ăi* or *Sfondéle* Beam Press of Corfu

purposely made thick and heavy to provide for a solid base and particularly in order to counterbalance the upthrust generated by the downward motion of the nuts and platen during pressing. In this sense, it is
quite different from the stone-beds of the screw presses (Fig. 6.12),
which were weighted down by the heavy crossbeam which effectively
counterbalanced the upthrust and therefore were made much smaller.
In addition, the *ăi* stone-bed was discovered in a central part of the

building away from the walls. Much space was required for the operation of the *ăi* (see below). Spatially, the *ăi* stone-bed differs from the stone-beds of the screw press which, being more compact and easier to operate, were placed alongside the walls of the workshops.

With the exception of a large millstone, nothing else was found in the workshop. It is very difficult to locate these monoliths without extensive excavation. When the *ăi* presses were destroyed, or replaced by more efficient types, the bulky stone-beds were buried in the earthen floors and forgotten. For instance, a few years ago two such stone-beds were temporarily brought to light by Nicholas Palaeológos in his Puladhes estate while repairing the floor of an old olive oil workshop destroyed by fire in 1870. They were incorporated into the new floor. (The presence of two or more presses in the same workshop is noted. We recall that Cato's workshop had four presses. This indicates

FIG. 6.7   The Stone-Bed *In Situ* of the *Ăi* Press at Sterni near Varypatadhes. The rod in the man's hand is one meter.

that the presses were low and slow yielding. Generally pulping was faster than pressing, and this presented production problems.)

The next step was to obtain evidence on the uprights which were presumably fitted in the slots of the stone-bed (Fig. 6.6, No. 2). Precise knowledge of their size and height would determine the overall size of the press, while the exact knowledge of their form and manufacture would give us leads as to the function and capabilities of the platen.

The oral traditions indicated that the uprights were invariably wooden. Thus the chances of finding them *in situ* were extremely slim, first because of their perishable nature, and second, because the ethnography has clearly shown that as soon as a machine becomes obsolete it is willfully destroyed and the wooden pieces find their way to the kitchen hearth. Needless to say, all the informants stated that they had not seen these items or any parts of the *ăí* press since they were children fifty years ago or more. Accident, however, conspired to save for posterity some of these uprights in the following way.

During the fieldwork I noticed that the doors of some old buildings in the village had thick wooden lintels partly carved into crude screws (Fig. 6.8). These items were photographed, measured, and drawn and then were shown to the old informants who recognized them immediately as the *adráchti* uprights of the *ăí* press. Subsequent search located several of these accidents of preservation on the island. The sizes indicate two variants: a small one that seems to belong to ancient winepresses and a large one which belongs to the *ăí* press. The upright shown in Figure 6.9 is typical of the latter. It was obtained from the door of a stable built in 1807 in the village of Kothoniki. The upright had served as a lintel to the stable door until the destruction of the building in 1967. It consists of a solid, roughly hewn beam of oak, complete and beautifully preserved in the wall of the old stable. It is 2.80 meters long and 0.18 × 0.14 meters in the section below the screw. The upper one third is gouged into a primitive screw 0.75 meters long, with fourteen roughly hewn sharp-edged threads with no flats at the crest. The major diameter of the threads is 0.15 meters, the minor diameter is 0.11 meters. The pitch is 0.08 meters. The helix angle and clearance are wide and irregular.

All these measurements indicate an extremely crude and technologically inefficient screw clearly contrasting with the sophisticated wooden screws of the screw press. These technical details further en-

FIG. 6.8   The Long Upright of the *Ăi* Press. The upright now serves as a lintel for the door of an old peasant house in the village of Synaradhes.

able us to reconstruct with accuracy the inner threads or female screw of the *sfondéle* nut (Fig. 6.6, No. 4). The lower part of the upright was firmly inserted in the square slot of the stone-bed. It was then locked into position with the aid of an iron wedge, about a foot long, inserted into a slot through the upright under the stone-bed (Fig. 6.6, No. 3; also see neat square slot, sized 0.6 meters × 0.10 meters seen toward the base of the upright in Fig. 6.9).

The accidental preservation and discovery of several uprights enable us to reconstruct, in conjunction with our knowledge of the stone-bed, the overall size and form of the *ăi* press. Yet, how could we envisage the exact shape and function of this press without a well-

FIG. 6.9   The Upright of an *Ăi* Press at Kothoniki. The rod in the man's hand is one meter.

documented knowledge of the platen? The chances of finding this item, however, were slim. Luck came to the aid of archaeology once more. A wooden platen was found, having this time been preserved in the form of a carpenter's workbench. We owe its preservation to the father of John Kardamis, ninety-four, from the village of Kamara. The original function of this workbench was totally unknown and unsuspected by the numerous descendants of Mr. Kardamis with the exception of the patriarch himself who, having been informed in conversation with my friend N. Pangratis of my research, recalled that when he was a child his father had told him that he had converted the platen of the family *ăi* press into a table. It withstood the hammerings and poundings of four generations and promises to take more if not willfully destroyed. We temporarily dismantled the workbench for study and photography, then we reverently turned it into a table once more!

The platen, called by the old informants *blándra*, or upper board, consists of a flat rectangular beam (the Roman *prelum*) hewn out of a choice piece of oak (Fig. 6.6, No. 5). It is equipped with two diagnostic cylindrical holes at either end. The holes are characteristically unthreaded (Figs. 6.10, 6.11), and they served a key function. The uprights were inserted into the two holes and kept the platen in position. Thus the diameter of the holes gives us the relative thickness of the upper part of the uprights. The distance between the two holes on the platen gives us the exact position of the two uprights and, by extension, the position of the two slots in the absent stone-bed. The Kamara platen is complete. It measures as follows:

Length	2.60 meters
Width	0.50 meters
Thickness	0.15 meters
Diameter of holes	0.24 meters
Distance between two holes	1.25 meters
Weight	180 pounds

The workshop where this platen was found and where it had operated in the past is now used as a storage building. It is reasonable to predict that if excavated the floor of this building will yield the original stone-bed.

We now have sufficient archaeological evidence for the recon-

FIG. 6.10
The Complete Platen of
an *Ăí* Press at Kamara.
The rod measures one
meter.

struction of the entire *ăí* press as it is shown in Figure 6.6, with the
exception of two elements, Numbers 4 and 6. The latter is a simple
lever not difficult to conceive, but the absence of Number 4 (the
sfondéle nut) is regrettable. Who knows? A specimen may be discovered some day buried in rubbish in some neglected corner or
backyard.

It can be readily seen that the *ăí* press is a mere elaboration of the
simple *lostós*, or weighted press (Figs. 6.3–6.5), particularly in terms
of the platen which is identical in all these types and moved up and

down the uprights in exactly the same way. But in the *ăi* the kinematic action of the platen was more effectively carried out by the transformation of the uprights into screws. In other words, the uprights mutated from mere supporting pillars into primary constructive elements directly involved in specific motions which caused the harnessing of more power because they now engaged the *sfondéle* nuts which screwed onto the uprights, thus forcing the platen down. This is the first application of the screw principle, albeit indirect, in the presses of Corfu. In other words, the *ăi* is an important developmental step in the direction of the ordinary screw press (Fig. 6.12). Technologically, the *ăi* press is much simpler than the screw press which required a thick crossbar containing, boxlike, the long inner threads or female screw (Clapham 1957, p. 382, Fig. 242). A similar situation has been described by Drachmann (1932, pp. 53–54, Fig. 13) in his analysis of the Roman presses:

FIG. 6.11
A Close-Up of the
Platen Shown in
Figure 6.10. Note the
unthreaded hole for
the upright.

FIG. 6.12   A Wooden Screw Press *In Situ* in an Old, Olive Oil Workshop at Kouramo near Kalafationes

When the screw was first used for the purpose of pressing, the inventor did not find all at once the way which is familiar to us all: that of using the screw directly on the thing to be pressed. At first it was used only to supersede the drum and the handspakes: it had to draw down the prelum.

Brönsted has reconstructed such a press. In his drawing the screw is fixed on the floor, and the nut, carrying four handles and thus forming a stella, travels down the screw, pressing down the end of the prelum, which has an oblong hole in it for the screw. That such a press is possible is shown by the fact that a press, built on this principle, is found at Fenis, near Aosta.

In the *ăi* press the carving of the crude screw (positive threads) on the uprights was done with a simple adz and chisel, while the *sfondéle* nuts (which I have not seen) were bulky chunks of hardwood about 0.75 meters wide and 0.30 meters thick, shaped into a rough nut containing at the center the female screw consisting of very few inner (negative) threads which matched, of course, the positive threads of the uprights.[8] The overall shape of the *sfondéle* nut was trianguloid with holes on each side for the insertion of a long curved lever of wood reaching almost to the floor (Fig. 6.6, No. 6). It is obvious that the entire *ăi* press was technically easy to manufacture, requiring little craftsmanship and no specialized knowledge or tools.

ACCESSORY EQUIPMENT

The only additional equipment necessary for the operation of the *ăi* press was a few wooden posts used when the press was loaded with the pulp and various wooden blocks (equivalent to the Roman *orbis*) placed between the platen and the pulp containers to facilitate pressing (even distribution of pressure on the pulp, elimination of the distance between the platen and the pulp containers, and addition of weight). We can distinguish: (*a*) Sturdy, but nondescript posts about 1.5 meters long placed between the platen and the stone-bed to hold the platen up during the stacking of the pulp containers on the stone-bed. Alternatively this could be done by holding the platen up with the shoulders. (*b*) Short cylindrical stumps and rectangular blocks.

8 The *sfondéle* nut shown in Figure 6.6, Number 4, was described in great detail by A. Anthis, eighty-two, from Kastellani. This informant operated an *ăi* press on the outskirts of his village when he was thirteen to fourteen years old. He stated that the *sfondéle* nut has three or four inner (negative) threads only, which could be cut easily from the outside with an ordinary carpenter's chisel and a mallet.

The stumps and blocks were about two feet long and functioned as wedges between the platen and the pulp containers very much like the wedges of the Pompeii press (Forbes 1955, p. 137; Brehaut 1933, pp. 27–28, n. 2). Now we are in a position to reexamine the vivid accounts of the informants about the actual operation of the monstrous *ăí*.

THE OPERATION OF THE Ăĺ PRESS

There is something ludicrous—and shocking at the same time—about the operation of the *ăí* press. No wonder the young generation of peasants listened to their elders with merriment and disbelief! The bulky machine was normally operated by four men in teams of two working on the two levers which turned the two *sfondéle* nuts. But all the males present in the workshop were invited to give a hand. "In the old days we slaved together," said the informants. Emphasis was on unison of motion. The men operating each lever worked in unison. The entire body of each operator acted harmoniously in a specific pattern of motions which we can follow in Figure 6.13, Numbers 1–6. The men stood close to each other and a few feet away from the long lever of the *ăí* (No. 1). Then in unison they extended the arms forward (No. 2), gently twisted their bodies to the right, swinging the extended arms as far back to the right as possible, "to gain momentum," like ballerinas (No. 3). Then, forcefully and abruptly swinging arms and body to the left (No. 4), they lifted and extended the right foot forward (No. 5) toward the lever—with the momentum gained— and yelling in unison "*ăíii!*" they "fell" together onto the wooden lever, striking it as strongly as possible with the right thigh (No. 6). Under the impact the lever moved forward, the *sfondéle* nut tightened somewhat, and the awkward platen went down an inch or so, pressing the pulp underneath.

The act was repeated for hours. To give some protection to their hips and thighs, the laborers wrapped themselves with several sheepskins which were presumed to absorb the severe shock caused by the full swing of the body against the cumbersome lever. It would be desirable to know what were the criteria of labor efficiency in those days! How forcefully should the laborer knock himself against the machine? Sarakomenos (1930, p. 202), without unfortunately giving any details, reports that hernias were customary but were conveniently attributed

FIG. 6.13   The Six Principal Movements Made by Operators of the *Ăi* Press

by the workshop owners to over consumption of olive oil. The master-ful rationalization is not devoid of humor and considerable ingenuity because, while it did nothing to discourage the strenuous effort, it warned against undue tampering with the precious oil supply.

In describing this idiotic operation, I cannot but wonder at the theoretical position of certain thinkers who deny the idea of progress. Once more we are reminded of Thomas Aquinas for his "Habet homo rationem et manum." Undoubtedly, the latter is evident in the *ăi* press, but one wonders about the former. As might be expected, the *ăi* press was very slow to operate. According to the majority of informants it required six to seven hours of continuous toil to press a *stémma*,

approximately 450 pounds,[9] of pulp whereas the wooden screw press
(not to mention later types) pressed the same quantity in three to four
hours, required half the number of workers, and yielded more oil because it pressed better. This means that the *ăí* often had to operate
constantly, day and night, to process the ripe olives. Delays caused
much of the fruit to rot and invariably produced very rancid oil. Moreover, the *ăí* simply did not press enough. The yields were low, and
much of the oil remained in the pulp which was given to the pigs or
used as fuel. This machine was not only cumbersome and harmful but
patently inefficient.

The *ăí* required much space. The long levers and the running,
pouncing, and tackling by a considerable number of operators required the machine to be in a central part of the workshop. Stone-beds
or their remnants found in the middle of ruined workshops generally
prove to be good indicators of an *ăí* press, whereas the screw presses
that defenestrated the *ăí* were smaller and easier to operate and were
placed more economically along walls (observed, for instance, at the
Vlassópoulos ruin near Haghia Marina, Kalafationes). Apart from
technoeconomic considerations, these attributes facilitate archaeological investigation and typology.

A NOTE ON CHRONOLOGY

At present it is not possible to date accurately the origin of the *ăí* press
in Corfu. It may have lingered since Hellenistic times. On the other

9 The current measures were not very accurate or standardized much beyond the local
level (characteristic of preindustrial activity). Also, confusions arise because similar
terms were used for dry or liquid measures. The quantity of olives deemed
requisite for one crushing operation (on the mill) was called *alessiá*. One *alessiá*
consisted of ten to twelve *moutzouria* of olives. Informants usually say that one
alessiá was equal to one and a half *mothi* (the Roman *modius* = 1.2 peck). In terms
of weight these measures were hopelessly variable because of the size and quality
of the olives, the degree of ripeness, freshness, water content, etc., or simply because of the way they were packed. Nobody really knew how much oil was produced by how many olives! Generally, one *moutzouri* was rated between forty and
fifty-two pounds. There is considerable consensus about the Venetian *moutzouri*
which equaled fifty-two pounds. A local *moutzouri* or the *Korakianítiko moutzouri*
was forty pounds. Informants supplement all this by stating that a common *alessiá*
was 450 to 500 pounds; a *korakianítiki alessiá* was 480 pounds; a *potamítiki alessiá*
was 620 pounds. The pulp produced out of one *alessiá* of olives was called *stémma*
or *zéma*. The contents of one *stémma* of pulp were scooped out of the mill and were
made to fill twelve reed baskets (later made of rope) which were stacked under the
platen, one on top of the other to form a column about 1.5 meters tall. Pressing
could then start.

hand we know of a similar press described by Vittorio Zonca near Venice in the sixteenth century (Beck 1900, p. 301, Fig. 363). This press is generally considered to be a simplified version of Hero's direct twin screw press which seems to have become known to the West in the sixteenth century through the circulation of an incomplete translation of Hero's work (the Pappus of Alexandria text; see Baldi 1601; also Bloch 1961, p. 70). We have seen that the Venetians successfully intensified the production of olive oil on the island of Corfu in the late sixteenth and early seventeenth centuries. It is possible that they introduced Zonca's type which became the progenitor of the *ăi* press of Corfu. During the eighteenth century the wooden screw press gained in popularity on the large estates and progressively displaced the *ăi* press (Sordinas 1971, pp. 14 ff.).

During this period many *ăi* presses were destroyed, and some of the *ăi* uprights were incorporated into buildings of that period. The *ăi* press lingered and continued functioning through the nineteenth and early twentieth centuries in the peasant inventories while the large estates were progressively replacing the wooden screw presses with various types of iron screw presses at first imported from Italy. The entire history of the olive oil workshops of Corfu presents considerable overlaps which render absolute chronologies meaningless if considered outside their social contexts. And precisely because of this, the established longevity of the *ăi* press presents considerable interest. Here are some unambiguous dates: The last *ăi* press in the village of Kastellani, built by Stamos Pangratis, the great-grandfather of Stefanos Pangratis from Kastellani, eighty-nine when I interviewed him in 1968, ceased functioning in 1892. And according to Spyros Gouliarmis Manghís, fifty-eight, from Kalafationes, the family *ăi* functioned until destroyed by his father in 1917. We can accept this date as a *terminus ante quem* of the *ăi* press on the island of Corfu.

MATERIAL CULTURE AND EXISTENCE

We have seen that the *ăi* press was progressively replaced by the more efficient and less cumbersome screw presses which had gained in popularity on the island since the eighteenth century. Further, we established from firsthand information and eyewitness reports that *ăi* presses operated on the island until the first quarter of the twentieth century. How can we explain the extraordinary longevity of a patently inefficient machine? What caused it to linger for so long in spite of the earlier introduction of better machines? Sociological deductions from the study of archaeology and the material culture are not very popular; neither can I do justice to a complex problem within the allotted space. In view, however, of the extraordinary eyewitness reports so amply corroborated by the archaeological finds and the ethnohistoric evidence, certain generalizations may not be out of order.

The phenomenon of the *ăi* is a curious instance not just of an anachronism or a laborious machine like, for example, the gigantic waterwheels or treadmills of antiquity, or simply an inefficient machine, but a veritable monster which required the laborers to *throw themselves* on it to make it work! What can we say of the social organization that tolerated or sanctioned the function of such a contraption for so long and so late?

The brutalization of the peasants of Corfu has already been alluded to in a previous paragraph. The inventories of the material culture indicate the crystallization of a passive symbiosis on the part of the traditional peasantry with an extremely poor level of technological organization. Ample evidence, to which only the barest reference can be made here (Partsch 1892, p. 271), shows clearly that for a long time —certainly until the turn of this century—the Corfu peasants, chained to an abject routine, were unable to modify significantly their technological patterns. Peasant routine was organized toward the barest and most marginal form of subsistence farming. No room was left for profit incentives or for cash values. Peasant existence was a culture of misery, characteristically referred to by the peasants as a life of "poverty and evil fate." The causes were diverse. To begin with, structural rules requiring equal inheritance and the giving of conspicuous dowries had caused the utter parcellation of the sparse and Lilliputian land holdings. But more important, unusually harsh taxation (beautifully documented in Andreades 1914)[10] left the freeholder with little cash if any at all throughout the long Venetian domination (1386–

10   The two-volumed monograph of Professor Andreades is a classic in social and economic history. The ethnohistoric documentation, particularly regarding the entire system of Venetian taxation of the Ionian Islands is excellent. Regarding the olive oil tax see Andreades (1914, Vol. 1, pp. 185–88, 211–93, Vol. 2, pp. 19–34, 206).

1797). During this long period the owners of large estates were able periodically to adopt costly innovations and equip their workshops with the wooden screw presses or other sophisticated machines of the time (Fig. 6.14). These were entirely out of reach for the peasants. The situation did not change in the nineteenth century,[11] although after the union of Corfu with Greece in 1864 a very slow process of depeasantization did start (Koty in Rose 1958, p. 340). But even then the bulk of the peasants remained at the mercy of the notorious practices of the petty oil merchants of the city, who advanced small credits in advance of the future crop always on their own usurious terms. This is only one instance of the historical enmity between the peasants and the city dwellers of Corfu. The peasants were regarded as fair game for ridicule and exploitation. The peasants feared and hated the citizenry and banded together very much like the Mexican all-embracing category of *nosotros los pobres* (Wolf 1966, p. 47; Redfield 1955, p. 133). The rivalry, much diluted by post–World War II mobility, persists still.

At the same time most of the peasants remained chained to the feudal system of Corfu, encumbered with harsh and demeaning obligations to absentee lords and more debts. The situation was terminated by the 1922 decree of the Pangalos government. Throughout this long period, the only cheap and plentiful commodity was labor (including the long-established, traditional, unspecialized craftsmanship which was adequate for the making of the *ăi* press). The women and children collected the olives, and the men, literally breaking their

---

11 Not that the wooden screw presses of the latifundia were much better. In the nineteenth century better screw presses were introduced from Italy ("Genoa presses"). In 1854 Damaskinos reported to the local Senate that "of the hundreds of workshops functioning on the island not more than four or five had good mills and presses." He concluded that the vast majority of workshops were equipped with machines that harnessed one fifth of the energy obtained by the four or five presses that had just been introduced. He stated that "the new presses yield one gallon more oil per each pressing operation," further adding that they provided other even more important advantages like speedier operation, better quality of oil, and humanization of labor (Damaskinos 1853, pp. 5–7). But the adoption of these innovations presupposed money. A note in the *Government Gazette of Corfu*, No. 257, p. 9, of November 28, 1835, estimated that the then "traditional" workshops of the large estates which were equipped with wooden screw presses cost one thousand *tallirs*, whereas workshops with "Genoa presses" cost two thousand *tallirs*. Needless to say, these estimates made no provision for labor, horses, ropes, baskets, containers, or maintenance. The money for this kind of investment was unavailable to the peasants, who had to be content with the *ăi* presses.

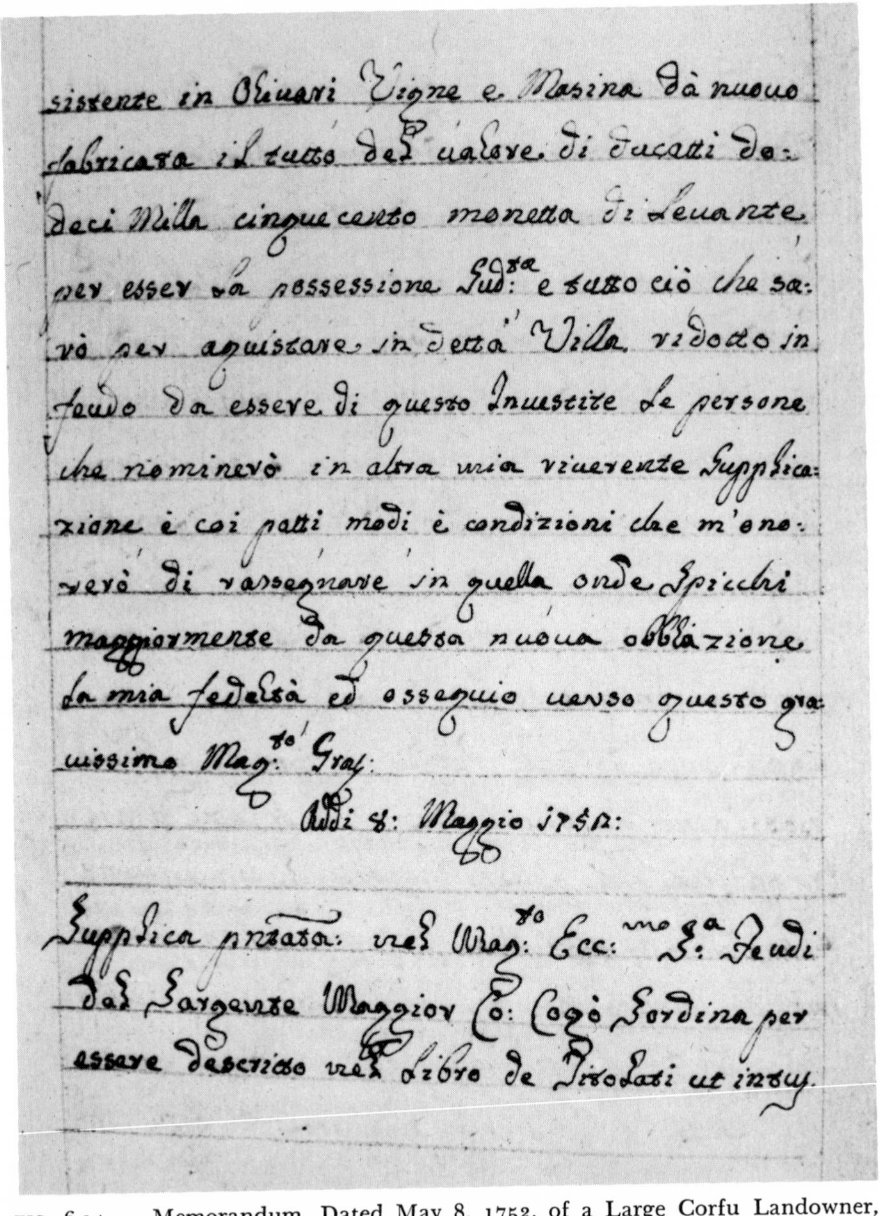
sistente in Olivari Vigne e Masina dà nuovo
fabricata il tutto del valore di Ducatti do:
deci Milla cinque cento monetta di Levante
per esser la possessione sud:ta e tutto ciò che sa:
rò per aquistare in detta Villa ridotto in
feudo da essere di questo Investite le persone
che nominerò in altra mia riverente Supplica:
zione è coi patti modi è condizioni che m'ono:
rerò di rassegnare in quella onde Spicchi
maggiormente da questa nuova obblazione
la mia fedeltà ed ossequio verso questo gra:
vissimo Mag:to Gra:

Addi 8: Maggio 1752:

Supplica presentata nel Mag:to Ecc:mo Sopra Feudi
del Sargente Maggior Co: Cogò Sordina per
essere descritto nel Libro de Titolati ut intus.

FIG. 6.14 Memorandum, Dated May 8, 1752, of a Large Corfu Landowner, Detailing the Modernization of His Workshop with New Machinery. The memorandum is in the Proveditori Sopra Feudi Infrascritti in Venice (original in the archives in Venice, Busta 1055, No. 57).

backs to obtain the precious oil, pressed the olives in low-yielding *ăi* presses. They loathed their lot and the machines that symbolized it. Yet there was no question of replacing them owing to lack of cash or reasonable credit. The situation engendered few incentives for the appearance or adoption of inventions which might maximize yields, save labor, and effect some tangible progress (Mumford 1963, p. 27; Lynn T. White 1962, p. 39). Or, in Firth's apt words, there was no "inducement for the improvement of material production" (1956, p. 11). In other words, the peasants of Corfu at this stage were laggard innovators because they lacked the potential for the pursuit of cash values and profit (Diaz 1967, p. 56). The interesting aspect of all this is that as soon as they realized that they could maximize yields for themselves they precipitated all sorts of changes (Blum and Blum 1965, pp. 43–44, 46; Rogers 1962, pp. 12 ff.; Sjoberg 1955, pp. 439–41; and compare with Barnett 1953, pp. 378–410).

For these reasons it is not at all surprising that the *ăi* press remained with the peasants of Corfu until the first quarter of this century while in their midst operated better, more efficient, and much more profitable machines introduced by the large and better organized estates 150 to 200 years earlier. The longevity of the *ăi* is a good example of technological lag and the attendant persistence of primitive craftsmanship, with the absence of capital outlays and the profit incentive.

Ironically, the term *ăi* has not altogether vanished from the present repertory of words. Its usage at present is limited to communication with the few remaining animate sources of energy on the island—horses, mules, and asses. The patient animals still perform their lowly duties under the stringent and peremptory command of their masters: "*Ăiii. . . !*"

REFERENCES CITED

Andreades, A. N.
   1914   *Peri tes Oikonomikes Dioikisseos tes Eptanissou epi Venetokratias* (On the Economic Policies of Venice in the Ionian Islands). 2 vols. Athens: Estia.
Baldi, B.
   1601   *Di Herone Alessandrino de gli Automati, Overo Machine se Moventi, Libri Due.* Venetia: Girolamo Porro.

Barnett, H. G.
  1953 *Innovation: The Basis of Cultural Change.* New York: McGraw-Hill.

Beck, T.
  1900 *Beiträge zür Geschicte des Maschinenbaues.* Berlin: Julius Springer.

Bennett, R., and J. Elton
  1898–1904 *History of Corn Milling.* 4 vols. London and Liverpool: Simpkin, Marshall.

Bloch, M. L. B.
  1961 *Feudal Society.* Chicago: University of Chicago Press.

Blum, R., and E. Blum
  1965 *Health and Healing in Rural Greece.* Stanford: Stanford University Press.

Bock, P. K.
  1969 *Modern Cultural Anthropology.* New York: Knopf.

Brand, C. M.
  1968 *Byzantium Confronts the West, 1180–1204.* Cambridge: Harvard University Press.

Brehaut, E.
  1933 *Cato the Censor on Farming (De Agricultura).* Columbia University Records of Civilization, No. 17. New York: Columbia University Press.

Chiotes, P.
  1865 *Historike Ekthesis Kai Engrafa peri Timarion Kerkyras.* Zante.

Clapham, M.
  1957 Printing. In S. Singer *et al.*, eds., *A History of Technology.* New York and London: Oxford University Press, 1954–58.

Coleman, J. C.
  1956 *Abnormal Psychology and Modern Life.* 2nd ed. Chicago: Scott Foresman.

Coon, C. S.
  1931 *Tribes of the Rif.* Harvard African Studies, Peabody Museum, Vol. 9. Cambridge: Harvard University Press.

Curwen, C. E.
  1941 More About Querns. *Antiquity* 15:15–32.

Dalton, G.
  1967 *Trial and Peasant Economies: Readings in Economic Anthropology.* New York: Natural History Press.

Damaskinos, A.
  1853 *Ekthesis tes epi tes Gheorghias Epitropes.* Corfu: Government Press.
  1864 *To en Kerkyra Agrotikon Zetema.* Corfu: Government Press.

Davy, J.
  1842 *Notes and Observations on the Ionian Islands and Malta.* 2 vols. London: Smith, Eder.

Diaz, M. N.
  1967   Introduction: Economic Relations in Peasant Society. In J. M. Potter et al., eds., *Peasant Society: A Reader*. Boston: Little, Brown.

Drachmann, A. G.
  1932   *Ancient Oil Mills and Presses*. Publications of Danske Videnskabernes Selskab, Archaeologiskkunsthistoriske Meddelelser, Vol. 1, No. 1. Copenhagen: Levin and Munksgaard.

Ellul, J.
  1964   *The Technological Society*. New York: Knopf.

Finlay, G.
  1856   *History of Greece Under the Ottoman and Venetian Domination*. Edinborough: Blackwood.

Firth, R.
  1946   *Malay Fishermen: Their Peasant Economy*. London: Kegan Paul, Trench, Trubner.
  1956   *Elements of Social Organization*. London: Watts.

Forbes, R. J.
  1955   *Studies in Ancient Technology*. Vol. 3. Leiden: E. J. Brill.
  1956   Food and Drink. In S. Singer et al., eds., *A History of Technology*. New York and London: Oxford University Press, 1954–58.
  1958   *Man the Maker*. London and New York: Abelard-Schuman.

Foster, G. M.
  1960–61   Interpersonal Relations in Peasant Society. *Human Organization* 19:174–78.
  1962   *Traditional Cultures and the Impact of Technological Change*. New York: Harper and Row.

Friedl, E.
  1962   *Vasilika: A Village in Modern Greece*. New York: Holt, Rinehart, and Winston.

Friedman, F. G.
  1953   The World of "La Miseria." *Partisan Review* 20:218–31.

Grasset de Saint-Sauveur, A.
  1800   *Voyage Historique, Littéraire et Pittoresque dans les Isles, et Possessions ci-devant Vénétiennes du Levant*. 3 vols. Paris: Tavernier.

Grimani, F.
  1856   *Relazioni Storico-Politiche delle Isole del Mar Ionio*. Venice: Cicogna.

Hammond, N. G. L.
  1967   *Epirus*. Oxford: Clarendon Press.

Heichelheim, F. M.
  1938   *Wirtschaftgeschichte des Altertums*. Leiden: A. W. Sijthoff.

Hoebel, E. A.
  1966   *Anthropology: The Study of Man*. 3rd rev. ed. New York: McGraw-Hill.

Hörle, J.
  1929 Catos Hausbücher. *Studien zur Geschichte des Altertums* 15:3–4. Paderborn.

Hultkranz, A.
  1968 The Aims of Anthropology: A Scandinavian Point of View. *Current Anthropology* 9:289–310.

Karavides, K.
  1931 *Agrotika*. Athenai.

Komiotes, M.
  1893 *Procheiron Dokimion peri tou en Kerkyra Susstematos tes Idioktessias*. Corfu: Koraes.

Legrand, E., and H. Pernot
  1910 *Bibliographie Ionienne*. 2 vols. Paris: Publications de l'École des Langues Orientales Vivantes.

McDonald, W. A.
  1969 *Progress into the Past: The Rediscovery of Mycenaean Civilization*. 1st Midland Book ed. Bloomington: Indiana University Press.

Matton, R.
  1960 Corfou. *Collections Institut Francais d'Athènes*. Athènes: Imprimeries de l'Institut Francais d'Athènes.

Mavrogordato, J.
  1931 *Modern Greece: Chronicle and Survey*. London: McMillan.

Mead, M., ed.
  1955 *Cultural Patterns and Technical Change*. New York: New American Library.

Mintz, S. W.
  1961 Pratik: Haitian Personal Economic Relationships. *Proceedings, 1961 Annual Spring Meeting of the American Ethnological Society*. Washington, D.C.: Smithsonian Institution. Pp. 54–63.

Moritz, L. A.
  1958 *Grain Mills and Flour in Classical Antiquity*. Oxford: Clarendon Press.

Mumford, L.
  1963 *Technics and Civilization*. 1st Harbinger Books ed. New York: Harcourt, Brace, and World.

Nix, L. M., and W. Schmidt, eds.
  1900 *Herons von Alexandria Mechanik und Katoptrik*. Vol. 2. Heronis Alexandrini Opera quae Supersunt Omnia (1899–1914). Greek, German, Arabic. Leipzig.

Nopsca, F., Baron
  1925 *Albanien, Bauten, Trachten, und Geräte Nordalbaniens*. Berlin and Leipzig: W. de Gruyter.

Partsch, J.
  1892 *He Nissos Kerkyra*. Trans. by P. Veja from German *Die Insel Korfu*. Petermans Mitteilunger, Vol. 19. Corfu: Nachamoulis.

Pierris, N.
  1966 *Bibliographie Ionienne*. Athens: Klisiounis. (Supplements Legrand 1910.)

Piggott, S.
  1965 *Approach to Archaeology*. New York: McGraw-Hill.
  1968 *Ancient Europe*. Chicago: Aldinè.

Pojago, G.
  1846–48 *Le Leggi Municipali delle Isole Ionie dall' Anno 1386 Fino alla Caduta della Republica Veneta*. 3 vols. Corfu: Kerkyra.

Porak, R.
  1943 *Un Village de France: Psycho-physioligie du paysan*. Paris: G. Doin.

Redfield, R.
  1955 *The Little Community: Viewpoints for the Study of a Human Whole*. Chicago: University of Chicago Press.

Releaux, F.
  1876 *The Kinematics of Machinery: Outlines of a Theory of Machines*. London: McMillan.

Robinson, D. M., and J. W. Graham
  1938 *Excavations at Olynthus, Part VIII: "The Hellenic House."* The Johns Hopkins University Studies in Archaeology, No. 25. Baltimore: The Johns Hopkins Press.

Rogers, E. M.
  1962 *Diffusion of Innovations*. New York: Free Press.

Rohan-Csermak, G. de
  1967 Ethnohistoire et Ethnologie Historique. *Ethnologia Europaea* 1: 130–58.

Rolt, L. T. C.
  1965 *A Short History of Machine Tools*. Cambridge: M.I.T. Press.

Rose, A. M.
  1958 *The Institutions of Advanced Societies*. Minneapolis: University of Minnesota Press.

Rostovtzeff, M.
  1941 *The Social and Economic History of the Hellenistic World*. 3 vols. Oxford: Clarendon Press.
  1957 *The Social and Economic History of the Roman Empire*. 2 vols., 2nd. ed. Oxford: Clarendon Press.

Sanders, I. T.
  1962 *Rainbow in the Rock: The People of Rural Greece*. Cambridge: Harvard University Press.

Santori, A.
  1852   *Storia dei Feudi nelle Venete Provincie*. Venice.

Sarakomenos, D.
  1920   *He Hellenike Elaea: He Kerkyraike Elaea*. Vol. 1. Athens: Sakellariou.
  1930   *He Hellenike Elaea: The Oil*. Vol. 2. Athens: Pyrsos.

Sathas, K. N., ed.
  1880–90   *Documents Inédits Pelatifs à l'Histoire de la Grèce au Moyen Age
            Publiés sous les Auspices de la Chambre des Deputés de Grèce*. Docu-
            ments tirés des archives de Venise. 9 vols. Paris.

Schweng, L. D.
  1962   An Indian Community Development Project in Bolivia. *America In-
          digena* 22:13–19.

Scrofani, X.
  1797   *Viaggio in Grecia Fatto nell' Anno 1794–1795*. 3 vols. London.

Sirakis, D.
  1925   Horismos Nomadhikes, Monemou kai Georgikes Ktenotrofeas. *Agricul-
          tural Bulletin of the Greek Agricultural Society* 12:651–777.

Singer, S., et al., eds.
  1954–58   *A History of Technology*. New York and London: Oxford University
            Press.

Sjoberg, G.
  1955   The Preindustrial City. *American Journal of Sociology* 60:438–45.

Smothers, F., W. H. McNeill, and E. D. McNeill
  1948   *Report on the Greeks*. New York: Twentieth Century Fund.

Sordinas, A.
  1971   *Old Olive Mills and Presses on the Island of Corfu, Greece*. Occasional
          Papers, No. 5. Memphis: Memphis State University Anthropological
          Research Center.
  1972   Ta Loutrouvia tes Kerkiras. To Historiko mias erevnas (The History of
          the Preindustrial Olive Oil Project in Corfu, with an Account of In-
          formants and their Contributions). *Deltion Anagnostikes Hetaereas
          Kerkiras* 9:7–16.

Sordinas, J. B.
  1911   *L'Olivier à Corfou*. Annual of School of Agriculture. University of
          Montpellier, France.
  1919   *He Elaea (The Olive Tree)*. Athens: Hellenike Georgike Hetaerea.

Stephanides, C. S.
  1948   Agricultural Machinery in Greece. *Foreign Agriculture* 12:250–53.

Sweet-Escott, B.
  1954   *Greece: A Political and Economic Survey, 1939–1953*. New York: Royal
          Institute of International Affairs.

Tanzer, H. H.
  1939   *The Common People of Pompeii*. Baltimore: The Johns Hopkins Press.

Theotokes, S.
1826   *Détails sur Corfou.* Corfou.

Typaldos, I. A.
1864   *He Feoudhokratea kai he Georgea Kata tas Ionius Nessous.* Athens.

Usher, A. P.
1954   *History of Mechanical Inventions.* 2nd ed. Cambridge: Harvard University Press.

Vickery, K. F.
1936   *Food in Early Greece.* Illinois Studies in the Social Sciences, University of Illinois, Vol. 20, No. 3. Urbana: University of Illinois Press.

Wace, A. J. B., and F. H. Stubbings
1962   *A Companion to Homer.* London: McMillan.

Weber, M.
1947   *The Theory of Social and Economic Organization.* Trans. by A. M. Henderson and Talcott Parsons. Glencoe: Free Press and Falcon's Wing Press.

Whipple, C. E.
1944   The Agriculture of Greece. *Foreign Agriculture* 8:75–96.

White, Leslie A.
1945   History, Evolutionism, and Functionalism: Three Types of Interpretation of Culture. *Southwestern Journal of Anthropology* 1:221–48.

1959   *The Evolution of Culture.* Paperback ed. New York: McGraw-Hill.

White, Lynn T., Jr.
1962   *Medieval Technology and Social Change.* Oxford: Clarendon Press.

Wolf, E. R.
1966   *Peasants.* Englewood Cliffs, N.J.: Prentice-Hall.

Wulff, H. E.
1966   *The Traditional Crafts of Persia: Their Development, Technology, and Influence on Eastern and Western Civilization.* Cambridge: M.I.T. Press.

Yerakaris, N. E.
1911   *Episkopissis tes en Kerkyra Idhioktessias.* Corfu: Kerkyra.

Chapter 7

A Multivariate Analysis of the Relationship of Artifactual to Cultural Modernity in Rural Buganda

Michael C. Robbins and Richard B. Pollnac

ABSTRACT   Those anthropologists who subscribe to a cognitive or ideational concept of culture see the material objects possessed and used by a people as distinct from that people's culture. From this perspective the question of the connection between the artifactual domain and the ideational or cultural domain becomes an open one. Since material objects lend themselves to exact quantification, the relationship between the domains becomes particularly amenable to empirical investigation.

In a survey of 109 household heads in a rural parish in Buganda, the authors collected information on the ownership of material possessions and on beliefs, aspirations, attitudes, and values. Items in each domain were coded as traditional or modern. When treated statistically, surprisingly little connection appeared between modern artifacts and modern cultural orientations. Those household heads who owned modern possessions did not always, or even usually, have modern beliefs and values. However, for those household heads under forty, a positive and significant relation did exist between artifactual and cultural modernity. Those heads over forty had an array of modern material objects but were usually less modern in their culture than were the heads under forty.

The results of this investigation support the concept that the material domain is distinct from the cultural one. The material domain may change with or without an accompanying movement in the cultural sphere. Thus, the investigation suggests that recent attempts to argue for a close, predictive relationship between the artifactual and cultural domains should proceed with caution.

174

Of fundamental concern to anthropologists working with material culture is the problem of discerning the nonmaterial social and cultural significance of material artifacts and remains. Anthropologists are not simply interested in the "things" themselves, but primarily in the amount and kind of information these things can provide about the culture, society, and behavior of their makers and users. Moreover, if we agree with Goodenough that "all we can see of a culture is its products and artifacts, the things people make, do, and say" (1966, p. 265), then it follows that everyone interested in learning about the culture of a population firsthand must eventually do so through the study of some form of its artifacts. If we exempt, for the moment, those who *do* archaeology, it appears that recently most anthropologists have neglected, rather seriously, the first of these three main information sources, *i.e.*, what people make and use. This seems especially unfortunate because the possession, use, and arrangement of material artifacts provide relatively permanent, objective data which can be both reliably and validly measured and documented (Pelto 1970, pp. 235–37; Lebar 1964; Kay 1964; Lewis 1969).

One of the great advantages to studying living populations is the opportunity to collect and intercorrelate data on not only what people "make" and "use" but also on what they "say" and "do." One is thus not only better able to reveal both the functional interrelationships of a community's material artifacts to its observable events, settings, and social relationships and differentiation, but also their cultural significance, that is, to examine the relationship of material artifacts to the ideational order of the individual members of a local population— their beliefs, attitudes, aspirations, values, ideas, preferences, principles of action, percepts, concepts, etc. In addition, these data, collected on living populations, can be of considerable value to prehistorians, who must use the information contained in material artifacts and their arrangements to understand the nature of the culture, society, and behavior of prehistoric populations. In large part, prehistorians depend on analogies of artifact-behavior-culture interrelationships of ethnographically known populations in making their interpretations. Furthermore, most prehistorians use the nature of material artifacts and their spatial distributions as evidence for social, behavioral, and cultural change through time.

Goodenough (1964, 1966, 1970) and others who subscribe to a

cognitive theory of culture have observed that because we learn about culture by studying its artifacts, we quite frequently and easily confuse artifacts with culture. That is, the artifacts themselves are often confused with the cultural standards, values, and concepts that guided their production. Moreover, the conceptual distinction between the phenomenal order of events, surroundings, behavior, and artifacts on the one hand, and the ideational order of beliefs, values, ideas, and principles of action of the members of a community on the other, becomes crucial for understanding the nature of change; for it is possible that change in one order will not correspond to change in the other.

As Goodenough (1966, p. 268) succinctly notes: "Observers commonly make the mistake of assuming that observed changes in material, behavioral, or social artifacts, and their arrangements in a community necessarily reflect a change in its members' culture: in their values, principles of action, and standards for getting things done."

Several anthropologists have recognized, and profitably employed, this distinction in their studies of the relationship of behavioral to cultural change. The works of Graves (1967), Rodgers and Gardner (1969), Inkeles (1966, 1969), Smith and Inkeles (1966), and Robbins and Pollnac (1969) are among the many that could be cited.

In fact, one anthropologist has gone so far as to call the "effective theoretical separation between cultural codes—cognitively based normative systems—and their enactment in behavior" one of the major recent breakthroughs in cultural anthropology (Keesing 1969).

A growing number of studies are being conducted on the relationship of material artifacts to social and economic patterns. A sample of recent ones include Chang (1968), Richardson and Thomas (1970), Laumann and House (1970), and Robbins (1966a). Far fewer studies have concerned themselves with the relationship between material artifacts and culture. Among these are the works of Segall, Campbell, and Herskovits (1966), Maxwell (1966), Robbins (1966b), Schensul, Paredes, and Pelto (1968), and Holloway (1969).

SCOPE OF THE PRESENT STUDY

We propose to examine the extent to which changes in certain aspects of the material style of life of a rural population in the Buganda region of Uganda can be used to explain (or predict) changes in certain aspects of the culture of its members. More specifically, we shall attempt to provide information on two basic questions:

1. Overall, are differences in the possession and use of certain modern material artifacts related to differences in the expression of certain attitudes, aspirations, beliefs, and values? That is, do individuals who possess modern material artifacts also express what we would define as modern beliefs, attitudes, and values?

2. Which material possessions offer the best prediction of the expression of which cultural items?

In our view, these questions warrant careful consideration if one recognizes both the multifunctional role of material artifacts and the variety of potential factors involved in their manufacture, adoption, maintenance, and use. On the surface it might appear that the possession and use of certain modern material items would constitute more accurate predictors of cultural modernity than others. For example, the use of wristwatches, Western clothing, and radios could perhaps be more easily construed as symbols and badges of modern cultural identities than, say, kerosene lanterns, bicycles, or metal roofs. But one cannot be sure. The opposite conclusion is possible or the use of either or both might merely reflect some other factor. That is, both of these kinds of items might be adopted and used simply because of their perceived utility as tools and functional equipment (or perhaps as indicators of socioeconomic distinctions) and not be related, at least in any significant way, to a change in the culture of their users. The essential point is that, in any given instance, whether artifactual change is in fact related to cultural change becomes questionable and must be answered by empirical research.

POPULATION AND PROCEDURES

Our fieldwork was conducted in Buganda, a former interlacustrine Bantu kingdom in Uganda (Map 7.1). The Baganda are a well-known East African agricultural population and several excellent accounts of their sociocultural system are available, such as Southwold (1965) and Fallers (1960), which are useful summaries and contain bibliographies. Although the Baganda retain a strong sense of their separate

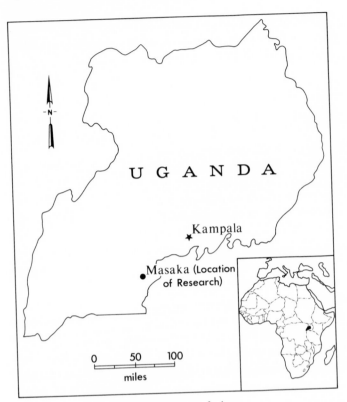

MAP 7.1   Uganda and the Research Area

cultural identity, they have eagerly accepted Western education, religion, and technology and, for the most part, seem committed to modernization: (Fallers 1961; Richards 1969; Kilbride and Robbins 1969; Kilbride 1970). Throughout our research, we were impressed by the considerable range of intrasocietal variation in modernization. For example, some individuals, educated in the West, owning automobiles and television sets, may live within walking distance of others who live in traditional thatched homes and wear traditional clothing. This marked range of variation provides an opportunity to explore several economic, social, and psychocultural concomitants of the relative extent of modernization and of the factors responsible.

The quantitative data which form the basis for examining the relationships of artifactual to cultural change are derived from responses to a social survey interview schedule. This schedule was administered in 1967 in Luganda to 109 household heads (57 females and 52 males), randomly sampled from a rural parish, Mulaka, near the town of Masaka. The households contained 519 individuals, approximately one fourth of the parish population. The interview schedules were designed to collect basic demographic, socioeconomic, and cultural information which could provide both a description of the population and data for assessing the modernization process occurring in this area. Included in the schedule were several items concerning the ownership of traditional and modern, personal and household, material possessions. The schedule also contained several questions which were constructed to provide data on both traditional and modern beliefs, aspirations, attitudes, and values. Both sets of items are described below.

It should be noted, however, that the present study is based on a secondary analysis of these materials. They were not collected primarily for the purposes of this chapter. The disadvantage of this, of course, is the potential danger that we made errors of omission and commission in the selection and use of both the material and cultural items. Had we gone into the field with the present objectives in mind, we would have collected more information of both kinds, including much more qualitative, or contextual, data from key informants, participant observation, and unstructured interviewing.[1] On the other hand, we feel we can quite confidently claim that we did not knowingly prejudice, or bias, our chances of objectively investigating these relationships because the data were not collected with the present purposes in mind. Nevertheless, the qualifications noted above place our study much more firmly in the exploratory, rather than in the definitive, category.

MODERN MATERIAL CULTURE

In Table 7.1 we have listed the material items used and their percentage distribution. A considerable amount of additional information on their availability, use, and meaning to the members of this population, as well as the social, economic, and cultural consequences of their adoption, can be found in Robbins and Kilbride (1972).

1   Additional fieldwork of this kind was conducted in 1969 and is reported on in part
    in Robbins and Kilbride (1972).

TABLE 7.1   Percentage Distribution of Material Items

Item[a]	Per-cent	Item	Per-cent
(12) clock	27	(23) concrete walls in main buildings	23
(13) watch	29		
(14) radio	39	(24) metal or tile roof on other buildings	40
(15) bicycle	48		
(16) drum	17	(25) photographs on walls	68
(17) motorcycle	06	(26) magazines	47
(18) automobile	07	(27) wears *Kanzu* at home or while visiting relatives and friends	78
(19) camera	06		
(20) iron	69		
(21) stove	47	(28) floor tile or concrete in main house	22
(22) metal or tile roof on main building	72		

[a]Variable identity numbers will be used for variable identification in subsequent tables.

The modernity of most of these items is quite obvious. Two traditional material items were also included. These refer to the possession of a Kiganda drum and a report by the respondent as to whether he (or her husband, in the case of a female) wears a *Kanzu*, a traditional ankle-length white gown worn by men, at home or while visiting relatives and friends (Pollnac and Robbins 1972). Material item responses were scored as either present (2) or absent (1). For the last two items (*Kanzu* and drum), we felt that negative responses could be interpreted as indicators of modernity.

CULTURAL MODERNITY

The items used to assess cultural modernity were selected on the basis of several considerations. Initially, they were selected because of both their face validity and the theoretical expectation that they would be valid predictors of attitudinal modernity. Furthermore, several similar items have been used in other studies conducted among the Baganda by other investigators (Doob 1960; Ainsworth and Ainsworth 1962); in other closely related interlacustrine Bantu populations, such as the Banyankole (Segall n.d.); and in other African and non-Western societies (Graves 1967; Smith and Inkeles 1966; Rogers 1969; Dawson

1967). These studies have shown that most of these items are reliable and valid predictors of other, more obvious, indicators of modernity, such as education, occupation, and exposure to mass media. Finally, our preliminary field research and several subsequent analyses of these materials had suggested that for the most part they had an acceptable degree of reliability and interrelationship with other, more ostensible indicators of modernization in our research community (Robbins and Pollnac 1969; Pollnac and Robbins 1972; Robbins *et al.* 1969).

Each cultural item is briefly described below, and the rationale for its inclusion is explained. Table 7.2 gives the percentage distribution of these items.

1. *If your daughter (or if you had a daughter) had a chance to go to the University, would you let her go?* A response of "yes" was coded modern (2); a response of "no" was coded traditional (1). This was based on the assumption that people's aspirations for a modern educa-

TABLE 7.2   Percentage Distribution of Cultural Modernity Items

	RESPONSE		
	Traditional (1)	*Modern* (2)	*More Modern* (3)
*Variable*a			
1 University Education for Daughter	06	94	
2 Husband and Wife Eating at Same Table	31	69	
3 More Than One Person Drinking from Same Straw	10	90	
4 Preference for Gourd or Glass	44	56	
5 Preference for Kiganda or European Dress	92	08	
6 Preference for Kiganda or European Doctor	42	58	
7 Delay of Second Child Until First One Weaned	59	06	35
8 Support for Poor, Helpless Clan Members	94	06	
9 Deceased Ancestors Can Harm People	43	02	55
10 Gratification Pattern	19	70	11
11 Self-Identity	57	28	15

aVariable numbers will identify variables in subsequent tables.

tion for their children (especially their daughters) would indicate the possession of modern values (Peskkin and Cohen 1967).

2. *Do you think it is proper for the husband and wife to eat at the same table?* Again, a response of "yes" was coded as modern (2), and a "no" was coded traditional (1). This question was constructed to determine if the respondent was accepting the modern emphasis toward the equality of sexual status (Peskkin and Cohen 1967; Levine 1970).

3. *Should more than one person drink out of the same straw?* "Yes" was coded as (1), and "no" as (2). Traditionally, many Baganda drank from the same gourd and straw as a symbol of social solidarity. Public health propaganda, however, has tried to discourage these practices for hygienic reasons. This item might determine if the person has been exposed to and/or has accepted this information.

4. *Do you prefer drinking from a gourd or a glass?* The response "gourd" was coded (1); a "glass" (2). The choice of a traditional Kiganda gourd for drinking rather than a glass is often used to symbolize that one is a "pure" Muganda (*Muganda wawu*). Moreover, one who refuses a gourd, or chooses a glass, is usually trying to indicate to others that he is both modern and refined.

5. *Do African women look more beautiful in Kiganda or European clothing?* A response "Kiganda" was coded (1), and "European" (2).

6. *Are there any diseases a Kiganda doctor can cure better than a European doctor?* If the respondent named any diseases, he was coded (1); if he stated there were no diseases, he was coded (2). This is admittedly a dubious item. We felt, however, that those who either did not believe there were any diseases that a Kiganda doctor could cure better, or who would not mention one, were reflecting either considerable exposure to modernity or a desire to present a modern impression of themselves to us during the interview.

7. *Do you believe that the second child should not arrive before the first child is weaned?* "Yes" was coded traditional (1); a response of "maybe," "possibly," "didn't know for sure," "couldn't say," etc., was coded as modern (2); and a definite "no" was coded more modern (3). This question was designed to measure whether people were adhering to, or expressing, traditional attitudes toward the customary postpartum sex taboo.

8. *Should poor, helpless clan members be supported?* "Yes" was

coded (1); "no" was coded (2). This question intended to measure whether people felt that, irrespective of a person's contribution, an ascribed membership in a kin-group nevertheless entitled him to support. A response of "no," it was felt, would indicate an emphasis on the relatively more modern form of economic individualism (Mboya 1969).

9. *Do you believe that deceased ancestors can do people harm?* Again, a response of "yes" was coded (1), a response of "not sure," "possibly," etc., was coded (2), and a definite "no" was coded (3). This question was aimed at determining whether people felt that traditional sources of social control in the form of deceased ancestral kin were important. We decided on an ordinal measure because of the corresponding belief that if a person denies the power of deceased ancestors, there is an even greater certainty that he will in fact be harmed. Therefore, those who feared to respond negatively or were unsure of how to respond seemed to be clearly intermediate.

10. *If someone gave you 1000 shillings* [approximately $743], *what would you do with it?* Several recent studies (Doob 1960; Graves 1967; Rodgers 1967; Pollnac and Robbins 1972) have noted that the tendency to voluntarily postpone more immediate desires in order to obtain more substantial future rewards is a characteristic of people beginning to modernize. Thus, if the response to the above question indicated that the expenditure or the use of the money would not yield immediate goal attainment but rather be postponed for future rewards, such as investment in farms, bank savings, school fees, goods for trading, etc., the response was coded (3) more modern, or deferred goal gratification. If the individuals indicated that they would buy a radio, cigarettes, or food, their response was coded (1) traditional, or immediate goal gratification. If the response was a combination of the two patterns, it was code (2) modern, or mixed.

11. The nature of a person's self-image as a modern person was based on his response to the question, *Do you consider yourself to be mainly: a traditional Muganda* (1), *a modern European-type person* (3), *or a "mixture"* (2)*?* This item was included because its more subjective nature allowed respondents to map *themselves* onto a modernity continuum and because one's self-image is a cognitive and motivational system of strong emotional concern. Several anthropologists have investigated and disclosed the crucial relationship of both

self-identity and reference group change to rapid sociocultural change (Berreman 1964; Parker 1964; Chance 1965; Goodenough 1966, Chaps. 8, 9; Wallace 1968).

THE RELATIONSHIP OF ARTIFACTUAL TO CULTURAL MODERNITY

The first step in the analysis was to determine whether there is any overall, significant relationship between the possession of material artifacts and the expression of modern cultural attitudes. Canonical correlation was used to examine this relationship. With canonical correlation one can determine the strength of association between two sets of variables and test the significance of this association. Canonical correlation also provides information that indicates the manner in which the two sets of variables can be combined to maximize their correlation. This information is provided in the form of loadings which indicate the degree to which the individual variables contribute to the canonical variates. This technique was selected for two reasons: first, preliminary factor analyses indicated that we could not assume that either the material or the cultural sets of variables could be reduced to a unidimensional scale; and second, canonical analysis is scale free and thus would not be affected by the mixture of nominal and ordinal scales present in our data.[2] The results of the canonical analysis are presented in Table 7.3.

As can be seen, this analysis indicates that the overall relationship between the possession of material items and traditional/modern attitudes is not statistically significant at the .05 level. The reason for this lack of statistical significance with a relatively high canonical correlation coefficient (.64) is that as the number of variables in each set is increased, the probability is also increased that some weighted combination of variables will be highly correlated by chance. See Bartlett (1941) for the rationale of this statistical test.

The contribution that each variable of the two sets makes to the maximum canonical correlation is also presented in Table 7.3. The loadings indicate that the attitudes concerning a husband and wife eating at the same table, the arrival of a second child before the first is

2   For a discussion of the mathematical rationale of canonical correlation see Hotelling (1936). For recent discussions of the application of canonical correlation see Koons (1962), Cooley and Lohnes (1962), and Rummel (1970).

TABLE 7.3   Relation of Modern Artifactual to Modern Cultural Items:
The Maximum Canonical Vector

Cultural Items		Material Items	
(4)	0.548	(27)	0.519
(5)	0.469	(14)	0.424
(7)	0.411	(21)	0.371
(2)	0.303	(19)	0.361
(1)	0.251	(26)	0.290
(11)	0.200	(28)	0.270
(9)	0.056	(24)	0.104
(8)	0.004	(20)	0.034
(10)	−0.007	(25)	0.020
(6)	−0.056	(23)	−0.123
(3)	−0.103	(15)	−0.128
		(16)	−0.142
		(12)	−0.177
		(13)	−0.219
		(18)	−0.222
		(22)	−0.250
		(17)	−0.374

Canonical Correlation = 0.64; $X^2 = 207.9$; $D_f = 187$; P⟩.05; N = 109

weaned, drinking from a gourd versus a glass, and Kiganda versus
European style clothing for women from the cultural item set, and the
radio, camera, stove, and wearing of a *Kanzu* from the material item
set, are the variables which contribute the most to the canonical vector
which explains most of the variance in the two sets. It should be remembered, however, that this association was not statistically significant at the .05 level.

Since the canonical analysis failed to indicate any overall significant relationship between the material and cultural variables, the
next step was to determine whether any of the dimensions derived by
means of the factor analyses mentioned above were significantly related. See Table 7.4.

Factor scores were calculated for each household on each factor,
and these scores were then intercorrelated.[3] The factor score correlation matrix is presented in Table 7.5. The correlations between the

3 For discussions of the calculation and use of factor scores see Robbins *et al.* (1969)
   and Rummel (1970).

TABLE 7.4   Orthogonally Rotated Factors (Varimax)[a]

| | Material Item Factor Analysis | | | | Cultural Item Factor Analysis | | | |
Variable	I	II	III	h^{2b}	Variable	I	II	h^{2b}
12	.253	−.289	.447	.347	1	.676	.069	.462
13	.081	−.536	.184	.328	2	.360	−.320	.232
14	.248	−.610	.221	.482	3	−.095	−.291	.094
15	.055	−.350	.263	.195	4	.140	−.629	.415
16	.004	.022	.249	.063	5	.010	−.203	.041
17	.054	−.408	−.157	.194	6	−.008	.123	.015
18	.402	−.301	.065	.256	7	−.054	.319	.105
19	.125	−.284	.063	.100	8	−.426	−.015	.182
20	.154	−.572	.202	.392	9	.127	−.060	.020
21	.302	−.678	.164	.578	10	.375	.064	.145
22	.232	−.185	.508	.346	11	−.035	−.415	.173
23	.788	−.143	.148	.663				
24	.405	−.226	.511	.476	Percent			
25	−.016	−.253	.586	.408	Total	8.7	8.4	
26	.124	−.024	.555	.324	Variance			
27	.219	−.180	.003	.080				
28	.787	−.149	.241	.700				

Percent
Total   11.5   13.0   10.4
Variance

[a]Initial communality estimates were squared multiple correlations. Final communalities are the result of a maximum of fifteen iterations.

[b]h^2 were calculated from the patterns presented. Criterion for number of factors rotated: eigenvalue of 0.7000.

Cultural and Material factors are extremely low, and although one correlation reaches statistical significance it accounts for only 9 percent of the variance in the factor scores of the two factors. Considering that Material Factor II and Cultural Factor II only explain respectively 13 and 8.4 percent of the variance of their respective data sets, the relationship does not have much predictive power.

Stepwise multiple regression was next applied to determine how much we could increase the amount of variance explained by increasing the number of factors used as predictor variables. The criteria variables were the two Cultural factors taken singly and the predictor variables, the Material Item factors, added in a stepwise fashion in

TABLE 7.5   Intercorrelations and Multiple Correlations of Material Item and Cultural Item Factors

	(1)	(2)	(3)	(4)
(1) Cultural Factor I	—			
(2) Cultural Factor II	−.046	—		
(3) Material Factor I	.086	−.173	—	
(4) Material Factor II	−.120	.300	−.096	—
(5) Material Factor III	.137	.021	.120	−.140

R 1.45 = .170 P⟩.05   R 2.34 = .333 P⟨.01
R 1.345 = .181 P⟩.05   R 2.345 = .335 P⟨.01
                               N = 109

terms of the amount of variance explained. The results of this analysis are also presented in Table 7.5. The multiple correlation between the Material Item factors and Cultural Factor I never reaches statistical significance at the .05 level, whereas the multiple correlations between the Material Item factors and Cultural Factor II are significant at the .01 level at each step. Although statistically significant, this multiple correlation accounts for only 11 percent of the variance, and, considering the amount of the variance in the data set explained by the factors involved, the relation, once again, is not very meaningful in terms of predictive power.

The final step in the analysis was to determine the relationships between the possession of specific material items and the expression of specific cultural attitudes. The results of this analysis are presented in Table 7.6. The results shown in Table 7.6 reveal essentially the same pattern of cultural and material item intercorrelation as the canonical, factor, and multiple correlation analyses presented and discussed above. In addition, however, it can be seen that the ownership of an automobile and/or motorcycle is also related to a few cultural items (Nos. 6, 8). These relationships, however, could quite easily be spurious because of the small number of motor vehicle owners (cf. Table 7.1).

In general, the results of this analysis support the others to the effect that there is little or no relationship between the ownership of modern material items and the expression of modern cultural attitudes. In fact, the few significant relationships that are present in Table 7.6 are close to the number that would be expected by chance.

TABLE 7.6   Intercorrelation (Phi) of Material and Cultural Items

Material Items	Cultural Items										
	1	2	3	4	5	6	7	8	9	10	11
12	.096	.112	.023	.024	.007	.080	.061	.070	.065	.080	.171
13	.018	.150	.110	.077	.020	.154	.078	.164	.171	.027	.190
14	.063	.189*	.103	.236*	.046	.134	.079	.140	.096	.168	.216
15	.029	.165	.076	.077	.020	.111	.066	.102	.109	.202	.053
16	.048	.031	.127	.015	.022	.150	.070	.045	.080	.082	.230
17	.030	.037	.014	.007	.008	.406*	.189	.402*	.028	.090	.141
18	.009	.081	.036	.067	.029	.351*	.140	.347*	.075	.119	.057
19	.030	.123	.014	.088	.271*	.047	.091	.063	.136	.044	.124
20	.049	.306*	.002	.175	.018	.123	.202	.105	.186	.146	.249*
21	.101	.298*	.089	.188*	.008	.120	.097	.120	.130	.123	.131
22	.071	.154	.093	.047	.052	.165	.086	.156	.132	.216	.137
23	.012	.212*	.002	.189*	.014	.168	.040	.143	.209	.139	.196
24	.006	.105	.128	.093	.028	.129	.110	.150	.117	.070	.118
25	.005	.279*	.070	.006	.024	.146	.151	.160	.166	.160	.188
26	.025	.113	.022	.055	.014	.095	.148	.091	.108	.058	.102
27	.114	.180	.079	.364*	.132	.104	.132	.082	.126	.063	.208
28	.004	.176	.012	.063	.004	.195*	.091	.150	.192	.050	.182

*Significant $P(.05$; $N = 109$

DISCUSSION AND CONCLUSION

Considering the two original objectives, the results suggest that in terms of the procedures we used: (1) There is little or no overall relationship between the ownership and use of certain modern material items and the expression of certain modern cultural attitudes in this community; (2) because little or no relationship was discovered between the material items on the one hand, and the cultural items on the other, and the relationships that were found could rather easily be attributed to chance, the question regarding the best predictor of cultural items from material items becomes inconsequential.

One possible explanation for these rather unexpected results can perhaps be found in the nature of the differential acquisition of material items within certain subgroups of the population. In this rural region of Buganda differences in occupation, cash income, land ownership, and formal education have all contributed to a rather marked socioeconomic stratification of the population which bears a strong relationship to age. Of interest here is the fact that there are, among the younger population, individuals with a modern outlook on life acquired from a good deal of formal education and exposure to other modernizing influences (*e.g.*, mass media exposure). Representative of this group would be primary school teachers, clerks, small business-men, medical assistants, etc. Although less affluent than the older rural elite, they nevertheless possess the desire and economic means to ob-tain a modern material style of life. Among this segment of the pop-ulation one can ostensibly observe a positive relationship between cultural and material modernity.

In contrast, most older members of the population are peasant farmers who adhere rather strongly to traditional Kiganda culture. They often have little or no education and speak only Luganda. On the whole, they have been comparatively less exposed to modernizing influences than the younger group. With the exception of a few older, wealthy, land-owning families, they tend to lack the economic means of obtaining an elaborate material style of life or participating as in-tensively in modern sociocultural activities. Moreover, their relatively small cash reserves are often put aside to provide for their children's and younger relatives' education. Nevertheless, through time, they have accumulated a rather impressive array of modern material items, particularly those which provide for a more comfortable and efficient life-style (*e.g.*, metal roofs, lanterns, bicycles, etc.). It is therefore among this subgroup that one observes the greatest disparity between cultural and material modernity. Given these considerations, we would suspect that the overall relationship between cultural and ma-terial modernity for the population as a whole has been obfuscated by the nature of these subgroup differences.

In an effort to explore this possibility, we subdivided the total sample into two subgroups based on age—those under forty (N=44) and those forty and older (N=65).[4] Using canonical correlation, the overall relationship between the material and cultural factors (cf. Ta-ble 7.4) was examined within each subgroup. The results of these sec-ondary analyses indicate, as expected, that among the younger group

4   Additional information on the socioeconomic stratification of this area and the rationale for using these age categories can be found in Robbins *et al.* (1969) and Kilbride (1970).

there is a positive and significant relationship ($R_C=.55$, $x^2=15.33$, d.f.$=6$, p$<$.02) between cultural and material modernity; whereas among the older group the relationship was not statistically significant ($R_C=.40$, $x^2=11.93$, d.f.$=6$, p$>$.05). These findings suggest that in the present case intrapopulation variation probably contributed to our inability to discover a relationship between material and cultural modernity for the population as a whole.

Perhaps the most significant lesson to be learned from this study is the potential and, in this instance, the very real hazards of making superficial inferences about one domain from the other. While our results are far from definitive and, of course, do not necessarily apply elsewhere, they do seem especially pertinent to research which attempts to use information concerning material culture to infer the nature of the nonmaterial culture of both past and present populations. Many archaeological investigators, for example, have called for caution with regard to making inferences from material to nonmaterial culture. Eoin McWhite (1956) presents a table of inferences arranged in a series of seven levels corresponding to the degree of abstraction involved. Level 7, the highest, is the psychological level which consists of "complex inferences from material culture to the behavioral and ideological culture of a social group or of an individual person" (p. 5). He warns that on the higher levels of his scale the inferences become increasingly hypothetical, and that at the highest level (Level 7), "intuition (in the popular sense of the word) replaces the more logical processes" (p. 6). Willey and Phillips (1958, p. 50) warn that "under special conditions even a primitive population may exhibit revolutionary changes in material culture without losing its identity as a society." Chang (1967, p. 35) agrees with this position and notes that "isolated and idiosyncratic shifts in stylistic tastes and fashions may occur on a grand scale irrespective of the social order which continues." In short, these theorists seem to agree that the degree of reliability in such inferences is in an inverse proportion to the degree of abstraction from the artifacts involved.

Recently, L. R. Binford (1968), after citing a number of authors who have subscribed to the preceding position, has attempted to develop an argument against this more cautious approach. We believe that the evidence presented here embarrasses Binford's position (although we do not deny the existence of a relationship between material and nonmaterial culture). David L. Clarke (1968, p. 359) has argued that the complex relationships involved have "tended to lead to either a desperate over simplification of the relationship or a denial of its existence." He feels that the solution to this problem lies in the field of social anthropology. The means by which social anthropology can help solve this problem have been exemplified by Ascher (1962), Goggin and Sturtevant (1964), Robbins (1966a), Heider (1967), Anderson (1969), and others. We feel that our present ethnographic example also supports the cautious position described above. Only with more ethnographic research which quantitatively assesses the empirical relationship between material and nonmaterial culture can we approach a solution to this problem. The solutions are beyond the stage of armchair speculation.

In conclusion, we would also like to suggest that our study supports the value of conceptually distinguishing the phenomenal order of a community's artifacts, events, and surroundings from the ideational order, or culture, of its members. This would appear to be especially important with respect to change. In this instance, there is clearly a lack of correspondence in the direction of change in the two orders for the population as a whole. We do not want to imply, however, that there could never be a strong relationship between them. Hypothetically, long-term sociocultural stability and isolation could potentially result in a stronger relationship between the two orders. Rather, what we want to stress is the necessity of examining the specific nature of possible relationships, in an empirical manner, prior to making generalizations about one from the other.[5]

5   We take this opportunity to acknowledge and express our gratitude for the generous support and assistance of several persons and institutions. In particular, we thank the Makerere Institute of Social Research, Makerere University College, Kampala, Uganda, for their help during our tenure there as research associates in 1967 and 1969. Our fieldwork in 1967 was supported by a grant from the Agricultural Development Council, Inc., and a National Science Foundation institutional grant administered by Pennsylvania State University. Our fieldwork in 1969 and the data analysis for both periods have been supported by the Wenner-Gren Foundation for Anthropological Research, a grant from the Graduate School Research Support Fund at the University of Missouri, and a Biomedical Sciences Support Grant Fr-07053 from the General Research Support Branch, Division of Research Resources, Bureau of Health Professions, Education, and Manpower Training, National Institutes of Health. We also thank Robert Benfer, John Bregenzer, Richard Diehl, James Gavan, Ward Goodenough, Philip Kilbride, Marvin Loflin, John Page, Pertti Pelto, and Ralph Rowlett for reading and commenting on various drafts of this paper.

REFERENCES CITED

Ainsworth, M., and L. Ainsworth
  1962   Acculturation in East Africa IV: Summary and Discussion. *Journal of Social Psychology* 57:417–32.

Anderson, K.
  1969   Ethnographic Analogy and Archaeological Interpretation. *Science* 163: 133–38.

Ascher, R.
  1962   Ethnography for Archaeology: A Case from the Seri Indians. *Ethnology* 1:360–69.

Bartlett, M.
  1941   The Statistical Significance of Canonical Correlations. *Biometrika* 32: 29–38.

Berreman, G.
  1964   Aleut Reference Group Alienation, Mobility, and Acculturation. *American Anthropologist* 66:231–50.

Binford, L.
  1968   Archeological Perspectives. In S. Binford and L. Binford, eds., *New Perspectives in Archeology*. Chicago: Aldine.

Chance, N.
  1965   Acculturation, Self-Identification, and Personality Adjustment. *American Anthropologist* 67:372–93.

Chang, K.
  1967   *Rethinking Archaeology*. New York: Random House.
  1968   *Settlement Archaeology*. Palo Alto: National Press Books.

Clarke, D.
  1968   *Analytical Archaeology*. London: Methuen.

Cooley, W., and P. Lohnes
  1962   *Multivariate Procedures for the Behavioral Sciences*. New York: Wiley.

Dawson, J.
  1967   Traditional versus Western Attitudes in West Africa: The Construction, Validation, and Application of a Measuring Device. *British Journal of Social and Clinical Psychology* 6:81–96.

Doob, L.
  1960   *Becoming More Civilized*. New Haven: Yale University Press.

Fallers, L.
  1961   Ideology and Culture in Uganda Nationalism. *American Anthropologist* 63:677–86.

Fallers, M.
  1960   *The Eastern Lacustrine Bantu (Ganda, Soga)*. London: International African Institute.

Goggin, J., and W. Sturtevant
    1964   The Clausa: A Stratified Nonagricultural Society (With Notes on Sibling
            Marriage). In W. Goodenough, ed., *Explorations in Cultural Anthro-
            pology*. New York: McGraw-Hill.

Goodenough, W.
    1964   Introduction. In W. Goodenough, ed., *Explorations in Cultural An-
            thropology*. New York: McGraw-Hill.

    1966   *Cooperation in Change: An Anthropological Approach to Community
            Development*. New York: Wiley.

    1970   *Description and Comparison in Cultural Anthropology*. Chicago: Aldine.

Graves, T.
    1967   Psychological Acculturation in a Tri-Ethnic Community. *Southwestern
            Journal of Anthropology* 23:337–50.

Heider, Karl G.
    1967   Archeological Assumptions and Ethnographic Facts: A Cautionary Tale
            from New Guinea. *Southwestern Journal of Anthropology* 23:52–64.

Holloway, R.
    1969   Culture: A *Human* Domain. *Current Anthropology* 10:395–412.

Hotelling, H.
    1936   Relations Between Two Sets of Variates. *Biometrika* 28:321–77.

Inkeles, A.
    1966   The Modernization of Man. In M. Weiner, ed., *Modernization: The
            Dynamics of Growth*. New York: Basic Books.

    1969   Making Men Modern: On the Causes and Consequences of Individual
            Change in Six Developing Countries. *American Journal of Sociology*
            75:208–25.

Kay, P.
    1964   A Guttman Scale of Tahitian Consumer Behavior. *Southwestern Journal
            of Anthropology* 20:160–67.

Keesing, R.
    1969   On Quibblings over Squabblings of Siblings: New Perspectives on Kin
            Terms and Role Behavior. *Southwestern Journal of Anthropology* 25:
            207–27.

Kilbride, P.
    1970   Individual Modernization and Pictorial Perception among the Baganda
            of Uganda. Ph.D. dissertation, University of Missouri, Columbia.

Kilbride, P., and M. Robbins
    1969   Pictorial Depth Perception and Acculturation among the Baganda.
            American Anthropologist 71:293–301.

Koons, P.
    1962   Canonical Analysis. In H. Borko, ed., *Computer Application in the Be-
            havioral Sciences*. Englewood Cliffs, N.J.: Prentice-Hall.

Laumann, E., and J. House
    1970   Living Room Styles and Social Attributes: The Patterning of Material

Artifacts in a Modern Urban Community. *Sociology and Social Research* 54:321–42.

Lebar, F.
1964   A Household Survey of Economic Goods on Romonum Island, Truk. In W. Goodenough, ed., *Explorations in Cultural Anthropology*. New York: McGraw-Hill.

Levine, R.
1970   Personality and Change. In J. Paden and E. Soja, eds., *The African Experience*. Evanston, Ill.: Northwestern University Press.

Lewis, O.
1969   The Possessions of the Poor. *Scientific American* 221:115–24.

McWhite, E.
1956   On the Interpretation of Archeological Evidence in Historical and Sociological Terms. *American Anthropologist* 58:3–25.

Maxwell, R.
1966   Onstage and Offstage Sex: Exploring an Hypothesis. *Cornell Journal of Social Relations* 1:75–84.

Mboya, T.
1969   The Impact of Modern Institutions on the East African. In P. Gulliver, ed., *Tradition and Transition in East Africa*. Berkeley and Los Angeles: University of California Press.

Parker, S.
1964   Ethnic Identity and Acculturation in Two Eskimo Villages. *American Anthropologist* 66:325–40.

Pelto, P.
1970   *Anthropological Research: The Structure of Inquiry*. New York: Harper and Row.

Peskkin, A., and R. Cohen
1967   The Values of Modernization. *Journal of Developing Areas* 2:7–22.

Pollnac, R., and M. Robbins
1972   Gratification Orientations and Modernization in Rural Buganda. *Human Organization* 31:63–72.

Richards, A.
1969   *The Multicultural States of East Africa*. Montreal: McGill-Queens University Press.

Richardson, M., and L. Thomas
1970   Behavioral Cycles and Land Use in Puntarenas, Costa Rica. Paper presented at the Southern Anthropological Society Meeting in Athens, Georgia.

Robbins, M.
1966a House Types and Settlement Patterns: An Application of Ethnology to Archaeological Interpretation. *Minnesota Archaeologist* 28:3–35.
1966b Material Culture and Cognition. *American Anthropologist* 68:745–48.

Robbins, M., and P. Kilbride
  1972 Microtechnology in Rural Buganda. In H. Bernard and P. Pelto, eds., *Technology and Social Change*. New York: Macmillan.

Robbins, M., and R. Pollnac
  1969 Drinking Patterns and Acculturation in Rural Buganda. *American Anthropologist* 71:276–85.

Robbins, M., A. Williams, P. Kilbride, and R. Pollnac
  1969 Factor Analysis and Case Selection in Complex Societies: A Buganda Example. *Human Organization* 28:227–34.

Rodgers, W.
  1967 Changing Gratification Orientations: Some Findings from the Out Island Bahamas. *Human Organization* 26:200–205.

Rodgers, W., and R. Gardner
  1969 Linked Changes in Values and Behavior in the Out Island Bahamas. *American Anthropologist* 71:21–35.

Rogers, E.
  1969 *Modernization Among Peasants: The Impact of Communication*. New York: Holt, Rhinehart, and Winston.

Rummel, R.
  1970 *Applied Factor Analysis*. Evanston, Ill.: Northwestern University Press.

Schensul, S., A. Paredes, and P. Pelto
  1968 The Twilight Zone of Poverty: A New Perspective on an Economically Depressed Area. *Human Organization* 27:30–40.

Segall, M.
  n.d. Personal communication.

Segall, M., D. Campbell, and M. Herskovits
  1966 *The Influence of Culture on Visual Perception*. Indianapolis: Bobbs-Merrill.

Smith, D., and A. Inkeles
  1966 The OM Scale: A Comparative Socio-Psychological Measure of Individual Modernity. *Sociometry* 4:353–77.

Southwold, M.
  1965 The Ganda of Uganda. In J. Gibbs, ed., *Peoples of Africa*. New York: Holt, Rhinehart, and Winston.

Wallace, A.
  1968 Anthropological Contributions to the Theory of Personality. In E. Norbeck, D. Price-Williams, and W. McCord, eds., *The Study of Personality: An Interdisciplinary Appraisal*. New York: Holt, Rhinehart, and Winston.

Willey, G. R., and P. Phillips
  1958 *Method and Theory in American Archaeology*. Chicago: University of Chicago Press.

Part Three

The Spatial Configuration

Miles Richardson

This section takes material culture and looks at its spatial expression, at how material items disperse and coalesce across the earth's surface to form distinctive configurations that reflect different histories and different societies. The first three articles trace the diffusion of artifacts, their incorporation and retention by social units, and their expression on the landscape. The remaining four articles take the spatial displays of several societies and ask how those displays relate to peoples' lives—to their attempts to make life more secure in the face of conflicting demands originating from the societies of which they are a part.

The man whose name is synonymous with the study of worldwide diffusion of material items is George Carter. For years he has been hammering on the wall of isolation that Americanist scholars have erected around the New World. In "Domesticates as Artifacts" he gives that wall an extra-hard blow. He convincingly points out that a domesticated hen is as much a part of man's material inventory as the pot in which the hen is cooked. And the great advantage of using domesticates as tracers of diffusion is that the main argument against diffusion—independent parallel invention—is blunted, for as the author says, "You can't reinvent a chicken." Not only does Dr. Carter use the presence and absence of several animals and plants to argue his case for transoceanic diffusion, he also draws attention to similarities in the linguistic and cultural contexts in which these animals and plants occur. The strength of such evidence rams hard against the wall of New World isolationism.

Complementary to the process of diffusion is the process of incorporation. As material items diffuse from one society to another, they do not simply move through like water through a metal pipe; they spread out into the society and become incorporated into it to the degree that the society (or its investigator) uses it to define the society's boundaries. Dolores Newton documents the final result of the incorporation process in her study of the hammock as an indicator of the boundaries between two Brazilian Indian tribes. Although the Krĩkati and the Pukobye intermarry to a degree and participate in each other's ceremonies, as shown by Dr. Newton's exhaustive examination of the data on hammock construction, the remaining social distance between the two is sufficient to support cultural diversity. The work of Dr. Newton bears directly on the archaeologist's problem of using material items to draw social boundaries.

Carter and Newton look at traits and their contexts. The next author, Fred Kniffen, looks at the changing landscape of a single area—southwestern Louisiana. He uses a number of traits to demonstrate the way that material cultures of different peoples interact with the same natural environment to produce dissimilar cultural expressions on the landscape. In so doing, Dr. Kniffen shows us how the cultural geographer uses material culture to study the dynamic interrelations between man and land.

The article by Thomas Schorr is a bridge between the previous three articles, which focus on diffusion and the landscape, and the next three, which turn our attention to the way that man utilizes the environment that he constructs around his activities. Like Kniffen, Schorr looks at the human landscape of a single area, Colombia's Cauca Valley, and, like Kniffen, he sees a portion of that landscape as arising out of the interplay between man and land. Yet Dr. Schorr quickly moves to the position that views much of the material, spatial, behavioral, and attitudinal displays as adaptations to the endemic threat of violence. He gives a vivid account of how local populations use both the natural and the material environments as devices to secure life and property against the recurrent physical violence that, according to Schorr, has plagued the area since before the arrival of the Spanish *conquistadores.*

Pearl Katz, in her "Adaptations to Crowded Space: The Case of Taos Pueblo," takes the material environment as a given and examines how the individual acts within its crowded confines. The Taos Pueblo population is not large nor is the density great, but because it is the residential and ceremonial center of the Taos Indians, the intensity of interaction is high. This intensity of social exchange, particularly within the Taos Pueblo house, produces behavioral responses that are strikingly similar to those of other crowded animals—such as the inhabitants of New York City.

A little way down the Rio Grande from Taos is the Pueblo of Picuris. Here Donald Brown shows the congruence between the Picuris social structure and architectural units. By comparing the social and architectural configurations of 1900 with those of the mid-1960s, Brown is able to trace how changes in social structure resulted in changes in the material and spatial configuration of the pueblo. Among other alterations, we find a growing secularization and an increasing orientation toward the national welfare system, each associated with a decline in traditional politico-ceremonial activities and a concomitant movement from the sacred, underground kiva to the secular, cement-block community center.

Although considerably removed both geographically and culturally from Picuris Pueblo, St. Helena Parish, Louisiana, is the subject of a companion piece by Milton Newton. Like Brown, Newton sees a congruence between social structure and settlement pattern. Socially, St. Helena Parish is considerably more diversified than Picuris Pueblo, but Dr. Newton carefully delineates the social components and ties them to their material and spatial expressions. From his examination arises a model of the Upland South courthouse town and its hinterland. Underlying both social structure and settlement pattern is the cultural configuration, shared by both whites and blacks, of a South greatly variant from the Anglo-Saxon plantation and its black proletariat. The male figure of this South is "action seeking," having a "high valuation of the ruthless fighter" and a "tendency to sudden rage," with egalitarian sympathies which lead him to respect the Robin Hood figures of Bonnie and Clyde.

Chapter 8

Domesticates
as Artifacts

George F. Carter

ABSTRACT   Domesticated plants and animals are artifacts in the sense that they are natural materials modified by man for his own purposes. They can be treated with all the usual form, function, and meaning analyses applied to other artifacts. They have the additional value that they avoid confusion concerning independent invention: plants and animals cannot be invented. Although both plants and animals suggestive of contact between the Old World and the New World have attracted some attention for centuries, only rarely have the data been treated simultaneously in both cultural and biological aspects, and surprisingly, only rarely has the full cultural context of plants and animal uses been examined. Some of the findings and possible future avenues of investigation for the coconut, hibiscus, sweet potato, chicken, turkey, and dog are discussed here, together with some asides on related cultural traits.

Domestic plants and animals are artifacts, for man has taken the natural material and modified it to suit his needs. A wild grass modified to yield an abnormal grain, a cow modified to produce quantities of milk, or a cobblestone modified into an ax are all part of man's material culture. The major difference is that man has somewhat more freedom in modifying the cobblestone than he has with a plant or an animal. Further, while one may argue that the ax function dictates the form (an only partially true statement since hafting is highly vari-

201

able) and hence that axes will independently come to be alike, one cannot so argue in the world of biology. Wheat, rice, maize have functional similarities but are biologically distinct entities with known homelands. They cannot be reinvented, and hence plants and animals often speak clearly as to place of origin and aid us greatly in determining where and when ideas flowed.

It is important to try to consider each item in context and as fully as possible. While space and time limit the treatment here, a feeling of context and complex is striven for by not separating the material too rigorously. This leads to some repetition, but it seems desirable that sweet potatoes not be considered apart from chickens and axes, both of which present evidence parallel to the chicken case. Too often the treatment of key items has been done in isolation, and then the isolated nature of the case has been used as evidence. See Kroeber's treatment of patolli-pachisi as a classic case, " . . . there are few possible counterparts . . . the context probability is against connection" (Kroeber 1948, pp. 550–51). He proceeds to discuss several other cases that supply a context (time counts by permutation, intoxicants, panpipes, bronze, lintel and corbel for thresholds, double-headed eagle, etc.), and then solemnly discards each as meaningless when "standing alone."

Fundamentally, we are looking at the problem of inventiveness of man. Is man basically inventive? Or is he better characterized as retentive? Anyone familiar with this question knows how difficult it is to deal with (Rowe 1966; Jett and Carter 1966). The problem of simultaneous invention in later times misleads us, though it shouldn't (Carter 1971), and even the treatment of cases like pachisi shows that the probability of independent invention can be interpreted so differently that opposite conclusions can be reached by serious scholars. Unpublished calculations by one of my students in consultation with mathematicians and psychologists led to an estimate of the odds against reinvention to be 1 to 10^{17}. Tylor, Lowie, and Kroeber were all impressed with the probability against reinvention, but Erasmus (1950) has presented an analysis that tends to explain it as a natural convergence.

Most of these difficulties disappear when plants and animals are the subject. They cannot be reinvented and the problem is reduced to the presence or absence. This is no small problem, as we shall see, but it is worth struggling with since clear examples of Old World plants or animals in America in pre-Columbian time or of New World plants or animals in the Old World can be decisive evidence for diffusion. Even one proven transfer of a domestic plant by man is important for it opens Pandora's box: if sweet potatoes, why not mathematics, architecture, pottery, or pachisi?

Interest in the question arose very early. Acosta in 1590 (1954) for one discussed the matter of animal relationships and noted that there were good reasons for thinking that there must be a land bridge in the northern Pacific: a remarkable use of zoology to hypothesize the existence of the Bering Strait bridge. It should not be forgotten that this included some cultural judgments. Acosta observed that quail and rabbits in America resembled those of Europe. While these might conceivably have been brought by men in boats, he judged that man would not have brought such things as tigers and poisonous reptiles.

Others followed, but with differing insights. Within one hundred years the matter of what was native and what was introduced by the Spanish had begun to be blurred, and Capa (1915), a Jesuit, took it upon himself to try to straighten this out by careful inquiry and observation. He found that in the case of most plants and animals he could tell which the Spaniards brought, for the natives had a Spanish word or its derivative for the particular item. For others, and to his surprise, this included the chicken, they had their own words. More than a century ago Alexander von Humboldt (1810) called attention to the use of the elephant headdresses among the Aztecs, marveling that a people in a land lacking elephants should nevertheless have representations of them. It is not suggested that elephants were carried but that ideas about elephants, including elephants in script, elephants in headdresses, and very probably, elephants in mythology, were. Thus plants and animals as artifacts and as clues pointing to influences and diffusions have long attracted attention.

PLANTS AS EVIDENCE

The Coconut. At the beginning of this century, the study of biological artifacts and their value as evidence for diffusion was reopened by O. F. Cook. He called attention to the sweet potato (1893), *Hibiscus tiliaceous* (Cook and Cook 1918), the coconut (1901), and other plants.

For these plants he offered evidence that they were of American origin and that they were pre-Columbian in the Polynesian world. He also added cultural evidence: in some cases the names were the same in America and in Polynesia.

The problem was becoming more complex. Cook had to show that the plants were identical in America and in Polynesia. This he could do, but he also had to show that they were not dispersed by natural means: drift, wind, animal transport. He could do this for the sweet potato, but not for *Hibiscus tiliaceous* whose seed is readily dispersed by oceanic drifts, or for the coconut whose seed has some waterborne dispersal potential. For the coconut Cook postulated an American origin and a man-carried dispersal over the Pacific. For the sweet potato and the *Hibiscus tiliaceous,* he called attention to the near identity of names in America and in Polynesia. Although the full significance of a biological entity with the same name in the Old World and the New World has tended to be glossed over, these two items alone should long ago have forced the admission of pre-Columbian trans-Pacific contacts.

However, an unfair burden was placed on Cook and others, for the field of anthropology had taken a hard position on the total independence of the Old World and the New World. For example, Burkhill (1935) : "Bretschneider considered that he had detected a mention of the sweet potato in Chinese works of the third and fourth century. The descriptions apparently fit well, *but it is impossible to believe* that the Chinese could have had at that time, so important a food crop, without sharing it with their neighbors, for which there is no evidence" (emphasis mine). Burkhill makes a gross assumption here: that useful plants must diffuse. Maize delayed for a thousand years or more in southern New Mexico before spreading to the Anasazi, and it never did spread into California proper. Turkeys were wild in the eastern United States, but that area never took up turkey keeping, although it was an area gaining ideas from Mexico where turkeys were domestics. How easily we make assumptions when they fit our preconceived notions! Clearly, Burkhill's underlying belief is that men did not carry plants, animals, or ideas across the Pacific. Tylor's position (1964, pp. 266–67) is also revealing: he rejected the whole Greco-Roman ceremonial complex as simply unbelievable despite archaeological evidence for a key part (concave mirrors).

Cook had real difficulties, and these can be summarized by using his examples. The coconut has all of its relatives in America and his hypothesis that the coconut therefore came from America was a logical conclusion, but not necessarily true. In this case the evidence has shifted. We now have paleobotanical evidence of coconuts outside America, and the coconut is considered to have originated in the area bordering the Indian Ocean. While this shifts the origin, it does not eliminate the problem. If the coconut was indeed in both Polynesia and America in pre-Columbian time, this fact has to be accounted for. The identity of the plant poses no difficulties if one has a specimen in hand. The problem is that there are no archaeological specimens in America. The argument then turns on literary references. These are notoriously difficult to use, and a scholarly donnybrook has ensued whose greatest value, now that the matter is settled, is as a source for insight into scholarly treatment (and mistreatment) of evidence. See Merrill (1954) for an ill-tempered and very revealing review of a half century of controversy, including the finding of a letter of one of Cortez' lieutenants describing groves of coconuts on the Pacific coast of Mexico. Since there is an unmistakable reference to coconuts growing on the Pacific coast of Mexico at the time that the first Spaniards reached that area, the question shifts: could the coconuts have reached America by drift, or does this imply human carriage?

To answer this, one needs a considerable amount of knowledge of winds and currents in the Pacific and a good set of experimental data on the viability of coconuts in seawater. The set of the winds and currents in the tropical Pacific is from east to west—from America to Asia. While there are brief reversals, and an equatorial countercurrent, none of these seem likely to deliver coconuts to America, for brief reversals will not accomplish two-thousand-mile drifts. The equatorial countercurrent is not persistent, and it flows at a small fraction of the speed of the overlying wind which blows in the direction opposite to the current. A floating coconut, subject to both wind and water, should move counter to the countercurrent and, hence, away from America.

Drift around the north Pacific seems totally out of the range of the viability of coconuts in seawater, though this is challenged, and the data on viability are conflicting. Heyerdahl's experiments indicated that floating coconuts lose their viability within a few weeks

(1952, p. 460). Krieger notes that although coconuts are of frequent occurrence in the drift arriving at the islands, they are found growing only where planted (1943, p. 18). Other experimenters argue for viability of up to a year.

The ocean current data suggest that the most likely way to get coconuts to America is via a drift from tropical waters either north or south to enter the westerly drift, then either across the southern Pacific or the north Pacific and equatorward along the American coasts. Such drifts are accomplished by some highly adapted seeds in the Atlantic, and these seeds regularly drift up on the shores of Great Britain. But I know of no data to indicate that coconuts from the Caribbean in any condition arrive on the coast of Europe, nor is there any evidence that western Pacific coconuts ever reach the northwest coast of America or the south coast of Chile. If coconuts do not regularly arrive at these way stations, there seems to be little chance of their achieving the additional, needed distance on to the tropical American coasts where they would have to arrive in viable condition for a natural transfer to America.

The coconut, then, illustrates a number of important points. Knowledge is subject to change. We did not originally know where the coconut originated, but this has now settled down as most probably in the Indian Ocean area. We had no clear evidence for its presence in pre-Columbian America, but this bitter controversy has been settled by the finding of a clear literary reference. We are still in the throes of controversy concerning the natural or human carriage to America.

Based on consideration of some of the physical factors, my judgment is that the coconut will prove to be humanly carried. This is an opinion, not a fact, and the separation of fact and opinion is vital for the progress of knowledge. Unfortunately, an opinion by an authority too often becomes fact. As examples, see Merrill and Tylor as cited by partisans of the antidiffusion school.

It is important not to lose sight of the context in which the coconut sits. The evidence for pre-Columbian voyages grows greater and greater, and with it the probability that man could have carried coconuts. It is also important not to lose sight of the fact that a coconut is a large fruit, that the shell is moderately durable, that the tree with its immense nuts is a striking art object and would be easily identifiable if realistically portrayed. And yet, despite the certainty that the plant was in America at the time of the Spanish Conquest, we seem to have no hard evidence outside the literary references, many of which are equivocal. Except for the letter from Cortez' lieutenant, we would still be arguing the case for the mere existence of the plant in pre-Columbian America. If it is so hard to prove the case for a large, durable fruit like the coconut, how much more difficult then for smaller, more perishable, less conspicuous plants!

Any thoughtful review of this controversy must stress the enormous difficulty of establishing facts and the immense influence of individual biases. To those committed to no transoceanic diffusion, coconuts were not American, were not in America before 1500, and could only drift to America if they were in America. For those so deeply committed, portrayals of coconut palms on American artifacts would likely be used to prove the post-Columbian age of the artifact! Are there portrayals of coconut palms on American Indian artifacts?

The opposite school of thought held that the coconut was American, had an equatorial pan-Pacific distribution by 1500, and had been carried by man, despite the fact that they can retain their viability while drifting some distance in seawater. As we have seen, the controversy has shifted about, and the only agreed fact at the moment is the pre-Columbian, pan-Pacific distribution. We could use investigations into names and uses, to see if these are alike on the two sides of the Pacific. While uses of artifacts and domesticates would be subject to argument of the "it's only natural" kind, names would not be. So far, no one seems to have examined these questions, but as some of the cases cited below show, names can give important insights.

The Sweet Potato. The sweet potato is an even more interesting case. It was very early noted as being present in both America and in Polynesia at contact times. It was also almost immediately noted that the name for the plant was the same in one part of America and in most of Polynesia. See Brand (1971) for a most extensive review of the literature. The sweet potato is normally reproduced vegetatively, and it was a discovery of the mid-century that it actually produces seeds at times. In the main the plant is a poor candidate for water, wind, or bird dispersal over vast oceanic distances. Even if such natural carriage were involved, there would remain the insuperable difficulty of the similarity of the names and the usage. The names are virtually identical (*kumar, kumara,* and variants), and this has been stressed abundantly.

For over seventy years it has occasionally been mentioned that a case can be made for *kumar* as a Sanskrit word. Cooley (1951) cites Christian in 1897 as comparing Sanskrit, Malay, Polynesian, and American words: "The various Polynesian forms of *kumara* ... form a curious chain of evidence. . . . c.f. Malay *'barat'* and Sanskrit *'barata'* (South India). . . . With *kumala* compare Sanskrit *kauwal*, the lotus, *kumthla* with *kumad* and *kumud*." Rivet carried these comparisons much further (see Table 8.1). Rivet's work shows that *kumar* and its related words were widely applied to various root crops in the Indo-Malayan and Papuan region. Just as *corn* in English meant any small grain, so in the Indo-Malayan realm, *kumar* was widely applied to root crops. Linguistically, one would have to attribute the word to a Southeast Asian origin if the normal rules were followed, for the word *kumar* in Sanskrit is obviously ancient there, because it has a very broad meaning distributed over a vast area. In America the usage is narrow: to one specific plant, in a limited area. The parallel is the word *corn*: ancient and very broad in usage (any small grain or any small, hard object) in English, a very narrow application in America (to one plant and then only in Anglo-America). Since the sweet potato, known in part of America by a Sanskrit name, is parallel to the maize-corn case, maize can be used as a model.

In Anglo-America the native population, especially along the Atlantic seaboard, was swept away quickly. The British settlers adopted some of the native agricultural plants but only rarely took over the native names. Squash, derived from the Algonquin, is one of the exceptions. They substituted a word of wide meaning, but with many agricultural meanings, for the principal new grain. This was also a case of a technological superior culture versus an undeveloped people. It was also a case of colonization with extensive replacement of the local population. To the extent that the model is applicable, some or all of these characteristics would seem to be expectable in the Ecuadorian region where *kumar* word forms were the name for the sweet potato. Perhaps this will seem less surprising now that Meggers, Evans, and Estrada (1965) have published their research in that area. Anyone familiar with Amerind mythology knows that this is also an area

TABLE 8.1   Sweet Potato Names in Oceania According to Rivet[a]

Place	Name
Maori, Mangareva, Tuamotous, Easter Island, Rarotonga	kumara
Tonga	kumala
Marguesas	kumaa
Samoa	umala
Tahiti	umara, umaa
Hawaii	uala, uwala
Mangaia	ku'a'ra
Fiji, Sa'a, Ulawa	kumaro
Ruk (Carolines)	kamal
New Guinea	kumala
Santa	uara
Java	kumadjang

[a]Rivet compiled comparable lists showing transfers of these names and yams and other root crops in Indonesia and India, constructed a second series of names also found for root crops in Oceania and Peru (*ubi, ebe, up, ep, ape* in Oceania; *kapa* and *apicu* in Peru), and pointed to further parallels such as *toki* (adz) in both Polynesia and Peru (Rivet 1956, 1957).

with very specific accounts of people coming from overseas and settling. While some of these accounts may well refer to people from Mexico, the sweet potato's name in this same area tells us that some of the people arriving there had Old World origins.

The sweet potato does not stand alone. The chickens of the western coast of America included races that are specifically Asiatic, primarily Indian. In the Amazon, Malay races of chickens are still commonly held by the Indians. Over a large area they are called by a Hindu name, and neither the egg nor the flesh is used. It is a case of non-European chickens, with non-European culture patterns, with non-European names, and with the whole complex pointing to a Southeast Asian origin, and ultimately to India (Carter 1971). The sweet potato's name in Ecuador fits a context of Asiatic contacts and carries suggestions of colonization. This context situation can be greatly expanded. The adz on the coast of Peru is identical in hafting detail (the variable aspect of such tools as axes and adzes) to Polynesian adzes and has the same name (*toki*) in both places (Beirne 1971). *Toki* has broad meaning in Polynesia, narrow in America, and is thus to be seen as another transfer of an Asiatic word to America. This by no means exhausts the list, but it should be sufficient to remove the word-plant linkage from the criticism "but if this were true, wouldn't you expect other cases?" There are many parallel cases.

The Hibiscus. The Hibiscus family is involved in a number of aspects of the diffusion question and offers opportunities for special insights. *Hibiscus rosa sinensis* is of particular interest. As the name indicates, the plant was originally thought to have a Chinese origin. However, it is an American hibiscus[1] as is shown by the form of the flower: designed for pollination by hummingbirds, a type of bird found only in America (Carter 1954; Van der Pijl 1937). Merrill (1912, p. 232, and repeatedly asserted in 1954) considered *rosa sinensis* to be a native of Southeast Asia, but this clearly is not true. It seems probable that the confusion arose because the plant was so anciently and firmly entrenched in Asia, and this suggests that the matter should be investigated.

One might well expect to find it portrayed in some pre-Columbian artwork. We know of none, but who has looked? Only rarely does anyone look at artworks with a set of cultural historical questions in mind and with the technological equipment to realize what he sees. De Prez (1935) recognized the kapok tree as represented in Javanese art before 1000 A.D., thus confirming Bakheusen Van der Brink's studies (cited by Merrill 1954) that had suggested a pre-Columbian diffusion. Also note that this fact was put on record in 1935 alongside the evidence for American hibiscus flowers in the same area, but it has gone largely ignored, the omission then being used as evidence of lack of context!

The difficulty of finding firm evidence for coconuts in America despite the fact that they *were* there cautions one on the use of negative evidence. While one would not want to overwork the dictum, it is certainly true that failure to find absolute evidence for a plant in an area in pre-Columbian time does not prove that it was not there. Neither of course does it prove that it was there. The greater danger is that the plant will be used to date the artifact in terms of the investigator's assumptions. The assumption that the portrayal of an American plant or animal in the Old World automatically means a post–

1   Hibiscus is distributed around the world, and there are Old World and New World forms. The situation is parallel to the amaranth. See Sauer (1950).

1500 A.D. date for that plant or animal's portrait is like going duck hunting and shooting your decoys.

The fact that the taxonomists considered *rosa sinensis* ancient in East Asia must have had some cause. What were the facts that led them to such a conclusion? The problem with the hibiscus group is again that it has not been adequately examined for names, usages, ritual, and mythology. For *tiliaceous* the name similarities (America: *majagua, mahoe*; Polynesia: *moaua, mao, mau, hau, fau, vau*) are clear signals that diffusion of ideas concerning the plant occurred whether the plant dispersal was natural or cultural.

The hibiscus flower deserves special attention, for it might yield some important evidence on cultural preferences. Were Merrill and others correct in stating that one would expect the major food crops to be the first things exchanged if a meaningful Old World-New World contact were made? Or is the overall picture more suggestive of exchange of specialty crops? In post-Columbian time, tobacco, rubber, cocoa, cotton, quinine, forsythia, dahlias, citrus, grapes, have been among the successful plant travelers. None are major food plants. Perhaps a better case can be made for more rapid diffusion of rarities, specialties, medicinals, and ornamentals than for major crops? I have suggested that this would not be unexpected, for a change of basic food crops involves vast populations and hence immense resistance would be expectable (Carter 1963). A parallel would be the rule in lexicostatistics that it is the hearth words that resist change. So, too, is it expectable that basic food crops would resist change, and such has indeed been the record even in relatively modern times.

It is odd that so fundamental a question as which crops did spread faster and farther after 1500 A.D. has had little attention, and as we have seen, much of that is clouded by assumptions. Wouldn't history-as-model be a useful device to apply? Admittedly we would have difficulty sorting out what is and isn't post-Columbian diffusion, but there would be enough clear cases to begin to establish some basic principles. How sad that so much polemic writing has been done and so few results of basic inquiry published.

Since this manuscript was written new data have appeared. The people of Nam Viet (southern China and northern Vietnam) are described in some detail by the northern Chinese, and this material has been surveyed and made available by Schafer (1967, pp. 201–203). In these descriptions the red-flowered hibiscus, a typical American type, is described in glowing terms especially in the ninth century. Even more interesting, the tradition of the people of Nam Viet in those times was that their ancestors had obtained this flower from the great rich land to the east, seemingly America. To compound this, they referred to the land as Fusang. Northern Chinese also knew of a great land to the east which they too called Fusang. While the northern Chinese fifth-century reference to Fusang as America has been derided and treated as if it were an isolated occurrence, Needham (1971) makes it clear that there are several Chinese references to a land to the east known as Fusang. He also recalls the vivid impact of Mexican archaeology on a sinologist by commenting that it was all *déjà vu*.

How extensive were these contacts? Needham's reaction records the obvious influence in art and architecture. The coconut probably was carried to America, the sweet potato and the hibiscus were carried back. What more? It was noted sometime ago that the kapok tree is portrayed in Java by 977 A.D. (De Prez 1935), and more recently Schafer (1970) has noted that in Tang time (600–900 A.D.) the people of Hainan Island spun and wove (!) kapok, and still do. Kapok (*Ceiba pentandra*) is an American tree. It would appear that we have hardly begun to examine this question.

So we have, as the discussion written earlier would lead us to expect, literary references to an American plant in Asia, a noneconomic plant (the opposite of E. D. Merrill's dictum), and in retrospect, O. F. Cook had the correct insight. Plants were carried. One can add that for at least some of southern Asia, America was seemingly known as Fusang.

The Grain Amaranths. To this, one can add the story of the grain amaranths. The amaranths are worldwide in their distribution, and prior to Jonathan Sauer's study (1950) one could make little sense out of the available data. His careful taxonomic study showed that all of the grain amaranths in both the Old and New World are American in origin and that the Old World amaranths, when used for food, are used as greens. Further, he found that the American grain amaranths were very widely distributed among the inland peoples of Asia: throughout the Himalayas, inner China, and so forth. The uses of the plant were at times very similar to the uses in America: the grain was popped; it was made into "popcorn balls" and consumed on special feast days.

The Chinese character that today represents the grain amaranth is known as early as the tenth century in China. The problem with the character is that it is impossible to prove that it has not changed meaning. It may have been named a similar grain in pre-Columbian time and then in post-Columbian time was borrowed to designate a post-Columbian new grain crop. On the other hand, the grain amaranth with an associated cultural complex is a most unlikely thing for the Europeans to carry to China. The grain amaranths were equal to beans and maize in prominence in the Aztec tribute lists and were so important in ritual and religion that they became a particular target for discouragement by the Spaniards. Since it was an important plant to the Mexicans but a plant to be discouraged by the Spanish, it is an unlikely candidate for Spanish diffusion. It is not a situation readily explained in terms of the Manila galleon or other post-Columbian situations. However, if the Chinese in pre-Columbian time were adopting American plants, why so insignificant a plant as the grain amaranth, and why are there not other plants and other evidence?

First, the amaranth was an important plant in pre-Columbian time and there are other plants in question, *e.g., Hibiscus rosa sinensis* and the sweet potato. Others will be discussed below. As for other evidence, it is extensive: record keeping by knots in strings, music (scales, instruments, and ideas, *e.g.*, the panpipe ceremonial complex and the association of sex gender with notes on the musical scale), art, and so forth, all transferred from Asia to America. The "other evidence" suggests that there should be more plant and animal evidence, and there is.

The Peanut. The peanut caught the attention of Oakes Ames (1939), an economic botanist, who recognized that the Chinese had a variant of an obviously American plant. He noted that a likely source in America was Peru, where this variant was prominent in archaeological levels. The role of climate of opinion is neatly measured by the fact that this passed almost unnoted. These observations may be about to take a dramatic turn.

We now have reports of archaeological peanuts from China (Chang 1968). Since this is of great importance both factually and for many theoretical considerations, I have written to Professor Chang for further details and have had a student, M. David Jones, do a research paper on the peanut question. The following draws freely from these sources. There are two archaeological sites in southeast China. At Chien-shang-yang, Wu-hsing, Chekiang, a site excavated in 1956 and 1958, two carbonized peanuts were found in a Lungshanoid association. They were identified by the Laboratory of Plant Seeds of the College of Agriculture of Chekiang, as *Arachis Hypogea L.* The second site was near the village of Shan-pei, northwest Kiangsi, and the archaeological association was again Lungshanoid.

In Chinese sources the introduction of the peanut is attributed to southern overseas origins. Chekiang is said to have obtained peanuts from Fukhien, its southern neighbor, toward the end of the sixteenth century. This does not mean that this was the time of introduction of peanuts to China, as some have seemed to assume, but only tells us when Chekiang got peanuts from Fukhien. Fukhien may have had peanuts for a century, a millennium, or more. Bretschneider quoted a Chinese source that attributed the introduction of the peanut to the Sung (960–1280) or the Yuan (1260–1368) dynasty, but Bretschneider rejected the dating, seemingly because he knew that the plant was American and hence that the date must be wrong (Burkhill 1935). It is obvious that no progress can be made when such circular reasoning is employed. Note that 900 is also the time when north China gets an American hibiscus from south China.

An archaeological find of peanuts in the Lungshanoid period would have seemed impossible only twenty years ago. Chang (1968) dates the Lungshan from 2000 B.C., persisting to 750 B.C. in the Yün-meng basin. The specific sites in south China suggest 2000 to 1500 B.C. dates. When art history studies (Fenollosa 1912) began to point out the Old Pacific art as basic to Shang, Northwest Coast America, Peru, and Mexico, we should have been alerted to the possibility of very early contacts with America. The 3000 B.C. dated pottery of seeming Asiatic origin in Ecuador indicates cultural impulses from the south islands of Japan (Meggers, Evans, and Estrada 1965). Ford's thesis (1970) that this contact was by a skilled maritime people should lead us to consider the possibility that the voyages to America were deliberate. If the peanut identifications and cultural associations are verified, then deliberate, two-way voyages of such ease that domestic plants could be carried is indicated. This reinforces the *kumar*-maize model which suggests not only rapid voyages, but colonization.

There are innumerable cautions here. Peanuts are not known in Peru at so early a date. We know so little of plants in Peru and Ecuador that this may not be a significant fact, but for the moment it would seem important not to overlook the discrepancy. The peanut is thought to have originated in Brazil, for that is the home of the majority of wild relatives and of the closest relatives of the domestic types. We have virtually no knowledge of the Brazilian agricultural contribution. Does it include manioc, peanuts, and pineapple? How old is it?[2]

It is necessary to remember that the earliest date game is a dangerous one. At the moment the earliest date for a domestic dog in the world is in Oregon, but no one seriously considers that this is the earliest domestic dog. It simply tells us that we will eventually find earlier domestic dogs somewhere in Eurasia. So, if the peanuts in China are correctly identified, and dated, we have a source for domestic peanuts to find in America at some date earlier than 1500 B.C., and the probable area of such a find is Brazil south of the Amazon. Meanwhile we can note the arrival of Asiatic potters on the coast of Ecuador about 3000 B.C. and their colonizing around the American shores in a manner indicating a boat-borne culture. Contact across the Pacific was underway, and plant exchanges cannot be ruled out even at these early time levels.

What we have here, moreover, is the suggestion of American plant complexes in the western Pacific, in Southeast Asia, and sometimes specifically in China in pre-Columbian time. Two plants in this group (maize and peanuts) strongly suggest that they were taken from the coast of Peru at a relatively early time, for the varieties in question are archaeologic rather than modern on the coast. The grain amaranth, on the other hand, by its ritual associations seems to have a Mexican origin. The sweet potato clearly was carried from America and spread at least throughout Polynesia and probably far beyond. The hibiscus in one or more forms was carried from America, and there are name similarities indicating cultural associations.

The gist of this incomplete coverage of the data (weeds, cottons,

2 Donald Lathrap (personal communication, 1973) believes that a strong case can be made for an early and important agricultural beginning east of the Andes.

and other plants have been omitted) is enough to suggest transfers of complexes. One could argue against this evidence by pointing out that the suggestions are vague as to time in Peru, diverse as to origin in America, and scattered in Asia. If the model one uses is that of a single contact with America, leading back to a single point in time and space in Asia, this might be a valid criticism. If, however, the real situation were one of multiple contacts spread over a great expanse of time and between varied points in America and Asia, then the present data would conform to the more complex model. Heine Geldern, for one, has argued for a complex model, though even his was too simple (too strongly focused on the area of Dongson influence in Southeast Asia over a relatively brief span of time) as the Jomon-like pottery in Ecuador now makes clear.

ANIMALS AS EVIDENCE

Domestic animals are artifacts and share in the useful quality that plants have in that they can never be assumed to have originated twice. No one can independently invent a Bactrian camel in America or a llama in Tibet, though men may independently or by stimulus diffusion domesticate a camel in each area. The American civilizations were peculiar in the slight development of animal domestications, and this was not due to any paucity of potential domestics. The guinea pig and llama and alpaca in the Andes, and the Muscovy duck and turkey in Mexico are an astonishingly poor showing given the resources of America. Wild equivalents of horses, cows, sheep, pigs, goats, and geese also were present but were not taken in hand.

The Turkey. The peculiarities are increased in some of the naming. Why should an American domestic be called either a Turk (the turkey), a Muscovite (the Muscovy duck), or a native of Guinea (the guinea pig)? The duck is not musky, and the Guinea associations at one time or another include guinea hen for turkey, Guinea wheat for maize, Guinea pepper for capsicum, as well as guinea pig, and the attributions were to African Guinea and not the Guianas. Jeffreys has made a powerful case for pre-Columbian maize in Africa (1953, 1963, 1965, 1971), especially on the Guinea coast. Was there a whole American agricultural complex there?

Only the English called *Meleagris* a Turk. All the other Europeans named this bird the Cock of India. They were quite specific: India and not the Indies. The Arabs made it crystal clear: *dyk hindi*, Hindu chicken. There is one report of a possible turkey bone from Hungary: in the fourteenth century level of the debris of the royal castle of Buda (Bokonyi and Janossi 1958). The Turkish literature is said to have many mentions of turkeys beginning in the fifteenth century.

It is a most slippery field in which to work, for the literary references are baffling in their use of names and it is often impossible to tell whether a peacock, guinea hen, or some other bird is being referred to. What is strikingly clear is that the naming of the turkey follows closely the pattern for the naming of maize. Both are attributed to an eastern Mediterranean origin and to a pre-1500 time period. For maize this is most effectively demonstrated by Finan's study (1950), in which he shows that Turkish wheat is clearly maize and that the pre-1500 maize is clearly not Caribbean maize. If the turkey belongs in this pattern, then it would seem to have been part of a complex of plants and animals from America that seemingly were carried across the Pacific, got into the hands of the Arab-Turk combination in the Indian Ocean area, and were being introduced into eastern Europe before 1500. If plants were being carried back and forth across the Pacific, and this is what the present picture strongly suggests, then it is not too surprising that animals would be carried (Map 8.1).

The Chicken. But if turkeys were carried across the Pacific from America, what might have been carried from Asia to America? The obvious parallel would be the chicken. In both cases the reason for carrying such fowl might be thought of as for food during the voyage. However, this would be to think of the situation in the twentieth century and strictly European culture pattern. The Asiatic pattern of use of fowl may have been entirely different from the fifteenth-century European use, and indeed we have good reason to think that it probably was. Chickens were not domesticated for flesh and eggs, but for divination. They had spread far indeed and much time had passed before they came to have what we call normal uses. For example, the Romans reported that Britons had chickens but did not eat them. Southeast Asians in part still disdain eating chickens or eggs. If Asians were carry-

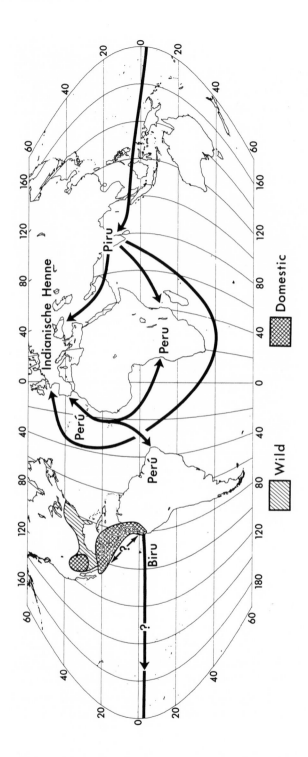

MAP 8.1   Linguistic Evidence for Diffusion of the Turkey

ing chickens across the Pacific, it is most likely that they were doing so for divination. If Asiatics brought chickens to America, an Asiatic pattern of uses would be expected. If chickens were brought by post-1500 Europeans, the Europeans' pattern of egg and flesh eating would be expected. The parallel to the grain amaranth is instructive: in Asia where it is probably pre-Columbian, it is a grain crop. In Europe it is variably a noxious weed or an ornamental, and such a use pattern does not support a European introduction.

The description of uses of fowl among some of the American Indian groups is very vague indeed.[3] Few ethnologists have reported on chickens and their uses, and it is only in correspondence or in conversation that I learn that chickens are still being kept mainly for prestige, for example in Valdivia and Chiloe, Chile (Gene Wilhelm, personal communication). In the Amazon, chickens are kept but they are not eaten nor are their eggs used, and just why they are kept at all is not reported. See for example McGovern's puzzled comments on the careful keeping of chickens in the upper Amazon for no discernible use (1927). Viva voce I learn that there are many naked-necked chickens in the Amazon. This is a Malay race. It is this area where a Hindu word for chicken is used for the chicken. (In passing, in Brazil the word *jangada* for a sailing raft duplicates the Tamil word for the identical craft.) Again we seem to be in the presence of a complex of biotic, linguistic, and other cultural traits: Asiatic chickens, with Asiatic name in use over a wide area. If Ford's thesis of a boat-borne colonization is correct, these may be elements of that complex. I suspect, however, that it is part of a later and specifically Indian or Indonesian colonization.

Among the Tarahumara and the Tepehuan in northwest Mexico, this same pattern is found: chicken keeping, but neither chickens nor eggs eaten (Pennington 1969). This appears to be a widespread pattern. It is clearly not a Spanish or a Portuguese pattern, for chicken eating and egg using were well developed in Greco-Roman times. If this were a European pattern it would have to have been diffused in very early times indeed. Limits are set on this by the time of spread of chickens into western Europe: mostly post-500 B.C. (eighth century in

---

3 Since this was written, my knowledge of chickens in America has advanced considerably; and I would state the case even more positively in terms of present knowledge.

Greece, 500 B.C. in Sicily, 200 B.C. in Rome). By the time of Christ the use of chickens in western Europe had become utilitarian in our terms for flesh and eggs: special breeds for flesh and for eggs as early as 300 B.C. in Greece. The time-and-culture complex then allows only a narrow span when chickens could be introduced from the Mediterranean without the flesh-and-egg-use pattern. A much longer period seems available in Asia where the chickens were domesticated and where the old patterns of no egg or flesh eating persisted longer.

Another way of looking at the chicken data is to ask what kind of chickens are in question? Twenty-five years ago with Edgar Anderson, I pioneered the concept of races of maize (Carter and Anderson 1945). Maize until then had been treated under the dictum "corn is corn," and I recall vividly the archaeologists at Santa Fe in 1935 trying to get some information from the maize experts on the meaning of the small ears of maize that were so distinctive of the early levels in the Southwest. They were repeatedly rebuffed with "maize is maize." This is botanically correct on the species level, but it overlooked the race concept. One could as well insist that man is man.

Chickens are chickens, *Gallus gallus*, and they all stem from the Indian-Indonesian area. But they also vary systematically as to race, very much as men and maize do. The sinitic race is plump, feather footed, phlegmatic, loose feathered, and lays brown eggs. Examples of this race appear in the earliest accounts of Central America. The Malay race is lightly feathered, often nearly naked, frequently naked necked. It includes very heavily muscled and quite large chickens, and the cocks fight on the ground. The Mediterranean race is light in build, naked footed, tightly feathered, lays white eggs, and fights in the air. There are associated differences in comb type, wattle color, leg color, and other characteristics that make treatment of chickens by race type a relatively easy matter. There are also peculiar variants that are clear marks of origin. These include such traits as black bones and black flesh and silkiness (imperfect feathers). The melanotic strains are centered in India as are the silky strains. The Japanese chickens are said to be more like Indian chickens than Chinese chickens, and the Japanese had silkies and other specialty chickens. If we knew the kinds of chickens that the Europeans had in the sixteenth century, we would be able to test the meaning of the Asiatic attitudes toward the chickens displayed among some of the American Indians.

Fortunately we have an exhaustive study of the European knowledge of chickens at just this critical time (1600), for Aldrovandri compiled a book with copious illustrations that shows just what the Europeans knew about chickens (Lind 1963).

The Asiatic types, even some of the Indian types, were unknown to the Europeans, one hundred years after Columbus' discovery of America. But what then are the chickens in the hands of the American Indians like? It has long been noted that the chickens of Chile and originally probably all of the west coast of South America are Asiatic in type. In their combs, tails, special forms of feather (silkies), colored-egg-laying traits, melanotic strains (black flesh and black bones), they are distinctly Asiatic. Most of these traits point to India, Malaya, or Japan. I have been informed that in the Amazon the naked-necked chickens are a common type. This would be a Malay race. This is also one of the types of chickens common among the Indians of the north-west of Mexico where the attitude toward the chicken is distinctly non-European: neither eggs nor flesh is eaten by the Tepehuan (Pennington 1969).

This is an Asiatic trait complex complete with Asiatic races of chickens! Since neither the trait complex nor these races of chickens could be derived from sixteenth-century Europe, one is forced to consider the question of pre-Columbian introductions. This question has been canvassed a number of times. Nordenskiold (1922) compiled an immense list of names for chickens in South America as part of his study of the distribution of names for Spanish introductions, such as steel knives, guns, and so forth. He assumed that the chicken was a European introduction, so when he found that the words for chicken did not conform to the patterns of the probably European-introduced items, he patiently rationalized his way out of all the difficulties. He assumed a diffusion rate approximately one hundred times that generally found for spreads of traits on the Neolithic level (Carter 1971; Doran 1971; Edmonson 1961). It is also approximately one hundred times the moderately well-documented rate of spread of the chicken in Eurasia. Nordenskiold never considered either the races of chickens or the culture pattern of noneating. When data suggest that the artifact in question is of Asiatic origin, is embedded in a culture complex of Asiatic type, and has a spread suggestive of an introduction in the early part of the Christian era (at least), it does not seem logical to assume that the artifact is a European introduction. And, most fortunately, since the chicken is a biological artifact, it cannot be explained away as an independent invention.

Names for chickens in Mexico supply even more interesting possibilities. Among the Tarahumara who eat neither chicken flesh nor eggs, the name for chicken is *totori* or *'otori*. This duplicates the Japanese name for domestic fowl, *totori*. The Aztec names for cock and hen turkeys are *huexolotl* and *cihuatotolin*. In these names it is clear that the root is *totoli* with only the linguistically simple change of *l* to *r* setting it apart from Tarahumara and Japanese. The question then becomes whether the turkey is being called a chicken or the chicken a turkey. Since the Aztec names were recorded by Sahagún, they are quite clearly not due to late Japanese influences. If the Japanese name is not an accidental sound and meaning duplication, a likelihood greatly decreased since we are dealing with Asiatic races and Asiatic uses, that is, a whole cultural complex, then it seems likely that both the idea of domestication and the name are transfers from Asiatic introductions to the American turkey.

A bit of reinforcement can be given to this by a survey of the names for chickens in the world. In the Old World, as a test case, it is easy to trace the English words for cock and chicken back through German to Sanskrit. *Kuk* becomes cock, and the diminutive *küchlein* becomes chicken. The time span is not less than 2,500 years. In America in the Amazon over a wide area, the name for the chicken is some variant of *karaka*. This is virtually identical to the Hindu word for one variety of chicken: the diminutive silky with melanotic flesh. Just such chickens are reported for the Pacific coast of South America (C. O. Sauer 1952). We lack any data on their presence or absence in the Amazon, but the presence in South America of the correct type of bird to fit the Hindu name seems significant. For all we know, such fowl are commonplace among the surviving Indian groups of the Amazon. It is only by a conversational accident that I know of the presence of the naked-necked Malay chickens in the Amazon, and if the worldwide survey of chicken names hadn't turned up a Malay name in the Amazon, there would have been no supporting evidence (Map 8.2).

The possibility of animal exchanges between the Old World and the New World has been neglected. The chicken has had a varied

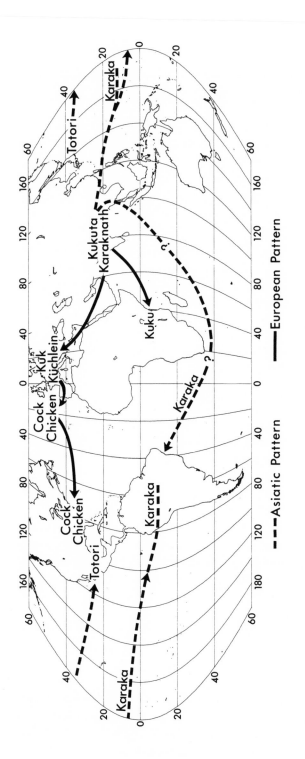

MAP 8.2   Linguistic Evidence for Diffusion of the Chicken

treatment; the turkey has been ignored. There seems to be no available study of the remarkable resemblances between the Mexican hairless and the Chinese crested (hairless) dogs. Nor do I know of any discussion of the cultural parallels: castrated, grossly fattened, and eaten. Yet this situation is more subject to scrutiny than most, for in Mexico this dog was frequently portrayed in pottery in its fattened state, and hence, not only the dog but the cultural trait of fattening should be readily traced in time and space. It offers a most intriguing opportunity.

Animal Distributions. There is often an implicit if not tacit assumption for complete diffusion for almost all traits once they enter an area such as North or South America. The evidence from plants and animals challenges the validity of this. Note for the domestic turkey in pre-Columbian America that it was a domestic from Panama northward toward the Pueblos. Beyond that, northward and eastward through the immense range of the wild turkey, the bird was eagerly sought for food but not kept as a domestic, and this was true despite the strong Mexican influences in the eastern United States. Similarly, the turkey did not spread into South America, with the possible exception of a small area on the Ecuadorian coast, despite the well-established and extensive trade that went on between Mexico and Ecuador and which led to the exchange of many cultural traits.

If the chicken was pre-Columbian in America, it surely did not attain a universal distribution. In South America it seemingly did not reach the Orinoco in pre-Spanish times for the Spanish are explicit in stating that it was not there, but that in going south from Venezuela, they saw the first chickens well over toward the Amazon drainage. The linguistic data confirm this neatly: in the Venezuelan area the word for chicken is of Spanish origin. In the Amazon it is seemingly a Hindu word over a wide area. In the Peruvian area it is a distinct word, *hualpa*, of unknown origin but of great significance since it was the name of the last Inca, Atahualpa, and of his uncle, Hualpa.

This kind of data is also significant for the case of the peanut in China. The Chinese account states that Chekiang got peanuts from Fukhien toward the end of the sixteenth century. The tendency to assume that since Chekiang was getting peanuts from Fukhien, Fukhien must recently have obtained them, can be shown to be a precarious conclusion. If the turkey in Mexico is a model, then the Indian in the present United States went along for millennia before taking up turkey keeping except in one limited area: the Pueblos. Or, for an even tighter model, maize appeared in southern New Mexico about 2000 B.C., but the adjacent Four Corners region didn't begin maize cultivation until about 1 A.D. We cannot assume instant, total, and complete diffusion. Further examples can be cited almost at random. Rice was exceedingly slow in reaching even the nearby islands off Asia, often not until 1000 A.D.

For the chicken-in-America question the meaning of the spot of Asiatic attitudes and Asiatic races in northwest Mexico is intriguing. Is this part of a separate introduction? Or was there a continuum of chicken keeping in pre-Columbian Mexico? For the edible dog: What is its distribution in time and space? What is its relation to a larger pattern of dog eating? Is it the only case of castration in America? It would be an interesting point since castration is widespread in the Old World and virtually unknown or at least very limited in the New World. If the Mexican hairless edible dog is related to the Chinese hairless edible dog, is this part of a China-Mexico exchange, and are the grain amaranth, hibiscus, and perhaps peanuts part of a complex?

If the exchange of turkeys and chickens across the Pacific is real, it would seem pertinent to ask what the limits on these exchanges might have been. Large animals such as elephants, horses, and water buffalo would be most unexpected. Not only their size but their food and water requirements would seem to create a limit. Pigs might be somewhat large for trans-Pacific carriage, and even in Polynesia they seem not to have been carried to all islands. Chickens were carried most widely, even to Easter Island, and this should prepare us for the possibility of their having been carried on to the coast of South America. A dog the size of the Mexican hairless would seem well within the size limit for transport, but large dogs might have been beyond the limit. Here, however, another set of problems is met: water craft and navigational skills. We have a great deal to learn and are hampered by the usual presuppositions. Fortunately, the work of Edwards (1965) and Doran (1971) are adding new dimensions to Heyerdahl's pioneering effort, and we begin to see the Asiatics as superior navigators equipped with sophisticated sailing craft. The junk needs to be renamed to avoid the connotations in English!

CONCLUSION

Plants and animals offer exceptional opportunities for studies in diffusion because they avoid the difficulties posed by the possibility of independent invention. They can be treated as artifacts with all the form, function, and meaning analyses normally applied in anthropology. They have been greatly neglected and rarely treated simultaneously as biologic entities, artifacts, and parts of cultural complexes. Nordenskiold would surely have reached different conclusions if he had been aware of the presence of Asiatic races of chickens known by an Asiatic name. The chicken-in-America question also changes when it is found that over wide areas, the Indian attitude toward the chicken is Asiatic rather than Mediterranean-European. We have hardly looked at the domestic animal field, but already chickens, turkeys, and one breed of dog emerge as possible pre-Columbian trans-Pacific transfers.

The plant situation is only slightly better understood, for with rare exceptions there has been little combining of biological, cultural, and linguistic inquiry. J. Sauer's study of the grain amaranths (1950), Stonor and Anderson's study of maize in Assam (1949) are among the rare exceptions.

It seems apparent that the Monroe Doctrine of Anthropology has been an effective barrier to scholarly inquiry into the plant and animal evidence bearing on pre-Columbian exchanges across the Atlantic and the Pacific. It is time that we utilized this important biological material much as we do other artifacts. It will very likely prove to be richly rewarding.

The biological data presented here favor the diffusion of artifacts rather than their independent invention. Man seems to be more retentive than inventive. Yet this paper has only covered a small portion of the total biological inventory of plants and animals utilized in the Old and New Worlds. All the remaining grains, flowers, fruits, poisons, and medicines need to be examined. As the examination of these remaining species proceeds, we may well find a very high percentage of paired plants, similar but not identical, appearing in cultural centers known to have exchanged specific plants, animals, and ideas in later times. Such a pattern would suggest that the cultural centers were in contact, via stimulus diffusion, at an even earlier date. This is a question that hovers like a cloud on the horizon. It will, I predict, loom larger in the near future, and the best area for testing the idea is likely to be in the domestic plant field.[4]

REFERENCES CITED

Acosta, P. José
  1954 *Historia Natural y Moral de las Indias* (1590). Madrid: Biblioteca Autores Espãnoles.

Ames, Oakes
  1939 *Economic Annual and Human Cultures.* Cambridge: Botanical Museum, Harvard University.

Beirne, D. R.
  1971 Cultural Patterning as Revealed by a Study of Pre-Columbian Ax and Adze Hafting in the Old and New Worlds. In C. L. Riley, J. C. Kelley, C. W. Pennington, R. L. Rands, eds., *Man Across the Sea.* Austin: University of Texas Press.

Bokonyi, S., and D. Janossi
  1958 Data About the Occurrence of the Turkey in Europe Before the Time of Columbus. *Aquila* 65:256–69.

Brand, D. D.
  1971 The Sweet Potato. In C. L. Riley, J. C. Kelley, C. W. Pennington, R. L. Rands, eds., *Man Across the Sea.* Austin: University of Texas Press.

Burkhill, I. H.
  1935 *A Dictionary of the Economic Products of the Malaya Peninsula.* Vol. 2. London.

Capa, Ricardo
  1915 *Estudios Críticos Acerca de la Dominación Española en América.* 4th ed. Vol. 5. Industria agrícola-pecuaria llevada a América por los españoles (1890). Madrid: Imprenta del Asilo de Huérfanos.

Carter, G. F.
  1954 Disharmony Between Asiatic Flower-Birds and Bird-Flowers. *American Antiquity* 20:176–77.

  1963 Movement of People and Ideas Across the Pacific. *Plants and the Migrations of the Pacific Peoples.* Tenth Pacific Science Congress. Honolulu: Bishop Museum Press.

  1971 Pre-Columbian Chickens in America. In C. L. Riley, J. C. Kelley, C. W. Pennington, R. L. Rands, eds., *Man Across the Sea.* Austin: University of Texas Press.

Carter, G. F., and E. Anderson
  1945 A Preliminary Survey of Maize in the Southwestern United States. *Annals of the Missouri Botanical Garden* 32:297–322.

4 I have presented in a lengthy paper the hypothesis of a single origin of agriculture at the agricultural origins symposium at the International Congress of Ethnology and Anthropology, Chicago, 1973. The symposium volume is to be published in 1974.

Chang, Kwang-chih
 1968   *The Archaeology of Ancient China.* 2nd ed. New Haven: Yale University Press.

Cook, O. F.
 1893   Food Plants of Ancient America. *Annual Report, 1893.* Washington, D.C.: Smithsonian Institution. Pp. 481–97.
 1901   The Origin and Distribution of the Cocoa Palm. *United States National Herbarium* 7:257–93.

Cook, O. F., and R. C. Cook
 1918   The Maho or Mahagua as a Trans-Pacific Plant. *Journal of the Washington Academy of Sciences* 8:153–70.

Cooley, J. S.
 1951   The Sweet Potato: Its Origin and Primitive Storage Practices. *Economic Botany* 5:378–86.

De Prez, Alfred Steinman
 1935   Observations sur la flore et la faune représentées sur les bas-reliefs de quelques monuments indo-javanais. *Revue des Arts Asiatiques* 9 (2): 60–61.

Doran, E.
 1971   The Sailing Raft as a Great Tradition. In C. L. Riley, J. C. Kelley, C. W. Pennington, R. L. Rands, eds., *Man Across the Sea.* Austin: University of Texas Press.

Edmonson, Munro
 1961   Neolithic Diffusion Rates. *Current Anthropology* 2:71–102.

Edwards, Clinton E.
 1965   *Aboriginal Watercraft of the Pacific Coast of America.* Ibero Americana. Berkeley: University of California Press.

Erasmus, Charles J.
 1950   Patolli, Pachisi, and the Limitation of Possibilities. *Southwestern Journal of Anthropology* 6:369–87.

Fenollosa, E. F.
 1912   *Epochs of Chinese and Japanese Art.* London: W. Heineman.

Finan, John J.
 1950   *Maize in the Great Herbals.* Waltham, Mass.: Chronica Botanica.

Ford, James A.
 1970   *A Comparison of Formative Cultures in the Americas: Diffusion or the Psychic Unity of Man.* Smithsonian Contributions to Anthropology, Vol. 11. Washington, D.C.: Smithsonian Institution.

Heyerdahl, Thor
 1952   *American Indians in the Pacific.* London: George Allen and Unwin.

Humboldt, Alexander von
 1810   *Vues des Cordilleres et Monuments des Peuples Indigenes de l'Amerique.* Paris: F. Schoell.

Jeffreys, M. D. W.
1953   Pre-Columbian Maize in Africa. *Nature* 172:965.
1963   How Ancient Is West African Maize? *Africa* 33:115–31.
1965   Pre-Columbian Maize in the Philippines. *South African Journal of Science* 61:5.
1971   Maize and the Mande Myth. *Current Anthropology* 12:291–320.

Jett, S., and G. F. Carter
1966   A Comment on Rowe's Diffusionism and Archeology. *American Antiquity* 31:867–70.

Krieger, W.
1943   *Island People of the Western Pacific: Micronesia and Melanisia.* Background for War Series, No. 16. Washington, D.C.: Smithsonian Institution.

Kroeber, A. L.
1948   *Anthropology.* New York: Harcourt, Brace.

Lind, L. R.
1963   *Aldrovandri on Chickens.* Norman: University of Oklahoma Press. (Trans. of *The Ornithology of Ulisse Aldrovandri,* originally published in 1600.)

McGovern, William M.
1927   *Jungle Paths and Inca Ruins.* New York: Century.

Meggers, B. J., C. Evans, and E. Estrada
1965   *Early Formative Period of Coastal Ecuador: The Valdivia and Machlilla Phases.* Smithsonian Contributions to Anthropology, Vol. 1. Washington, D.C.: Smithsonian Institution.

Merrill, E. D.
1912   *A Flora of Manila.* Manila: Bureau of Printing.
1954   *The Botany of Cook's Voyages.* Vol. 14. Waltham, Mass.: Chronica Botanica.

Needham, J. N.
1971   *Science and Civilization in China.* Vol. 4. Cambridge: Cambridge University Press.

Nordenskiold, E.
1922   *Deductions Suggested by the Geographical Distributions of Some Post-Columbian Words Used by the Indians of South America.* Comparative Ethnological Studies, Vol. 5. Göteborg: Elanders boktryckeri Aktiebolag.

Pennington, Cambell
1969   *The Tepehuan of Chihuahua.* Salt Lake City: University of Utah Press.

Rivet, Paul
1956   Early Contacts Between Polynesia and America. *Diogenes* 16:78–92.
1957   *Les Origenes de l'Homme Americaine.* 6th ed. Paris: Gallemard.

Rowe, J. H.
1966   Diffusionism and Archaeology. *American Antiquity* 31:344–47.

Sauer, C. O.
   1952   *Agricultural Origins and Dispersals*. Isaiah Bowman Lecture Series. New York: American Geographical Society of New York.

Sauer, J. D.
   1950   The Grain Amaranths: A Survey of Their History and Classification. *Annals of the Missouri Botanical Garden* 37:561–632.

Schafer, E. H.
   1967   *The Vermillion Bird: Tang Images of the South*. Berkeley and Los Angeles: University of California Press.

   1970   *Shore of Pearls*. Berkeley and London: University of California Press.

Stonor, C. R., and E. Anderson
   1949   Maize Among the Hill Tribes of Assam. *Annals of the Missouri Botanical Garden* 36:355–96.

Tylor, E. B.
   1964   *Early History of Mankind*. Edited and abridged by Paul Bohannan. Chicago: University of Chicago Press.

Van der Pijl, L.
   1937   Disharmony Between Asiatic Flower-Birds and American Bird-Flowers. *Annals du Jardin Botanique de Buitenzorg* 48:17–26.

Chapter 9

The Timbira Hammock as a Cultural Indicator of Social Boundaries

Dolores Newton

ABSTRACT   The delineation of tribal boundaries is a perennial ethnographic problem. The significance of tribal designation varies through time as well as by custom from region to region. Two Timbira tribes are studied here regarding the strength of the boundary which separates them. These tribes have intermarried to some extent during this century and have an ongoing participation in each other's ceremonies. The extent to which they have culturally merged is here gauged on the basis of a quantitative analysis of one artifact which these tribes have in common: the hammock. Results suggest that the Krikati and Pukobye are still sufficiently socially distant from one another to maintain a significant cultural diversity. This study suggests that this method might be fruitfully applied to other ethnographic contexts in which social documentation is inconclusive, as well as to the familiar archaeological context where documentation may be lacking altogether.

The data for this study are drawn from a field and museum study of the artifacts of the Gé tribes of central Brazil.[1] The discussion will

---

1   The fieldwork for this study was done between September and December of 1968, under a Wenner-Gren Foundation Museum Fellowship. The fellowship also permitted me to visit museums in Europe and Brazil which had major collections of Gé artifacts. The kind assistance of many individuals in these museums and of Sr. Edson Soares Diniz, who assisted me in the field, is acknowledged. My initial fieldwork with the Krikati was carried out from September, 1963, to June, 1964, under

focus on two Timbira tribes, the Krĩkati and the Pukobye, and on one artifact, the hammock. The problem entails an interpretation of the significance of variation found in this artifact within each tribe and between these tribes. There is some question of their status as separate tribes, which I intend to show can be resolved with the aid of artifact analysis. The hammock lends itself to this method of analysis, because it is a relatively simple artifact, but which, nonetheless, yields crucial data about the relationship of these tribes.

ETHNOHISTORY AND TRIBAL DEFINITION

The designation of tribal units and their boundaries is a perennial ethnographic problem. Nowhere is that problem more difficult than in the case of the Gé groups in general and the Timbira in particular. Names occur once or twice in written records, and then disappear. Other names occur without identifiable precursors; and one is left the task of working out the amalgamations, separations, and extinctions of the groups. Even in cases where there is continuity in the tribal designation, there is frequently an unspecified amount of absorption of other peoples.

The names of the Krĩkati and the Pukobye appear for the first time in the nineteenth-century records, during a century which saw the Timbira tribes pacified and reduced in numbers by war and disease (Nimuendajú 1946, p. 4). There is little doubt that the social upheaval of this time was responsible for dislocation and mixture of remnant tribes, which resulted in the redrawing of social boundaries.

The Krĩkati were first mentioned in 1844, at which time they were located along the Tocantins to the west of their present site (Map 9.1). Then in 1849–1854 they were at the mission station near the present town of Imperatriz. From this time to the next mention of them in 1919, when they were found in their present location at the Pindaré headwaters, their whereabouts and situation were unaccounted for.

the auspices of the Harvard Central Brazil Project directed by David Maybury-Lewis, and in company with Jean Lave. I give my thanks to Janet Siskind for her encouragement well larded with good advice and to my husband, Jefferson Fish, whose advice on the statistical analysis and on matters of coherence and style was indispensable.

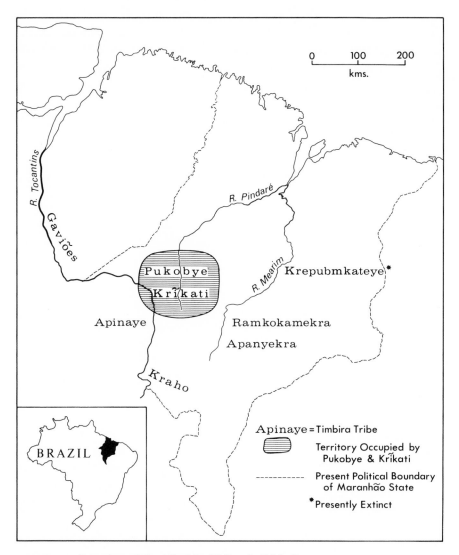

MAP 9.1   Location of the Timbira Tribes in This Century

The Pukobye were first noted at the turn of the eighteenth century on the River Grajaú and its western affluent, the Santana (or
Santa Ana), in the area to the east of that which they presently occupy.
Although the Krīkati and Pukobye histories seem to indicate a greater
geographic separation than at present, Nimuendajú suggests that the

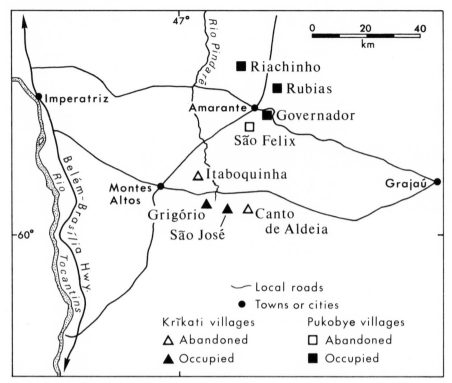

MAP 9.2   Krīkati and Pukobye Villages

early sources may have confused them and included Krīkati in their accounts of Pukobye (1946, pp. 16–19).

The present Krīkati are in two villages near the Brazilian town of Montes Altos, and the Pukobye are divided among three villages near the town of Amarantes. Both local groups are in the west-central part of the state of Maranhão (Map 9.2). These village clusters are separated from one another by a long day's journey on foot and from other Timbira tribes (Apinaye, Ramkokamekra, Apanyekra, and Kraho) by distances of many days' travel at least. The Pukobye and Krīkati today intermarry with one another. Intermarriage occurs between them with greater frequency than it does with any other tribe, although marriage with other Timbira is still more common than that with the more distant Gé tribes, or with the nearby Tupian groups or with Brazilians. In any case, endogamy of the village cluster remains the preferred and actual form of marriage.

The Krĩkati and Pukobye today share one set of names for themselves and for each other: the Krĩkati are called *Põkateye* (people of the savanna) and the Pukobye are called *Irobmkateye* (people of the forest). Insofar as these tribal names are descriptive of their respective environments, it is of interest that Nimuendajú, some forty years ago, recorded the exact opposite for the Pukobye. At that time, the Pukobye were *Põpeykateye* (people of the true savanna). Several other Timbira groups, Krĩkati, Krepubmkateye, and occasionally Ramkokamekra, also used the term. Thus, the Pukobye can be placed at an earlier time in the savanna area to the east of their present, forest location (Nimuendajú 1909–40, p. 40, 1946, p. 18).

But, in addition to this territorially based change of tribal designation, even the term "Pukobye" has also become functionally moribund, although still recognized by some older people. Although this need for continuity in names is obviously not one which the Timbira share, I have chosen to retain Pukobye for the sake of continuity in the labeling of local groups. By contrast, the Krĩkati still use Krĩkati as their most common self-designation, while recognizing in the alternate terminology that they are also Põkateye, "people of the savanna." Village names are another source of identification. Pukobye and Krĩkati occasionally use village names to refer to each other. Some of them even name people by reference to a particular village which has ceased to exist.

Finally, it should be noted that there is no term used by Krĩkati or Pukobye which refers to both of these groups together. It is curious that the weight of opinion from outside sources is that these are but local groups of a single tribal entity, in spite of the indigenous terminology which points up only differences. Let me indicate what these sources are. Regional Brazilians as well as Apinaye use a single term, Gaviões, to designate these local groups, with no distinction made between them. In a publication of the Conselho Nacional de Protecão aos Indios (Malcher 1962–64, p. 143), settlements of both groups are lumped under the designation "Caracati" (Krĩkati). This information comes from a survey which must have been done during the period of 1935–1945, judging from the names of the villages given. Finally, Nimuendajú designated these local groups as "Krĩkati Pukobye" (1946, Map 1) in the wake of the mixture which he observed of Krĩkati with Pukobye in 1928–1929. Since this occasion is the only documented instance of more than minor mixture between these groups, it is worthwhile to consider the details.

The 1919 census lists 273 Krīkati and only 52 Pukobye (Nimuendajú 1946, pp. 17, 19). Nimuendajú's visit to both of these groups ten years later provided population counts of 80 Krīkati and 270 Pukobye.[2] In the interim between these counts, the Krīkati had been in protracted conflict with a local rancher and had begun to disperse from that settlement area. They abandoned the last village of Canto da Aldeia in 1930, and Nimuendajú believed them to be extinct as a group after that time (1946, p. 17).

The Krīkati did not, in fact, disappear after that crisis. They did disperse for a few years (some even attached themselves to Brazilian homesteads in small family groups) but by 1935, at the latest, they had united again only a few miles from Canto da Aldeia in a village called Itaboquinha. Working with life history data on the adult Krīkati, I could confirm the continuity of the present population with that of the dispersed village. In these life histories it is interesting that there was no mention of even brief sojourns with the Pukobye, since we know from Nimuendajú that a substantial number did go there. On the occasion of his visit to the Pukobye in 1929, Nimuendaju noted that "the true Pukobye have dwindled to very inconsiderable numbers, the majority of the people now inhabiting Pukobye settlements being members of other tribes, notably Krīkati refugees" (1946, p. 19).

From the above information we must conclude that the Krīkati who migrated to the Pukobye area, whatever their number, did not return. There is reason to believe, however, that the numbers were not as great as the population counts would lead us to think. Although the figures imply that some two hundred persons changed from the Krīkati to the Pukobye locality in ten years, other evidence indicates that this is unlikely. First of all, the present population sizes are quite similar, and it is not likely that this would be the case had so many Krīkati left their area and not returned. Secondly, even Nimuendajú believed the 1919 count of Pukobye to be on the low side (1946, p. 19). Finally, it

2   The date of Nimuendajú's visit to these groups is indicated incorrectly in his *The Eastern Timbira*. It is probably due to an error in the translation of the original German manuscript. The error is on p. 17 of the above book, where it is said that he visited the Krīkati the year after the 1919 census. This is contradicted both in the following discussion of the Pukobye (p. 19) and in the museum collections, which he made of all these tribes and which are dated 1928–1929 in his own hand.

seems likely that by the time of Nimuendajú's visit in 1929 (by which time he had already recorded large numbers of Krĩkati with the Pukobye) the Krĩkati had already begun to disperse locally, so that those who had done so would have been missed in his count.

The conclusions that emerge are that the Pukobye did experience some increased influx of Krĩkati in the late 1920s but without any equivalent mixture of Pukobye with the Krĩkati in their area. This formulation presents difficulty only in one regard: the Krĩkati today also claim to be a mixture of many tribes. They say that the real Krĩkati are very few, as do the Pukobye in regard to the true Pukobye among them. But, there is no documented mixture of other tribes with Krĩkati in any significant numbers. However, persons for whom there was general agreement that at least one parent had been true Krĩkati, were all above sixty years old. The difficulty in explaining the unaccounted-for mixture could be resolved if the mixture took place during the last century, when there were no records for these tribes.

Population data collected in 1968 will shed light on the extent of Pukobye and Krĩkati mixture in this century. As the data in Table 9.1 show, presently three times as many Krĩkati-born persons live among the Pukobye than Pukobye-born persons live among the Krĩkati. In Table 9.2, the Pukobye village data are broken down by age category. Krĩkati-born persons in the two oldest categories are the only ones who might have come to the Pukobye area during the period of Krĩkati harassment before 1930. Those over fifty years might even have come as young adults, while those under fifty must have come as children with their kin, if they were there before 1930. It is significant that the highest ratio of Krĩkati-born persons to Pukobye-born persons in the Pukobye area comes from the over fifty years category. It suggests that the mixture of the two groups was greater for people of marriageable age in the 1920s and early 1930s than for persons of marriageable age any time after that (except perhaps for persons presently in their twenties). I have also included the comparable Krĩkati village data in Table 9.3. In summary, we can see that the population data are consistent with the above conclusion that the most sizable influx of Krĩkati into Pukobye villages was during the crisis period before 1930. It is, furthermore, clear that the mixture between these tribes has gone on for at least the past two to three generations.

One might be tempted to use this ongoing mixture as evidence to

TABLE 9.1   Summary of Krīkati and Pukobye Population Data, 1968

Krīkati Villages:	No. of houses	Total Population	Persons of Pukobye birth
São José	17	158	2
São Grigório[a]	5	46	2
Totals[b]	22	204	4
Pukobye Villages:			Persons of Krīkati birth
Governador	11	140	13
Rubias	2	30	1
Riachinho	3	26	0
Totals[b]	16	196	14

aThis is actually no longer a village, but five houses now in three places all within forty minutes' walking distance of one another. Quarreling among these households is the cause of the village separation, and at this point it threatens to send one family off to live with the Apinaye where they have relatives.

bThe total population figure includes Krīkati or Pukobye and all other persons of origins other than that specified. In the case of the Krīkati this includes one Apinaye and several others with one Apinaye parent, as well as the noted Pukobye; and in the case of the Pukobye this total includes a Xerente and two persons with one Guajajara parent.

TABLE 9.2   Age Distribution of Population in the Pukobye Area, 1968[a]

Age Range	Years of Birth	No. of Pukobye[b]	No. of Krīkati[c]
50 & over	before 1920	11	3
40–49	1920–1929	23	1
30–39	1930–1939	29	3
20–29	1940–1949	27	6
10–19	1950–1959	31	1
Totals		121	14

aCount is for villages of Rubias and Governador only.
bBorn in Pukobye area and living in Pukobye area.
cBorn in Krīkati area and living in Pukobye area.

support the view that the Krīkati and Pukobye are really one tribe. However, this mixture continues to be numerically slight. Moreover, while some kindred feelings do exist between the tribes, they tend much more to see themselves as different. Thus, while the Krīkati readily acknowledge themselves to be a mixture of many groups, they do not especially stress the Pukobye. Furthermore, during the period of harassment, there were Krīkati who did not seek asylum with the Pukobye. One such woman said that she was too afraid of the Pukobye to even visit their villages.

The descent patterns of these two groups also function to maintain their discreteness. There is no lineal descent. Nor is there a precise rule which assigns people to a given group if they are of mixed parentage. It is, rather, a combination of parentage and birthplace which provides the basis of identification. If one marries into his natal group, the issue of his identity is essentially settled. The significance of this pattern is that in spite of the intermarriage, there are no persons born and living in one area who hold, by virtue of a unilineal descent rule, membership in the opposite group. The above pattern of group identification serves well for my purposes of classification of individuals as Pukobye or Krīkati. Some classification must be made, in order to compare the products of individuals who belong to one group with those of the other. In the population tables, persons are classified as Krīkati or Pukobye on the basis of birthplace, since they were all raised in the area where they were born.

Although individuals may change their location, they do not erase the cultural learning that has taken place during the first fifteen years of life. Therefore, individuals who have changed tribal areas as adults (*i.e.*, on the occasion of or after their first marriage) are still considered to be cultural products of the group in which they were born and raised. The children of these individuals, if they were born and raised in the second area, would be considered products of that area. The in-

TABLE 9.3   Age Distribution of Population in the Krīkati Area, 1968

Age Range	Years of Birth	No. of Krīkati[a]	No. of Pukobye[b]
50 & over	before 1920	23	1
40–49	1920–1929	20	1
30–39	1930–1939	30	2
20–29	1940–1949	19	0
10–19	1950–1959	41	0
	Totals	133	4

[a]Born in Krīkati area and living in Krīkati area.
[b]Born in Pukobye area and living in Krīkati area.

fluence of the parents might well cause certain deviations in the behavior of their children vis-à-vis the new cultural milieu. Nevertheless,
the cultural forms which the adopted group evolved would be determined in part by these added elements. Turning now to a specific set
of cultural behaviors, that of hammock making, let us see if these behaviors can be used to gauge the extent of cultural and social overlap
between these Timbira groups. In a word, to what extent do material
cultural differences delineate social distance and, therefore, define
social boundaries?

HAMMOCK ETHNOGRAPHY

It is a common ethnographic generalization that in aboriginal times
the Gé tribes limited their use of the hammock to a temporary frond
variety which they made while on trek. At some time in the past the
Krĩkati and the Pukobye all but replaced the frond variety with cotton ones, and presently they use the cotton hammock not only on treks
but also for daytime resting and nighttime sleeping in the village.

The date and circumstance that led to the adoption of the cotton
hammock are not known. Nimuendajú reported that three of the
Timbira groups (Pukobye, Krĩkati, and Krepubmkateye) owned a
fair number of hammocks, but that "nearly all of them have been obtained in barter from the nearby Guajajara" (1946, p. 42). He does
not give the origin of those hammocks which were not bartered, and he
further states that "to date the Timbira have not manufactured a
single cotton hammock" (1946, p. 42). Personal accounts from the
Krĩkati and the nearby Guajajara, comparison between Timbira and
Guajajara hammock forms, the age distribution of Timbira hammock
makers, and linguistic evidence contradict the conclusions reached by
Nimuendajú. Indeed, these data suggest that the Krĩkati and Pukobye
have made some hammocks for at least sixty years.

However, the majority of the people still do not regularly use the
hammock. The ratio of hammocks to the total population is 1:4, and it
is rare that more than one person sleeps in a single hammock. Most
people still use platform beds or mats on the ground, both of which
are more typical of the Timbira than is the hammock.

The use of cotton, it is generally agreed, is an aboriginal trait of
all the Timbira. Generally, this use has been limited to decoration,

and so the utilitarian nature of the hammock is distinctive. It also requires more cotton cordage than any other object. In all villages, women grow the cotton, remove the seeds, and spin the cordage (Fig. 9.1). Women also make the actual hammock. All women over the age of thirteen are potential hammock makers. There are no specialists in this skill, although some women appear to be more frequent producers than others.

In general appearance, the hammocks made by both groups are identical. They are string or net hammocks, in contrast to the solid fabric or woven varieties characteristic of Brazilian and some distant Indian tribes (Figs. 9.1, 9.2). These string hammocks are made by wrapping a continuous strand around two posts set vertically in the ground. The distance between the posts is the length of the finished hammock. A rope, placed through the loops formed around the post at either end, provides a means of suspension. Spaced out along the length of the hammock, there are between six and twenty transverse rows of twining (made across the width of the hammock) which hold the longitudinal strands in each stitch, and each adjacent row encloses the same longitudinal strands (Fig. 9.3). There is no particular time of the year designated for hammock making. The construction process itself takes only a few hours, although these hours might be spread over two or three days while other activities are pursued as well. The spinning, similarly spread out, might take a month or two.

TRIBAL DIFFERENCES IN HAMMOCK CONSTRUCTION

The Krīkati and the Pukobye are identical with regard to all aspects of the social context surrounding the hammock and hammock construction: the functions of hammocks, the ratio of hammocks to people in a village, the fact that women make them, and so on. Yet despite this similarity in context, Krīkati and Pukobye do not make identical hammocks. So that I could specify with precision the variations that occur in hammock construction, I noted the following variables for each hammock:

1. Raw material (*buriti* frond, *tucum*, or cotton)
2. Technique of twining (S twining, Z twining, and countertwining)

FIG. 9.1   Seated on a hammock, a Krĩkati woman spins cotton.

FIG. 9.2   Hammock Being Constructed on a Frame in the Krīkati Village of São José

    3. Twist of the cordage (S or Z)
    4. Total length of longitudinal strands
    5. Total width of hammock at the center transverse rows
    6. Number of transverse rows
    7. Space between transverse rows and between transverse rows and end loops

Of the seven dimensions, two statistically separate Krīkati and Pukobye hammocks. These are (2) technique of twining and (3) twist of the cordage. While the other five dimensions may yet reveal internal configurations within each tribe, they do not relate to the issue at hand: differentiation between the two tribes.

In its simplest form, twining is done with two transverse strands which enclose a warp (or longitudinal strand) and then cross each other before enclosing the next warp, and so on until all of the warps are engaged. Figure 9.3, parts *a* and *b*, illustrate two forms of this simplest twining. In *a* the strands cross each other in a left over right direction, and in *b* the strands cross each other in a right over left di-

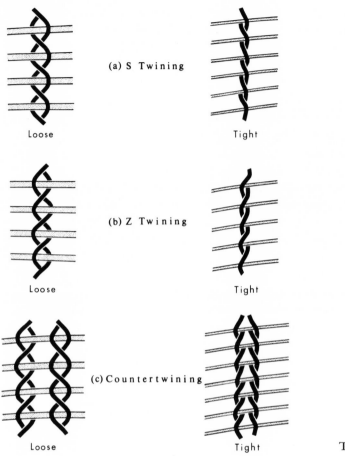

(a) S Twining

Loose

Tight

(b) Z Twining

Loose

Tight

(c) Countertwining

Loose

Tight

FIG. 9.3
Types of Twining

rection. These two forms are called S twining and Z twining respectively, because wrapped strands suggest the forms of these letters. The combination of a row of S twining and a row of Z twining done close together results in a third type: countertwining (Fig. 9.3 c).

All three types of twining occur in both Pukobye and Krīkati hammocks, but in different proportions. The Krīkati preference is for countertwining, and the Pukobye preference is for S twining. For some reason, not as yet clear, the Z twining is of minimal occurrence in both groups. Table 9.4 summarizes the relevant data and includes the chi-square test of significance. These results indicate that the Pukobye and Krīkati populations are distinct in this trait. Having excluded already the possibility that such a difference might be based on factors of social context or use, it must be concluded that this is a difference in cultural preference. In this case, the preference for a given type of twining is assumed to reflect a preference for certain motor behaviors.

In the Timbira tribes under discussion, and in most other Brazilian tribes with which I am familiar, cotton cordage is commonly two-ply. These two (or more) plys can be twisted in one of two directions, usually indicated by the letters S or Z which graphically suggest the right-left and the left-right slant of the respective twists. The direction which occurs is simply a matter of the direction in which the spindle is rotated. As the Timbira spin cordage, a spindle whose shaft is rotated by pulling it back along the leg and allowing it to spin in the resulting clockwise direction (looking down from above), will produce an initial Z twist of the first ply. Two plys with an initial Z twist will naturally twist together into an S direction. Since the two plys are usually twisted together with a spindle, the cordage gains additional tightness in the process.

The above description indicates the direction of twist in two-ply cordage, made by a right-handed woman who begins the first twist by pulling the spindle back, in a clockwise direction, along her right leg. The rest of the procedure follows from this beginning. By contrast, the final twist of the cordage is reversed (*i.e.*, Z) either if the woman is left-handed and works along her left side, or if she makes the initial twist by pushing the spindle forward along her leg in a counterclockwise direction. Of course, if she is both left-handed and pushes the spindle, the cordage is an S twist.

Table 9.5 presents the cordage twist data which I collected on 90 percent of the hammocks in Pukobye and Krīkati villages. This table excludes hammocks of mixed S and Z cordage. Such examples might

TABLE 9.4   Krīkati and Pukobye Twining Preferences

| | | Type of Twining | | |
	Countertwining	Z Twining	S Twining	Totals
Krīkati	25	3	4	32
Pukobye	13	1	19	33
Totals	38	4	23	65

$X^2 = 14.57$ and p⟨.005

TABLE 9.5   Krīkati and Pukobye Cordage Twist Preferences

| | Cordage Twist | | |
	Z Twist	S Twist	Totals
Krīkati	17	8	25
Pukobye	8	14	22
Totals	25	22	47

$X^2 = 4.7$ $p < .05$

result from a few women spinning the cordage for a hammock which one woman makes, or from repairing a hammock with cordage that differs in twist from that of the original. Since original and repair cordage cannot always be distinguished, I found it necessary to exclude hammocks of mixed cordage from this comparison. The distribution of cordage twist types between the two tribes is statistically significant.

One might ask whether the two traits which distinguish between the tribes actually constitute a single phenomenon. If this were so, we would expect that the tribes' respective preferences would occur together. But as we see in Table 9.6 this is not the case. The cordage twists of both groups are distributed among the twining types in direct proportion to their frequencies in the sample. As a matter of fact, given the low N in each case, the complete lack of association between the two is striking.[3]

The choices that the two tribes make between Z and S cordage cannot be explained on the basis of utilitarian factors, as both types of cords apparently are equal in strength. Likewise, the choice between S and Z twining of the transverses is not based on strength factors. However, countertwining, because it has four strands, is stronger than either S or Z types, both of which have only two strands. The extra strength of countertwining may explain its popularity among the Krīkati. The transverses need the extra strength as they are the first parts of a hammock to wear out. Conversely, Pukobye, who use less countertwining, often double the strands for each element of the S-

3 The fragmentary evidence from the museum collections suggests that this is not a recent phenomenon. Unfortunately, all but one of the hammocks which Nimuendajú collected in 1928–1929 were destroyed in World War II, and no descriptive records were left. The surviving hammock from the Krīkati (Museum für Völkerkunde, Dresden; cat. no. 44566, original no. 338) is the same in all details as the present-day ones. This hammock also shows the nonassociation of the dominant cordage and twining types: its cordage is S twist and it is countertwined.

twined transverse, and so achieve a strength equivalent to that of countertwining.

Both the Pukobye and the Krĩkati seem aware that the transverses wear out easily, because both sometime use heavier gauge cordage for the transverse twining than for the longitudinal strands. However, neither selects the logical alternative of setting the transverse rows closer together. Although I did not question them about the point, both groups may prefer a relatively wide spacing of the transverse rows. Janet Siskind reports (personal communication) that although the Panoan-speaking Sharanahua make both string and solid-fabric hammocks, only string hammocks are used by women with babies. In the string hammock, when the baby urinates, the strands can be held apart thus preventing the urine from wetting the hammock.

THE HAMMOCK AS A SOCIAL BOUNDARY MARKER

Because the different styles of twining and cordage manufacturing that the Krĩkati and Pukobye use have no utilitarian value, the variations between the two tribes are not the results of greater or lesser degrees of technological development. Although we cannot assume it, it seems likely that the Krĩkati and Pukobye acquired the hammock independently of one another (but from a similar model).[4] The data are in

TABLE 9.6   Comparison Between Cordage Twist and Twining Types in Krĩkati and Pukobye Hammocks

| | | Type of Twining | | |
	Countertwining	Z Twining	S Twining	Totals
Krĩkati Cordage				
Z Twist	12	2	3	17
S Twist	6	1	1	8
Totals	18	3	4	25
Pukobye Cordage				
Z Twist	3	0	5	8
S Twist	4	0	10	14
Totals	7	0	15	22

4 Since this paper considers only the Krĩkati and Pukobye, the influence of other tribes on cordage twist and twining is not discussed. However, it may be stated with confidence that the two tribes have influenced each other more than any other tribe has influenced either of them.

TABLE 9.7   Percentages of Twining Types and Cordage Twist in Krĩkati and Pukobye Hammocks

	Krĩkati	Pukobye
Twining Types		
Countertwining	78%	39%
Z Twining	9%	3%
S Twining	13%	58%
Totals	100%	100%
Cordage Twist		
Z Twist	68%	36%
S Twist	32%	64%
Totals	100%	100%

harmony with such a conclusion. The best explanation for the present frequency distributions is that of a movement of individuals from one tribe to another. The diffusion of traits without the actual exchange of people is more likely when one trait is superior to the other or when one group of people is more powerful than the other. Neither is the case in this instance. Moreover, the traits under consideration are a part of a nonconscious motor activity and this makes them less available to conscious manipulation than traits of a conscious kind.

The high percentage of countertwining and Z cordage twist among the present Krĩkati argues that originally the Krĩkati had only these two techniques (Table 9.7). In similar fashion the data suggest that the Pukobye had only S twining and S cordage twist. Furthermore, the Krĩkati in contrast to the Pukobye have higher proportions of the presumed original traits. For example, the ratio of countertwining to S twining among the Krĩkati is approximately 6:1, while the ratio of S twining to countertwining among the Pukobye is less than 2:1. These proportions suggest a higher movement of traits and people from the Krĩkati to the Pukobye than from the Pukobye to the Krĩkati. If such is the case, then there should be more Krĩkati individuals living with the Pukobye than Pukobye individuals living with the Krĩkati. Indeed, this is the case. Table 9.1 shows there are fourteen Krĩkati living with the Pukobye and only four Pukobye living with the Krĩkati.

We would expect that the longer the alien hammock makers have lived with a tribe, the greater would be the proliferation of their type of hammock. So, given the higher frequency of the Krīkati traits of countertwining and Z cordage among the Pukobye, we would expect to find more old Krīkati among the Pukobye than old Pukobye among the Krīkati. Tables 9.2 and 9.3 indicate that this is true; there are three Krīkati over fifty living with the Pukobye and only one Pukobye over fifty living with the Krīkati.

Among both the Krīkati and the Pukobye, some women will use one technique for one hammock and another for the second hammock. This lack of consistency is higher among the Pukobye than among the Krīkati (Table 9.8). More Pukobye use two or more techniques than do the Krīkati. These data also support the idea that movement of traits is principally from Krīkati to Pukobye. Because of the higher proportion of Krīkati women living among the Pukobye, would-be Pukobye hammock makers have a higher frequency of alternate models for constructing hammocks. The women who remain in their natal households provide one model for the beginner while incoming women provide another. The higher inconsistency among Pukobye hammock makers would seem attributable to their greater opportunity to learn both models.

An alternate to the explanation that accounts for variation in hammock making as being due to tribal differences would be that such variation reflects variations in the age of the makers. Such an explanation might hypothesize that twining techniques are essentially fads that new generations pick up or drop. Although plausible, such an explanation does not fit the data on the Krīkati and the Pukobye. As Tables 9.9 and 9.10 show, no connection exists between the techniques of twining and the age of the hammock maker.

TABLE 9.8   Consistency of Twining Types in Hammocks Made by the Same Woman[a]

| | Repetitive Hammock Making | | |
	All Examples Same Type	Examples Differ in Type	Total
Krīkati	6	2	8
Pukobye	1	6	7

[a]Because of the small N, no statistical comparison is possible.

TABLE 9.9   Distribution of Twining Types by Age of Maker, Krīkati
(São José)

Age of Maker	Countertwining	Type of Twining Z Twining	S Twining	Totals
50 & over	5	0	1	6
40–49	5	1	1	7
30–39	6	1	1	8
20–29	7	0	0	7
13–19	3	1	0	4
Totals	26	3	3	32

TABLE 9.10   Distribution of Twining Types by Age of Maker, Pukobye

Age of Maker	Countertwining	Type of Twining Z Twining	S Twining	Totals
50 & over	2	0	3	5
40–49	3	0	3	6
30–39	2	0	3	5
20–29	4	1	6	11
13–19	1	0	2	3
Totals	12	1	17	30

CONCLUSIONS

Among the Krīkati and Pukobye, two techniques employed in hammock construction have a distribution that is statistically related to tribal membership. These techniques, the method of twining and the manufacture of cordage, have no utilitarian value. Their distribution seems to reflect motor habits learned within the context of the tribe. The explanation that best fits the existing data hypothesizes that the Krīkati originally utilized the techniques of countertwining and Z cordage twist and that the Pukobye employed S twining and S cordage twist. Subsequently, an exchange of people and, therefore, techniques between the two tribes occurred, but with a greater flow from the Krīkati to the Pukobye than in reverse. This explanation receives support from the facts that presently more older Krīkati live among the Pukobye than the reverse, that more Pukobye hammock makers use several techniques than do Krĩkati ones, and that hammock trait preferences do not vary according to the age of the maker.

This explanation agrees with the sparse documentation available and with what informants express regarding the distinctiveness between the two tribes. The fact that informants are not aware of the tribal differences in the types of twining and cordage making discussed does not lessen the relevance of these items in distinguishing tribal boundaries. The cues that the informants use to distinguish between the tribes are those not always accessible or immediately recognizable to a nonnative. In contrast, material items are readily observable; the anthropologist can collect them and measure them with greater ease and accuracy than he can gather and measure attitudes and opinions. The analysis of material culture adds another dimension to the solution of a multitude of ethnographic problems. The present study shows its value in solving a particular kind of recurrent ethnographic problem: determining the social boundaries of tribes.

REFERENCES CITED

Malcher, José M. Gama
  1962–64   *Indios, Grau de Integração na Communidade Nacional, Grupo Lingüístico, Localização.* Conselho Nacional de Proteção aos Indios, n.s. Publicação Nº 1. Rio de Janeiro: Ministério da Agricultura.

Nimuendajú, Curt
  1909–40   *Unveröffentlichte Sprachaufnahmen.* Ms. in Museu Nacional, Rio de Janeiro.
  1946   *The Eastern Timbira.* University of California Publications in American Archaeology and Ethnology, Vol. 51. Berkeley.

Chapter 10

Material Culture in the Geographic Interpretation of the Landscape

Fred B. Kniffen

ABSTRACT   Cultural ecology is a meeting ground between anthropology and geography, although the goals of the two fields are quite different. Anthropology seeks to gauge the significance of the environment for culture; geography is concerned more with the importance of culture for the environment, what man is doing to the earth.

The material details of the landscape are the geographer's lore. The cultural geographer must first group systematically the forms constructed by man in living on the earth. Idealized conclusions regarding cultural processes and history thus derived must be checked against the reality of functioning areas. One area so checked, the prairie of southwestern Louisiana, revealed that woodland invaders fared poorly; at the same time, the Spanish-American range cattle complex from open grasslands and farmers from the midwestern prairies did well.

Throughout the two thousand years of its existence as a recognized field, geography has had a primary concern with the material aspects of the earth's surface. Maps, the immemorial tools and records of geographic undertakings, were in their earliest form crude realistic representations of natural and cultural features. Even in geography's diversification away from simple landscape description, an interest in the landscape's material form per se has never been lost. In fact, to those in other disciplines, geography has appeared to be so materialistic and descriptive, so little concerned with cultural values, as rarely to be counted among the behavioral sciences. Some geographers are satisfied with this exclusion; others are not.

Be that as it may, a concern with the relationships between man and nature has been an inescapable consequence of geography's preoccupation with the earth's surface. The degree of concern with man-land relations has varied from an extreme environmental determinism almost to a cultural determinism, where man's activities seemingly take place in a natural vacuum and only spatial distribution is a considered natural quality. Long before culture was formalized as a series of concepts, geographers were dealing with certain aspects of culture, naturally those tying man to earth, those related to natural qualities such as space, location, distribution and to environmental qualities such as climate, terrain, and resources. It was, then, cultural processes related most closely to environment that got geographers' attention: invention, diffusion, adaptation. Such significant considerations as value systems, subjective perception, and the like, were early neglected.

Modern cultural ecology is regarded by some geographers as an invasion of a geographic field by anthropologists. Certainly cultural ecology is a meeting ground that should profit from multiple attention. Furthermore, while there is partial concurrence of observational data and methodological approach, it appears that the goals can be clearly differentiated.

Geography sees its results negatively in alterations of nature and positively in settlements, primary production, transportation networks, and similar phenomena. Culture for the geographer is a means to an end, the understanding of the landscape, the landscape that is a blending of natural and cultural qualities. For the anthropologist, culture is the end. He sees how environment may shape culture. He finds ultimate results in the nature of culture itself.

Geographer and anthropologist can agree that nature is important in cultural expression. They can also agree that where a restrictive nature necessitates cultural adaptation, the nature of the adaptation is derived from cultural processes, not from natural processes. As George Carter so aptly expressed it, "The role of the environment is determined primarily by the culture of the man. The same physical environment plays an entirely different role for the farmer, the manufacturer, the hunter, the pastoralist" (1966, p. 57). Carter might have added that farmers with different cultural backgrounds may use the same physical environment in quite different ways.

Today the geographer better deserves a place among behavioral scientists. This is because of his increasing interest in what might be termed the psychological aspects of culture as they motivate behavior with respect to the land: value systems, environmental perception, the whole range of cultural rationale. Still, geography students of land-scape likely need not become as deeply versed in the intricacies of culture as is the anthropological culturologist. It is difficult, however, to say just what about culture the geographer can disregard. One might assert that surely social organization is of no importance to the student of the material landscape. Then it is pointed out that there commonly is a direct relationship between social structure and struc-ture of the settlement pattern, the latter of primary importance to the geographer. And, does selectivity among the facets of culture, one might say, fragmentation, bias the investigator's conclusions to the point of inaccuracy? Are the results of such selective approach solid and worthwhile? Judgment must rest on the quality of the geogra-pher's work.

The material forms constituting the landscape are the geogra-pher's basic lore. The cultural geographer deals primarily with the occupance pattern, the marks of man's living on the land. He finds his data, his evidence, in buildings, fields, towns, communication systems, and concomitant features. His procedure parallels that of the system-atic botanist in discovering types and groups of related types. As a geographer he is ever cognizant of quantity and distributions; to show them he constantly employs the map, the symbol of his profession. From his organized material data the geographer draws conclusions re-garding cultural patterns, processes, sequences, value systems, all di-rected toward explaining the landscape.

It is important to keep in mind that the cultural geographer em-ploys an evidential approach that basically studies material things. As with archaeology, many of the things studied belong to a practically undocumented past. Only by first considering the material forms can subjective values be discerned. One does not start with subjective con-cepts and values. He ends with them after considering the evidence in material expression. In light of this position, one may take issue with Amos Rapoport's criticism of Henry Glassie's failure to relate house form to value system, hence missing "the important question—why things were as they were" (Rapoport 1969, p. 44). Glassie, like this writer, evidently believes that material form must come first, that only from the evidence thus revealed can subjective values be discerned. This approach has worked very well. What other is there that can derive and substantiate conclusions on subjective matters?

Type occupance patterns are the product of technological capacity, cultural norms and values, and natural environment. Their basic functioning components are determined by man's elemental animal needs: shelter, food, water, communication. Regardless of degree of cultural complexity, satisfaction of animal needs takes priority over all other needs that are culturally acquired rather than biologic. Culturally sponsored traits such as disposal of the dead may become spatially universal and so, like animal needs, parts of the universal occupance pattern. The occupance pattern, composed of the material forms arising from the satisfying of man's needs, is the standardized structure to be utilized in both individual and cross-cultural studies.

While we may be slaves to the thinking of the Greeks, we have found no approach to the study of natural phenomena superior to their systematic consideration, credited to Aristotle. Kroeber includes culture with natural phenomena when he states: "This is the idea of culture . . . as something entirely a part of nature, wholly an evolutionary development within nature, and therefore to be investigated by the methods of fundamental natural sciences" (1953, p. xiv). Certainly this injunction applies to the geographer's consideration of certain aspects of material culture.

When studying any aggregation of material culture, the constituents must be sorted into their mutually commensurate categories. The categories are those from the complex of man's universal activities that mark his occupance of the land. They begin with man's basic animal needs and functions—food, water, shelter, communication—and expand to include material evidence of his culturally acquired traits, such as religion, government, recreation, and the like. Traits, complexes, and culture types are in turn set up in the rather rigidly idealistic terms necessary in a systematic approach. Isolated departures from the norm are largely disregarded, be they the product of historical accident, environmental differentiation, or other cause. And material fact is initially of more concern than process or causation.

Process and causation come into their own when the results of idealistic systematic study are set against the reality of regional consideration in the culture area. Now there are seen in anomalies within the ideal systematic structure the results of environmental differentiation, historical accident, and evolving cultural values. Here, it is hoped, one gains notions of the nature of culture change as it is expressed materially, of what environmental adaptation means, of the invention of new traits. He should be able to detect from the material cultural expression of the landscape ongoing trends in its development. The projection of trends into the future is prediction. Accuracy of prediction is the final test of the study's worth. All the steps from ideal systematic study to the reality of regional consideration must be gone through to attain the ultimate goals of understanding how systems of material landscape expression come about and predicting their future. There is no shortcut.

The points made above may be more telling if put to the test of actuality, to an existing regional culture area. The one selected for illustration is the prairie region of southwestern Louisiana, a region of distinctive natural environment, diverse cultures, and experiencing significant historical happenstances. It is possible in retrospect to evaluate the roles of nature and culture and to detect in their material expressions auguries of the future. No account of the slow accumulation of data and their ordering is rendered here. Rather, a finished study is assumed, or at least sufficient progress to describe the material patterns of the successive cultures that have occupied the prairie region.

THE PRAIRIE

The prairie region occupies some four thousand square miles of southwestern Louisiana, about a twelfth of the state's total area (Map 10.1). To the south is the lower-lying and treeless marsh, and beyond, the Gulf of Mexico. To the east is a lower-lying and forested swamp. Abutting the triangular-shaped prairie to the north are pine hills. The prairie surface is of low relief, sloping gently southward to marsh and Gulf. The several major streams of the region follow the slope from north

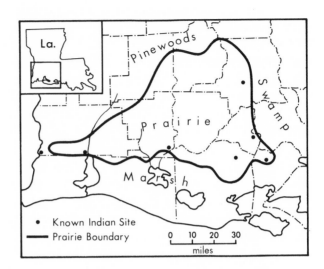

MAP 10.1
The Prairie Region
of Louisiana

to south. Along the streams are gallery woodlands. The interfluves are tall-grass prairies.

The soils composing the natural-levee ridges bounding both Recent and Pleistocene stream channels are light in texture and readily arable. The much more extensive interfluve soils are heavy, with an impervious hardpan lying a foot or so below the surface. They are most difficult to cultivate, "too wet to plow one day; too dry the next," and defy all but modern means of tillage. They can likely be grouped with the vertisols described by Duffield as too refractory for primitive farmers (1970). Prairie rainfall is moderate to heavy, with hot summers and high evaporation. Winters are mild but subject to the occasional sweep of cold north winds. Animal life in the prairie has never been truly abundant. For example, bison probably did not appear in the area until mid-seventeenth century.

INDIANS IN THE PRAIRIE

The gathering-hunting-agricultural economy of both prehistoric and historic Indians did not find a favorable milieu in the prairie. Occupied sites were not dense, and they were situated along streams and at the margins of the prairie where it joins the richer marsh and swamp (Map 10.1). One migrant group from the wooded East, the Koasati, found refuge at the northern edge of the prairie in the fringing pine forest. Indian woodland cultures with dependence on agriculture did not find receptive conditions in the prairie, while the prairie was not rich enough in its own right, in gathering and hunting potential, to invite adaptation on the part of woodland cultures.

EARLY EUROPEAN OCCUPANCE OF THE PRAIRIE

European cultures first entered the prairie in two major thrusts, French agriculturists from the east and Spanish herdsmen chiefly from the west. The French brought with them the settlement pattern so nicely adapted to the riverine terrain of wooded eastern Louisiana. Land was divided into the customary long-lot strips fronting on the prairie streams and extending back into the open prairie, commonly for a mile and a half (Map 10.2). A road followed the stream bank; to its sinuous course were oriented the fields and the dwellings of the inhabitants, usually the half-timber house of older Creole French Louisiana (Fig. 10.1).

Trees were cleared from the lighter soils of the rivers' natural levees. On them were grown corn, cotton, beans, and other subsistence crops. "Providence" rice[1] was grown without artificial irrigation in the natural shallow ponds that dot the eastern portion of the prairie. Wheat did poorly in Louisiana, and distance from the Mississippi River precluded dependence on imported wheat flour. As a result, the prairie French accepted corn bread as a staple food, something the river French never did. In time, cattle reared on the prairies became the cash crop of the prairie French, a crop capable of making its own way eastward to water transportation.

Spaniards introduced the cattle complex characteristic of Spanish America into prairie Louisiana. The latter then became the eastern-most extension of what was a continuous distribution of the complex through Texas and into Mexico. Animals, implements, structures, terms, usages were those of Spanish America. Spanish land grants in grazing areas were large rectangular *sitios*. Centrally located in the grant were the headquarters of the ranch and the home of the pro-prietor. Dispersed over the grant were corrals, natural ponds pre-served as watering places, and sheds open to the south for protection

---

1   "Providence" rice is a hardy rice that will grow with little special care.

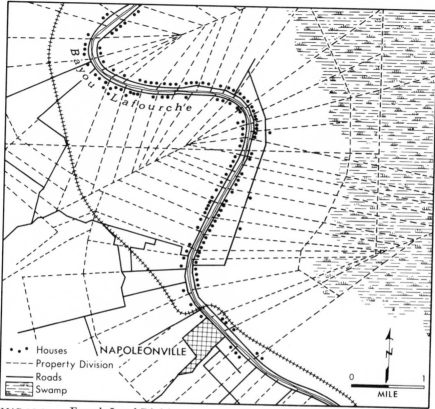

MAP 10.2   French Land Divisions

against wintry blasts. Trails ran at random over the unfenced prairie
(Map 10.3).

The careful, professional, and well-regulated animal husbandry
of Spanish America stood in marked contrast to the comparatively
haphazard usages of the Anglo-Saxon, piney-woods cattle complex.
The latter advanced from the eastern seaboard with the American
frontier. It got hardly, if at all, into the prairie, but it passed through
the bordering pine hills to the north into eastern Texas. The Spanish-
American cattle complex, nurtured in open grasslands, readily adapted to natural conditions in the prairie. The piney-woods complex, an
adjunct to field agriculture, did not.

Many of the prairie French became in time thoroughgoing cattle-
men. They seem to have brought few changes to Spanish-American

FIG. 10.1   Creole Half-Timber House

practices. There were a few concessions to linguistic differences, as when *rancho* became *vacherie*, and *tarabilla*, a simple Spanish device for spinning horsehair, became French *tarabi*. Today the traditional and largely Spanish-American practices survive among French-American cowboys on the vast unfenced marshes of coastal southwestern Louisiana.

LATE EUROPEAN OCCUPANCE OF THE PRAIRIE

There was no great change in the occupance patterns of the prairie until the 1800s, when the completion of a railroad line across the prairie was the revolutionary event that initiated radical alterations. First, the American rectangular land survey, introduced after the Louisiana Purchase and applied to the great bulk of the prairie which had not been previously surveyed, asserted itself. It found an ideal setting in the flat-lying lands. The haphazard trails over the open prairie disappeared before straight section-line roads and square turnings (Map

10.4). New towns were plotted in systematic rectangular patterns oriented to the railroad or to the cardinal directions. The old French strips along the streams were overwhelmed by the greater mass of the new system, and the Spanish *sitio* grants were largely obscured.

Those who took the lead in the postrailroad development of the prairie were largely settlers from the American prairie Midwest. They were appreciative of the possibilities of prairie soils for agriculture, and they saw in the low cost of Louisiana lands an opportunity for economic gain. They brought with them a whole cultural system of land occupance, of material installations and practices. Their houses were imports from the Midwest and strange to the older French inhabitants of the prairie. There were the older Midwest I house (Fig. 10.2) and the square, two-story house with pyramidal roof (Fig. 10.3). The barns similarly were constructed after the fashion of Midwest types. Farmstead building clusters were dispersed, spaced on the order

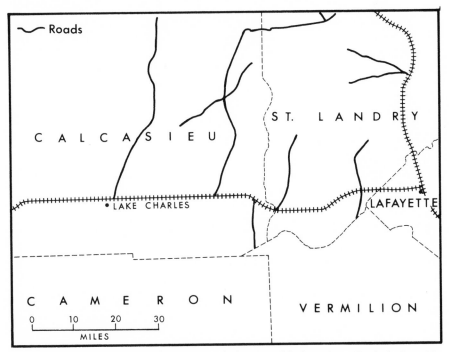

MAP 10.3   Random Road Pattern of the Spanish-American Period. In 1884 the Spanish-American pattern of roads continued to meander across the Louisiana prairie.

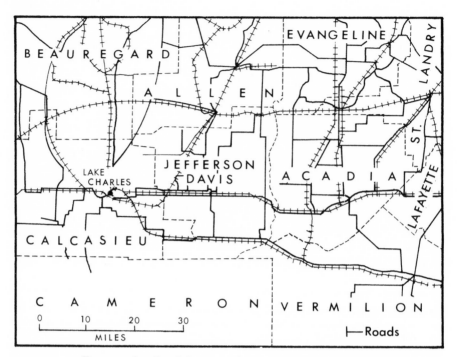

MAP 10.4   Rectangular Road Pattern of the Anglo-American Period. By 1917, rail lines and rectangular roads of the Anglo-American culture had dissected the flat countryside.

of one each quarter mile along the rectangular grid of roads. Wind-mills, wells, adequate highways, and cultural precedent moved farm centers from along streams to the open prairie road grid. Windbreaks of quick-growing trees were planted to protect farmstead buildings. All contributed to the distinctly midwestern character of the landscape (Fig. 10.4).

Agricultural crops and practices went through a period of trial before a successful system was developed. The midwesterners first visualized a corn-hog-grain economy like that with which they were fa-miliar. Somehow it was not highly successful. Finally, the midwestern-ers found in a local crop, rice, something that did well and to which they could adapt readily their accustomed agricultural practices. In-stead of following the unique methods of growing rice developed by the French along streams of the Mississippi system, prairie rice was grown just as were wheat and other grain crops in the Midwest. It is true that annual floods played an essential role in the production of river rice and were not duplicated in the prairie, but cultural precedent was responsible for the introduction of midwestern reaper, binder, and steam thresher to the growing of prairie rice.

One new technique the midwesterners had to learn was irrigation. Irrigation is not essential to the growing of rice, but it serves an important function in keeping down contamination by weeds. The haphazard methods employed by the French in producing "providence" prairie rice for subsistence did not suffice in the new commercial era. The midwesterners devised an irrigation system nicely adapted to existing conditions of soil and terrain. The southward-flowing streams, and subsequently, wells, provided water that could be pumped into main canals constructed on the high natural banks of the rivers. From the main canals, gravity carried water to the fields through lesser canals. Low levees were constructed to hold water to the required depth in the fields, while the impervious hardpan prevented the loss of water by downward seepage.

Not only the fields and farmsteads took on a midwestern character, but so did the villages and towns. The latter invariably followed

FIG. 10.2   Midwestern I House

FIG. 10.3   Midwestern Square House

a rectangular pattern, and the smaller towns along the railroads were dominated by tall grain elevators and water tanks: both pattern and structure are reminiscent of the grain-growing sections of the North. It is important to note that no single factor, such as soil type, terrain, or cultural influence, was accountable for the distinctive prairie occupance pattern. It may be pointed out that in northern Louisiana, also surveyed in the rectangular land-office system, rough terrain led to an irregular road system, indifferent soils to spotty agricultural utilization, and an Upland South culture to quite different building types and farmstead complex. A midwestern culture met a familiar natural and a permissive cultural setting in the prairie; it is interesting to conjecture what its fate might have been in hilly, forested northern Louisiana.

With the passage of time, field methods in growing prairie rice have changed to parallel developments in northern grain-growing techniques. Horses and mules have yielded to tractors, and binders and threshers to combines. The field surfaces have been graded to make field levees simpler. Airplanes are commonly used for seeding and fertilizing. Combining rice while it is still damp has necessitated the addition of driers, tall, bulky structures standing beside the grain elevators. And modern transportation has caused less dependence on railroads, while modern highways cut across the old grid pattern and eliminate square turnings. Stock and hay barns give way to machinery sheds. Good soil management dictates the regular fallowing of fields and their use as improved pasture for beef cattle. Once again beef cattle, though in quite different guise, are a significant landscape item.

But, there is additionally a more subtle change in the occupance pattern, a change attributable to the introduction of different cultural values. They come with a movement of French Louisianians from farther east into the prairie. Materially, their presence is evidenced by different house forms, smaller fields with abnormally wide headlands, a variety of crops rather than exclusive rice culture. The change is no

FIG. 10.4   Midwestern Type Landscape on the Louisiana Prairie. (Photo courtesy of Louisiana Department of Commerce and Industry.)

FIG. 10.5   Modern Acadian House

recrudescence of the older French settlement pattern along the prairie streams. Land patterns remain essentially those of the midwestern period, while the new house form is Acadian rather than Creole in lineage (Fig. 10.5).

The accounts of successive settlement patterns appearing above are chronicles of agricultural uses of the land. Shortly after the beginning of the present century, petroleum, the first discovered in Louisiana, became an added item in land use of the prairie. Petroleum has its distinctive forms in planned and regular arrangements in oil fields, refineries, and company towns. The petroleum installations appear to exist in harmony with agriculture in the prairie, yet completely alien to it. The two are contiguous, but without transitional forms or blending of any kind. One seems not to influence the other. Values are different without being antagonistic.

RETROSPECT

Examining the spectrum of human occupance of the prairie, one views a constant nature, the significance of its qualities varying with and dependent upon the technology and values of the several occupying cultures. Historic accident has determined the presence of specific cultures. There has been slower evolution between revolutionary events such as shifts in political boundaries and the coming of the railroad.

Understanding of the area has been reached through examination of the material evidence of man's occupance. Settlement forms, houses, fields, roads, towns, have been sorted into their several categories. The types belonging to each category have been arranged in temporal sequence. The resulting seriation has revealed what at any specific time are relict forms and what is newly emerging. As one can thus see the sequence of change for the past, so can he detect present trends and venture to look into the future. Certainly he can see the decline of the older Midwest pattern, even after making due allowances for evolutionary change. He can foresee the continuing expansion of the newer French culture, even if in doubt as to its evolutionary changes.

Finally, it may be pointed out that, not surprisingly, the two cultures initially most successful in the natural setting of the prairie were those nurtured in similar natural conditions elsewhere: Spanish-American range cattle rearing and midwestern prairie grain farming. And, as a corollary, the distinctive cultures of the prairie have not expanded outward into forested Louisiana.

REFERENCES CITED

Carter, George F.
  1966 What They Say About Cultural Geography. *Philippine Geographical Journal* 10:57.

Duffield, Lathel F.
  1970 Vertisols and Their Implications for Archaeological Research. *American Anthropologist* 72:1055–62.

Kroeber, A. L.
  1953 Introduction. In A. L. Kroeber *et al.*, eds., *Anthropology Today*. Chicago: University of Chicago Press. Pp. xiii–xv.

Rapoport, Amos
  1969 Review of Henry Glassie's Patterns in the Material Culture of the Eastern United States. *Landscape* 18–3:44.

BEHAVIORAL ADAPTATIONS AND SOCIAL STRUCTURE

Chapter 11

The Structure and Stuff of Rural Violence in A North Andean Valley

Thomas S. Schorr

ABSTRACT   The material and spatial configurations of human activity in the central Cauca Valley of Colombia are the expressions of an ecological system, one component of which is a complex of adaptations to the persistent threat of physical violence. Violent acts against life and property—collectively known as *la violencia*—are often attributed to Colombia's political feuds; yet, violence is endemic to the area and the record of its occurrence extends back to pre-Columbian times. As a consequence, inhabitants have evolved material, spatial, behavioral, and attitudinal configurations, each of which must be analyzed within the contexts of the others, in order to comprehend the totality of this adaptive design for survival.

The combined effects of land form, floods, soil types, disease, economic activity, and recurring hostilities in the region have led to the concentration of settlements between the protruding spurs of the cordilleras. These communities present only a single, easily defended entry to hostile groups. Settlements located away from the protective embrace of the mountains are limited to sparse groups strung along the natural levees of the Cauca River. Each population cluster is a closed grouping; within it, house-compound construction and composition, material arrangements, and the handling of movable property and goods are all reflections of strategies adopted for defense and security. Intertwined with this is a complex of expressive behavior which includes fear and suspicion, reticence, secretiveness, precautionary restraints on activities, wakefulness, sobriety, deference, and distrust of everyone not in a direct *confianza* relationship. An elaborate intelligence network, incorporating the mass media, itinerant service specialists, and close personal ties, provides continuous information about the possibility of attack. Overall attitudes are maintained and are structured to prepare the individual for the worst at any time.

These physical, behavioral, and attitudinal responses to physical threat, while elaborate, are nonetheless *normal*, composing an adaptive organization which increases the survival chances of human populations in an ecosystem threatened with recurrent violence.[1]

Throughout the history of the central Cauca Valley and stretching back as far as prehistoric reconstruction can infer, the occurrence of sudden violence at the hands of others has been a fact of everyday life. The earliest historical accounts describe an alternating state of peace and war among the tribes of swidden cultivators who inhabited the valley and neighboring uplands. All of them indulged in raids, surprise attacks by day and night, plundering, crop burning, kidnapping and cannibalism against their neighbors, and when the Spaniards came, against them as well. These hostilities were nothing more than periodic cycles of a predatory type of economic symbiosis (Wagner 1960, pp. 15, 19), institutionalized among competing populations, and serving to regulate their numbers and dispersal with respect to fluctuations and limitations in the available resources. This kind of violent competition among specialized populations has been a hallmark of the valley and of the Colombian nation as a whole that has persisted into recent times in the garb of party-political strife.

Excellent accounts written by specialist and lay authors provide multifaceted interpretations of Colombian violence, its demography, economics, politics, and psychology. And new chapters are being written every day (see Fals Borda 1968; Fluharty 1957; Gutiérrez 1964; Guzmán *et al.* 1962; Lievano Aguirre 1968; Payne 1968; Ramsey 1973; Schorr 1973*a*, 1973*c*; Williamson 1965). For the most part however, studies of violence in Colombia have deemphasized the analysis of variables that have contributed to its persistence, in favor of interpreting incidents and periods of strife as necessary for the solution of specific conflicts of interest which have arisen from time to time. I prefer to shift from the ontological levels at which violence in Colombia

1   "Stuff...1: materials, supplies, or equipment used in various human activities: as a. *obs*: military baggage: IMPEDIMENTA b.: bullets or shells fired from a gun: PROJECTILES ⟨were throwing broadsides at him...and *stuff* was going past him from both sides and killing—Ira Wolfert⟩" (Webster's Third New International Dictionary).

customarily has been viewed and to analyze it as a continuously re-curring cycle generated by a complex of interrelated conditions that occur as a part of the structure forming the general ecological system of that part of the world.

The people of the region recognize three kinds of threats to exis-tence. These were intensified during the years from 1946 to 1953 and came to be referred to collectively as *la violencia*. The threats are clas-sified according to the motive that gives rise to the violent act: (1) poli-tics, (2) banditry, and (3) vengeance. The three are not mutually exclusive classifications; for example, hired bandit groups may kill as mercenaries, for political reasons as well as for robbery, in order to sustain themselves. The bandits, however, do act continuously in an organized, professional way, whether at the command of political interests of a national sort or as of late, answering to international interests in fomenting terror and subversion. Individuals engaging in part-time violence may perform killing only rarely, in an answer to a political call, for instance, and may otherwise spend most of the time as respected members of a community, engaged in economically produc-tive endeavor. During the intense, Conservative-Liberal conflicts of fifteen to twenty-five years ago, law-abiding citizens were recruited into bands for organized sallies against towns of the opposite party. Besides these organized, quasi-military groups serving specific orders, there are those who, in criminal, psychopathic manner, rob and kill *para divertirse* (for the fun of it). These individuals may participate in all three classes of violence, operating within organized groups, or on their own, for their own ends anytime they choose. Those who par-ticipate frequently in violence and especially killing are referred to as *pájaros* (birds), a word which carries sexual connotations in this region of Latin America as it does elsewhere. The vengeance motive operates on a more casual basis and can be perpetrated at any time as a retali-atory gesture against specific incidents of past violence or against in-sults to one's interest: real, imagined, or contrived.

Combining all of the possible motives for violence, however, produces a situation in which its occurrence becomes random and fre-quent, with or without prior warning which might give an oppor-tunity for life-saving maneuvers in the face of an attack. Because of the long-term persistence of these threats to existence, imminent vi-olence becomes an unremitting expectation, reflected in the frequently voiced phrase, *"En el momento menos pensado, algo sucede"* (Just when you least expect it, something happens). It is a normal expectation, to which local populations in normal response have organized a complex of material and spatial arrangements, together with their associated behavior, attitudes and expectations; these can be teased apart from the total fiber of adaptive relations and identified for the ways they enhance survival and continuance.

CONDITIONS IN THE STRUCTURE OF LOCAL EXISTENCE

Contrary to the contentions of many, the spatial organization of society cannot be meaningfully comprehended without an understanding of the totality of ecological relationships in which specific societies are involved, adaptively through cultural means. Universals that can be recognized and related to panhuman behavior independent of contact and exchange among societies are very simple indeed (Morrill 1970); and recently developed, worldwide regularities of any complexity can be traced to the temporal process of culture-adaptive unification among communicating societies, a very recent evolutionary phenomenon that has linked together ecosystemic cycles throughout the extent of the earth's biosphere. Comparative analysis of the ecological cycles that take place within regional systems—including geophysical, biological, and human sociocultural components—show how unique the resulting material and spatial structures of societies can be (see Barth 1956; Bennett 1969; Conklin 1961).

Elsewhere, I established in detail the ecological interrelationships involving human populations in the central Cauca Valley (Map 11.1), especially as they have formed a matrix for persisting strife (Schorr 1965, 1968, 1973*a*). The products of a population's adaptation to existence under these conditions occur replete throughout its organization, even incorporating into the individual microcosms of its members. Some of the unique manifestations are easier to recognize than others and bear close examination here; among these are the physical characters of social organization, constructional modifications, and the related, consistently adaptive behavior of the populations responsible for these patterns.

A close scrutiny of the geographical situation shows that the populations of the region are peculiarly located in only two zones.

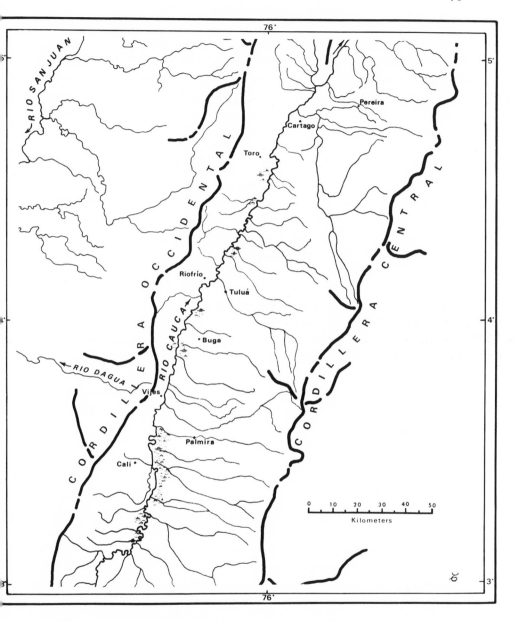

MAP 11.1 The Broad, Flat Plain of the Central Cauca Valley. It lies at an elevation of about 950 meters above sea level and, during the Pleistocene, formed an enclosed lake, sealed except for the precipitous gorges to the north and south which channeled the flow of the river.

Each zone presents conditions which, together with the activities of the populations inhabiting them, produce settlements consistently structured in two ways: larger, semicompact settlements of eight hundred to two thousand inhabitants occur within the folds of the valley walls (Fig. 11.1), while smaller, ribbon settlements of eight hundred or less populate the natural levees on the west side of the Cauca River. The larger settlements are located very precisely in relation to a dependable water supply—usually a mountain stream—and a protective enclosure formed by the cordillera and its spurs. In every case, these habitation centers have been founded on a platform of bajada—outwash and erosional debris—strategically nestled up against the sharply rising mountains at an elevation slightly above the flood zone of the valley floor and contained on each side within spurs of the mountains that extend outward toward the valley bottom. Thus, the mountains enclose the settlement protectively on three sides and present only a single, easily defended entry on the open side, therewith providing for long-term security against the recurring attacks of hostile groups. Another defensive advantage of being situated at a level above the valley floor is the advanced warning provided by early visual sightings of potential assailants, reducing the chances of being caught offguard by a surprise attack, which might otherwise occur without a moment's notice (Fig. 11.2). The present, predominantly Conservative party inhabitants of one of these communities, Guayabal by name,[2] recall only too well the frequent flights at dusk of women and children, up into the safety of the mountainous interior, while men armed themselves and occupied the strategic positions of defense—the tips of the spurs to the north and south, the bridge—where they waited out the night and the days to come, prepared for an attack by vengeful Liberals seeking to even the score of violence.[3] The smaller, riverside settlements are confined to the narrow, natural levee on the west bank of the Cauca River where drainage is good over the fertile alluvium. The opposite bank is largely unoccupied because of the river's slow, migratory trend across the floodplain toward the east (Fig. 11.1). Even on the west bank, frequent flooding, higher ambient temperatures, endemic dis-

---

2   Except for the correct identification of the Cauca Valley, pseudonyms are used throughout this paper.

3   Most of the data included here come from settlements on the west side of the Cauca River, which today are of predominantly Conservative party membership.

FIG. 11.1 Guayabal, *upper left*, and Guayabalito, *upper right*, are built into mountain folds above the floodplain, while La Florida, *below center*, supports itself upon the fertile levee of the Cauca River.

FIG. 11.2   This view over Guayabalito extends past the north spur of the hamlet and along the western cordillera toward the open valley beyond. The canal was constructed recently for drainage and irrigation.

eases, and lack of protection from predatory groups have kept settlements sparse and spaced out.

    Methods of cultivated food production have changed very little over the years intervening between the conquest and the modern agricultural development programs; they still show an adaptive fit that corresponds to the dual settlements pattern. The people of the bajada practice infield-outfield cultivation while those of the riverside till

permanent, infield plots. In addition to gardening the ample yard surrounding their *casa*,[4] inhabitants of the upland settlements cultivate
land in the mountains. Until recently, upland populations applied the
indigenous slash-and-burn, digging-stick technology in cultivating the
outfield plots and, in parts of the region, it is still employed to produce
the seasonal staples of maize (*Zea mays* L.), beans (*Phaseolus* spp.), and
squash (*Cucurbita maxima* Duchesne, hubbard squash or *zapallo*, and
other species including calabashes). The perennial yuca (*Manihot
dulcis* Pax.), arracacha (*Arracacia xanthorrhiza* Bancroft), and plan-
tain (*Musa* spp.) are cultivated wherever they will grow—on the fallow
or uncleared portions, amid other crops, in fields of their own, and
around the *casa* (Map 11.2). A small version of the *casa*, having no
more than a sleeping room and a cookroom, accompanies those mountainside plots beyond the first ridge of foothills. These are constructed
on a prepared platform of earth at a convenient spot on the rugged
terrain so as to be near the field (Fig. 11.3).

Because the family's main residence remains in the settlement
below, the climb up to the plot is a daily task during the few weeks
spanning the semiannual sowing season. Periodically, other trips are
made for weeding and furrowing. However, it is always desirable to
return home, down below to the security of the family and the settlement before nightfall. For this reason then, the mountain plot is usually never any farther than can be reached by a climb of from one to
two hours (Fig. 11.4). Only at harvest time does anyone stay overnight
at the mountain farm. Then they will go as they have gone for centuries, sometimes with the greater portion of the extended family, and
remain the number of days necessary to complete the harvest, using the
strength and endurance of every able-bodied person aged six years and
over, male and female alike, with beast of burden, to lower the produce down the precipitous slopes to the main house. This operation is
completed as quickly as possible, for security is at its worst during
these times. People constantly fear raids and theft of the newly har-

---

4   The word *house* is an inadequate gloss for the local concept, *casa*, which encom-
passes a bounded area of land and the various constructs on it inhabited by a family,
including the main house, a cookhouse (sometimes located apart), a wash trough
with connected water storage tank (*lavadero*) separated from the main house, an
outhouse (not always present), animal pens for pigs and chickens, a garden for fresh
produce, flowering plants, and ornamental shrubbery, the total *casa* fenced to indicate the extent of its boundaries (Map 11.2).

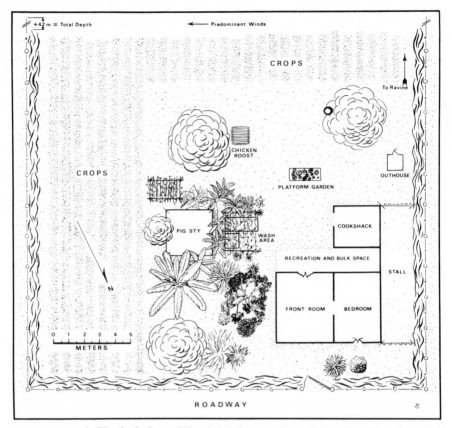

MAP 11.2   A Typical *Casa*. The inhabitants of rural hamlets like Guayabal structure the *casa* to include everything necessary for their privacy, protection, and sustenance.

vested crops. A single person will never stay alone in the mountains under any circumstances. Rather, a group of two or three always remains if it becomes impossible to transport the entire harvest of the day down the mountainside before the early valley sunset conceals everything in darkness. Below, wives and children, who have been sent ahead under the protection of a male escort, are safe in the nearness of neighboring friends and relatives.

At the riverside, large plots cultivated for the same staples surround the *casa* and extend down the slope of the levee to a line where soil conditions of poor drainage and high salinity limit further use of the land. Permanent, infield cultivation is possible here because of the extraordinary fertility of the alluvium soil of the levee and the convenience of bucket irrigation during the long, dry summers. The riverside settlements were additionally specialized as ports; gradually, this function yielded to the development of more efficient forms of land transport. Riverside *casas* are composed in the same way as those of the uplands except that their surrounding fences are much more durable (Fig. 11.5). Where barbed-wire fencing is common for upland *casas*, heavy *guadua* slats (*Guadua angustifolia* Kunth.) are put to use below in the construction of protective palisades.

By far, the majority of the rural population inhabits these settlements interspersed among the folds of the mountains and along the banks of the river. Apparently, they have lived in this fashion since long before the conquest, for the structuring of space in many of the settlements is the result of adaptation to an existence within the totality of these conditions through the extrasomatic extensions of a pre-Columbian technology. The present layout of trails and roadways presents testimony in its organic, veinlike tracings, originated solely to accommodate pedestrians in the absence of wheeled transport or

FIG. 11.3   This isolated house in the western cordillera, some two hundred meters above Guayabal, is occupied seasonally while the owner clears his outfield for planting.

FIG. 11.4   The daily climb to reach the outfield usually starts before dawn for these two *compadres*. Each shoulders a long *barretón,* the metal-tipped digging tool preferred for cultivating the steep slopes.

beasts of burden. Ancient formations similar to these occur all over the world and are recognized to be typical of "large numbers of pedestrians given freedom of movement in limited areas" (Esher 1966, p. 156). In the uplands, they follow the principal runoff channels or otherwise conform to features of topographical relief as these give access to resource centers (Fig. 11.1). Their plans can be easily differentiated from towns established or modified by the Spaniards, all of which show the well-known characters of the grid street layout and a central plaza planted with tall trees and bordered by conspicuous civil and religious buildings (Fig. 11.6).

A peculiar, spatial configuration visible in the plans of Guayabal and Guayabalito bear this out, but show moreover how macroecological relationships have worked to produce unique, spatial organizations for each one of these two adjacent settlements. The configuration of roads and paths in each community resembles a funnel, the only difference being that they are oppositely oriented to one another (Fig. 11.7). The Guayabal pattern funnels upward into the higher elevations of the mountains while that of Guayabalito is reversed, leading in a downward direction onto the valley floor. Correspondingly, the economic activity of the people of Guayabal centers on mountainside cultivation while that of Guayabalito two kilometers away on the other side of the spur, focuses upon the cultivation of terrain immediately below the settlement; few people in Guayabalito have work in the mountains. Furthermore, the meander scars of former river activity that are still visible on the floodplain indicate that at some un-

FIG. 11.5   The riverside *casa* usually features a sturdy fence for additional security in the open surroundings of the valley plain.

FIG. 11.6   The town of Toro, with its grid layout, principal plaza, market square, and tree-lined boulevard, shows the imposition of Spanish design upon a restrictive terrain.

FIG. 11.7   The peculiar funnel pattern of roadways in Guayabal and Guayabalito represents a centuries-old specialization of these hamlets to local resources.

determined time in the distant past, the Cauca River flowed in a bed
that took it hard by Guayabalito, at a distance of no more than four
hundred meters from the lower fringe of the settlement. A short distance upriver, a wide turn in the same scars tells that the river flowed
by Guayabal at a greater distance of 1.3 kilometers (Fig. 11.1). As is
still the case in many actual situations in the valley, there was once a
permanent marsh between Guayabal and this former course of the
river, vestiges of which have persisted as lagoons into recent years.
Hence, given these local conditions, inhabitants of Guayabal came to
seek cultivation opportunities above them in the mountains while
their neighbors in Guayabalito at one time cultivated the riverbanks
and engaged in water transport. Long-term tectonic activity[5] worked
to change the river's course by slowly elevating terrain on the west
side, and as the river responded by moving eastward over time and
space, it gradually separated from the settlements. What remains today
are only the physical traces of this early relationship left in the mean-

5   Colombia averages approximately twenty-five major earthquakes each year.

der scars, the settlement plans, field boundaries,[6] and the persisting economic orientation of each settlement.

The growth of these settlements evidently began about a nucleus of dwellings staked out on the bajada or levee and spaced by the surrounding plot. As the density ratio between people and land increased in the upland settlements, the fan area became fully occupied, and the population extended upward on the slopes. On the riverside, expansion progressed along the levee, halting at low points likely to wash out during flood stage. In both zones, the cultivable land has fragmented over time through inheritance practices until minimally sized plots support the greatest numbers of family members possible under the reigning circumstances, producing the *minifundio* tenure pattern. On the floodplain away from the mountains and the river, poor soils, lack of drainage, frequent floods, and parasites provided conditions suited only to pasturage, casual livestocking, and the *latifundio* pattern associated with this type of adaptation (see Schorr 1965 on how the Spanish introduction of livestock filled a hitherto unoccupied niche over the zone of the floodplain).

DEFENSIVE ARRANGEMENTS AND CORRELATED BEHAVIORAL ADAPTATIONS

The structure of space and material arrangements only gain meaning when they are related to the ongoing, concrete behavior of individuals and of populations. As I demonstrated in another context having to do with methods for the study of sociocultural change:

In essence, then, the physical modifications and reconstructions which a population introduces upon the landscape are tangible representations of those aggregate, human behavioral procedures that make up the "epiphenomenon" of organized social systems. An analysis of the characteristics of this physical signature in the context of the total ecology ... will yield interrelated patterns of information about many of the processes that contribute to the generation or restriction of change in the group. This "external" analysis of the system's characteristics over time, to be complete, must be combined with "internal" investigations such as those suggested by Barth (1967), into the way time and resource allocations are

6 Field boundaries still persist to indicate the river's former course even over portions of the terrain where surface remains of the old channels have become totally obliterated through erosion and human activity.

changed by the members of the society and become institutionalized. Neither "external" nor "internal" views alone can provide the totality of information needed for an understanding of the processes of social change (Schorr 1973*b*).

This applies not only to the analysis of the gross structure and material modifications of settlement networks, as the preceding section has demonstrated, but it can also be used to understand the structure and material arrangements present in smaller sectors of individual, family, and neighborhood life. Firth (1951, p. 42) recognized these smaller material features, together with language, as "social media" providing elemental apparatus for expressing, carrying on, and preserving the thought and action that makes up social relations within the community. A few examples from the region of study show how material arrangements embody a history of defensive and security strategies on the microlevel.

All houses within the structure of the rural hamlets are built adjacent to roadways and access paths, but few of them have entrances which open directly onto the road. Even in those instances where houses have been built with a principal door fronting the road, the door has invariably been filled in and sealed over (Fig. 11. 8). In this way, anyone entering the house compound must do so by first entering the surrounding yard, which is always enclosed by a fence, and then approaching the house by passing completely around it so as to gain access to the interior from the side *opposite* the roadway. Doing so requires that the entering person remain in the open within the house compound, exposed for a lengthy period of time to the risk of attack by one or more vicious dogs. This approach to the house additionally forces the entering person to be identified by passing in full view of the cookhouse, the center of activity during the daylight hours (Map 11.2). In effect, there is no concealed access into the house compound, anyone entering is highly visible and therefore vulnerable. For this reason, local people, even among friends, usually hesitate before entering a house to avoid the possibility that an unannounced visit might be taken as an intrusion. To advise those within of the entry and to allow time for the usual personal grooming as well as an opportunity to restrain the dogs, a visiting individual will prefer to stand waiting outside the principal gate and to call to those on the inside, remaining there until the forthcoming response invites entry.

In addition, a garden of ornamental plants, shrubs, and trees is arranged and cultivated so that it effectively conceals those daily activities of the family that occur in the vicinity of the house. Cooking, washing, eating, work, and entertainment spaces are baffled from view by arrangements of ornamental vegetation, effectively shielding the family's routine activities from the scrutiny of outsiders, providing a screen against a direct line of sight useful to armed intruders, while at the same time serving as a blind from which those on the inside can survey passersby and other goings-on perfectly hidden from view in the thick camouflage (Fig. 11.9, Map 11.2).

During the after-dark hours and before bedtime, bright lights outdoors and in the house are avoided. Most of these communities are not completely electrified, and very few people aside from store owners possess the readily available gasoline lamps of high luminosity such as the Coleman, preferring rather to operate when necessary by candlelight. Even candles are shielded behind a door and are never placed in

FIG. 11.8   As a security measure, the main roadside entrance to these living quarters (see Map 11.2) has been sealed, limiting access to a single door on the opposite side of the building.

FIG. 11.9   The arrangement of ornamental vegetation around the building in Figure 11.8 and in this house across the street conceals activity in the yard but allows a view of the roadway and the snowcapped volcano Ruiz to the east.

the center of a room where they might be viewed from an open window or portal. The reason given for these precautions is that a very bright interior blinds those on the inside from seeing out into the dark. Someone could stand outside in the open night, take careful aim, and shoot to kill anyone indoors illuminated by the light, without that person ever perceiving the presence of the assailant. Even a dim candle can produce a hazard if placed in view from the outside, for it silhouettes anyone standing in front of it, thus providing an easy target.

At bedtime, all valuables are taken into the sleeping area, including tools, cookhouse utensils, quantities of food, and unfinished laundry. Doors are locked and buttressed from the inside with tables, chairs, shovels, or anything appropriate. Windows are similarly closed with tight-fitting, wooden hatches and are barred. Because chickens, and especially hens, are highly prized, even above beef and other meats as a relished food particularly on occasions of ceremony, they are the most expensive source of flesh protein. Hence, chicken thieving at night is perhaps the most common of the petty threats to livelihood, and structures and behavior are geared to minimize this threat. The special structure consists of a platform roost, elevated by some three meters above ground level and completely enclosed by sharpened *quadua* pickets (Fig. 11.10). At the age of a few weeks, cockerels and pullets are patiently trained individually to ascend a ladder and enter the roost at sunset, after which the ladder is withdrawn and stowed within the main house. The arrangement makes it impossible for any-

FIG. 11.10   An elevated, fortified chicken roost of *guadua* protects the birds by night. During the day, the chickens nest and lay in the living area of the yard.

one to attempt chicken stealing without running the risk of producing a lot of noise in the process of scaling this kind of fortified roost. Besides the presence of one or more vicious watchdogs, the head of the house is conditioned to awaken instantly at the slightest rustle of feathers or nonrandom cluck and to go out with bared machete in hand to kill the thief unfortunate enough to be caught.

No one stays in a house alone at night if it can be avoided, and single people will always go to stay with others. If there is something of value on the premises which must be guarded, then the responsible individual will be joined by someone else. Adolescent males are quick to offer to stay with a lone individual, and it is even acceptable for boys to stay in the houses of older women during the night. People will voluntarily visit and stay with others without having to be asked, if they know that a person would otherwise be alone. Once safe inside and the house sealed for the night, it is uncommon for persons to go out again except to inspect when there is a suspicion of trespassing. After turning in, it is rare that a family will even respond to a friendly call from the outside, in spite of the fact that the voice might sound like that of a well-known friend or acquaintance. The possibility is too real that bandits or other attackers may be out there, lying in wait, intent on robbery or vengeance, and imitating a friendly voice to gain access to those inside. If an attack is suspected, then those within the house will shout for help from neighbors, who will always answer the call, well armed and ready for a fight.

THE STRUCTURE OF COMMUNICATIONS
ABOUT VIOLENCE

Any structure of vigilance and defense, to be effective, must have access to intelligence. Communications about possible violence and other threats to and within the settlement are transmitted over a number of channels. Newspapers and radios provide information concerning the state of violent or threatening activities in other regions that might feasibly involve the settlement at some time in the future. Of the two daily morning newspapers available in the region, *La Nación* and *La Voz del Oeste*, only the latter is regularly delivered in the small Conservative settlements, even though distributorships for both newspapers exist in all of the principal towns serving the area. *La Nación*

FIG. 11.11   Family and friends gather at the sale of threshed maize to hear what news the buyer brings.

is considered to be the better newspaper for overall information and is especially recognized for its coverage of agricultural affairs. In addition, *La Nación* is also a mainline Conservative newspaper while *La Voz* is recognized as Liberal by the Conservatives, despite its claim to being nonpartisan. However, *La Voz* attracts all of the readership in the area because it gives play to reports on violence, a treatment which borders on sensationalism in the reportage of individual incidents in all their gory detail, well illustrated with photographs. *La Voz* arrives just before noon in the small hamlets, in time to be read over the lunch hour. The first question usually put to a person reading the newspaper is, "How many murders and robberies were there yesterday?"

The appearance of itinerant merchants, service specialists, and official representatives creates another principal channel through which communications about violence enter the hamlets. Many events that go unreported in the newspapers travel this way, for much of the rural acts of violence are isolated enough to escape notice of the press as well as to go unrecorded in the official tallies. Visiting shoe repairmen, dentists, cloth merchants, agricultural buyers, rural services extension agents, political officeholders, and the like always attract a few neighbors who will question the visiting individual about the occurrences and details of violent incidents (Fig. 11.11). Mention of the names of people affected by violence is always a feature of the discussion. Usually, someone in the group will know the victimized person directly, through acquaintance, or indirectly through hearsay or kinship ties. There is an intensity of interest and the tone of the conversation carries a grave fascination that is characteristic of no other topic. Visiting relatives and friends from other parts also provide this kind of information.

Communications about activities *within* the settlement, when not sensed directly, usually travel along the lines of *confianza*, the closest possible relationship of complete trust and reliance that can exist between two individuals, in which they are bound to discuss everything without reservations and to maintain complete confidence over the information that is shared (Fig. 11.12). Knowledge of anything which happens in one part of the hamlet passes quickly along the lines of *confianza*, through encounters with friends or visits, so that there is nothing that takes place that can be construed in the least way as threatening to security, which the hamlet as a whole does not find out about on short notice. Children also play important parts as intelligencers of local affairs. And as in Mexico (Hotchkiss 1967), likewise in this region of Colombia, children visit and spy on others and report back everything to their parents and friends of the family. Children are encouraged, trained, and rewarded for reporting to the parent or other trusted adults everything that has occurred or that was said about persons outside of their presence. Adults spy somewhat also, but not as effectively as children. However, in this respect, they too continue this detailed reporting to those in the confidence relationship. It is considered expected and routine, regardless of the possible consequences that may result when the interested party, upon hearing the information, then evaluates it and decides to take vengeful action over a harm done, either real or imagined.

Adding to this is the refined use of sense organs on the part of the individual. Long-distance vision and hearing are common, and people are able to scrutinize others, discern significant sounds, and detect subtle odors at distances of hundreds of meters. This acuity in the use

FIG. 11.12
Amigos de Confianza

of the senses is practiced continually from childhood onward, with parents and friends setting the example, and involves nothing exceptional on the biological side of the sensory apparatus, only training in their sharpened use to a degree seldom achieved in other environments. Accompanying this long-distance sensing ability is the practice of local people to notice every physical characteristic possible about a person and to use these as a basis for inferences concerning the person's interests, motives, provenience, immediate intent, and expectation. Shoes, socks, or lack of them, spectacles, haircut, facial expressions, state of cleanliness, articles of apparel and their condition, parcels, suspicious bulges, direction of travel, time since last seen, and the like are all scrutinized for some indication of the individual's state of being and immediate purpose.

VIGILANT ATTITUDES AND PRACTICES

No system of communications about threats against life and property can be so complete as to provide for 100 percent security. Because of this, a set of cautious attitudes, beliefs, and practices are regularly held and used as guides for behavior. Above all is the belief, as mentioned earlier, that something bad will happen when it is least expected. When something detrimental actually does take place and initial communications fly, the very worst is always expected to have happened. For example, when a few small bombs went off in four rural capitals on Tuesday, September 24, 1963, as a part of a terrorist plot timed simultaneously to disrupt activities in these four cities, people of the small hamlet of Guayabal felt the repercussion intensely. Radio broadcasts and later the newspapers gave accurately detailed information of the happenings, emphasizing that no one suffered personal damages, that the destruction of property in these cities was slight, and that life continued as usual; still, the inhabitants of Guayabal imagined that *la violencia* had broken out in full force, this time the work of Castro-Communist-inspired terrorists. It was rumored that numerous loved ones working in these cities had fallen dead, victims of the bombings, and it took anguished days to corroborate, through ties of kinship, the initial radio and newspaper reports that absolutely no one was hurt in any of these places as a result of the incident.

Another consistent belief associated with unfortunate happenings of this sort always places the locale of the violent act much closer to the people receiving the news than is actually the case. For example, a misfortune occurring fifty kilometers away in the city of San Carlos became confused when transmitted from one person to the next and was eventually understood by local inhabitants as having taken place in the town of Pescador, only nine kilometers away.

Except where *confianza* and kinship ties operate between individuals from different settlements, people of one rural hamlet usually view those of the next hamlet up the road as really despicable, very violent people who are never to be trusted, while by comparison they will always represent themselves to visitors as being healthy, sound, simple, good, and trustworthy people. This is nothing more than a cover designed to present the most favorable image of themselves;

their evaluations of self and others are quite accurate, and there exists a sliding scale of relative trust and reliance which is at its best within the family and then extends outward in diminishing expectations to persons of *confianza*, casual friends, acquaintances, people known to sight, and at the limit of least trust, to complete strangers. Seldom will anyone traveling away from their home settlement stop on the road to assist an unknown person in distress, wounded, dying, or dead, for fear that those responsible for the mishap might still be in the vicinity and would not hesitate to inflict harm again in order to prevent discovery. Nor is it advisable to stop and assist in the case of an accident or a signal from a roadside traveler, for these incidents have always proven to be the most dangerous in that the person asking for help could easily turn into an assailant.

It is of little surprise, then, to encounter an all-pervading attitude of fatalism (Fig. 11.13). Peasants complain continually to each other about their miserable condition of poverty and deprivation, of the insecurity of a life of mistrust and the threat of imminent harm to the individual, his family, his kind, or his interests. Most are quick to voice the belief that they will never be rid of these trials, but that only in the other world will any reward be forthcoming, when the death that has always threatened eventually liberates them from earthly misery and carries them aloft to the other side (Fig. 11.14). Fatalism, in this sense, is psychological preparedness for the unremitting threat of extinction, for tomorrow may very well never dawn.

ADAPTATIONAL CONTINUITY

The world of the valley peasant faced with this kind of continuous threat to existence is a curious one, but it is nonetheless *normal* for the population, comprising a unified totality of adaptive organization that heightens survival chances given the reality of violence in local life. The zonal distribution of populations, settlement structure, house-compound construction and composition are all designed to afford maximum security and are intertwined with behavior expressing fear and suspicion, reticence, precautionary activities, wakefulness, sobriety and deference, distrust of everyone not in a direct *confianza* relationship, tension geared and maintained at a high level by the news media, fascination over violent and harmful occurrences, vigi-

FIG. 11.13   Two sisters in mourning reflect quiet resignation over condolences sent upon the death of their younger sister.

lance and resignation about expecting the worst at any moment, and an all-pervading fatalism. A subsequent part of the analysis extending what has been set forth here (Schorr 1973c) necessarily treats the psychodynamics of socialization practices as they are expressed under these conditions, for they produce the set of behavioral manifestations that integrate the society and maintain it adaptively within the total ecological system. This extension of the analysis is crucial for the understanding of why and how sociocultural adaptations persist or change. The foregoing presentation has examined only what are essentially defensive strategies that work together to adaptively cope with survival in the face of persisting strife. However, the key to the internal structure, which systematically fosters the strifeful manner in which these societies and their parts interact within the larger ecosystemic network and stimulates the production of violence as a solution for a problem of scarce resources, lies in the norms and practices of socialization. These same small societies, which are adapted defen-

FIG. 11.14   The *sabila* (*Aloe vulgaris*), a medicinal plant believed to ward off evil and bring prosperity, is adorned with red carnations and used to hold condolences on an altar to the recently deceased girl.

sively for survival under strifeful conditions, also work offensively to produce strife within the group, as well as against competitive groups, through a complex interplay of fear and anxiety over the satisfaction of the most basic biological needs: food and sex. The equilibrium[7] that results in the system maintains an optimum balance between the available resources, their distribution in time and space, and the populations in need of them.

The relationships set forth in this analysis only emerge when it is understood that environments to which populations must adapt are not to be conceived of simplistically as the nonhuman surroundings, nor should any analysis of ecosystemic relations be confined solely to the ties that relate a given human group through energy cycling to the nonhuman components of the environment. Rather, analysis of the system must include conditions of persistence and change that are a result of specific kinds of behavioral relations among segments of the human population itself. Each segment, bounded in a particularistic way, has to adapt to the presence of every other segment (Barth 1969). Hence, the particular conditions of the total ecological system, involving relations among the geophysical, biotic, and sociocultural components, together give rise to the pervading adaptational configurations present in the material, spatial, and behavioral organization of society. In the case of the Cauca Valley, these adaptive traits, upon analysis, are seen to be inextricably interrelated in the need to maintain security in surroundings of limited resources and continuing vulnerability to violence and early death.[8]

REFERENCES CITED

Barth, Fredrik
   1956   Ecological Relationships of Ethnic Groups in Swat, North Pakistan. *American Anthropologist* 58:1079–89.

7 By "equilibrium," the reader should not understand "static" or "changeless," for equilibrium systems defined by parameters that continually change in value are well known in the real world.
8 Portions of the fieldwork upon which this paper is based were supported by grants from the Foreign Area Fellowship Program; the U.S. Public Health Service (Research Grant No. TW–00143, ICMRT award) through the National Institutes of Health, Tulane University, and the Universidad del Valle (Cali); and the University of Pittsburgh, Faculty of Arts and Sciences. A preliminary version of the paper was presented at the sixty-ninth annual meeting of the American Anthropological Association, San Diego, California, on November 21, 1970, and contains in summary a few paragraphs which were presented elsewhere (Schorr 1973*b*).

1967 On the Study of Social Change. *American Anthropologist* 69 (6):661–69.

Barth, Fredrik, ed.
1969 *Ethnic Groups and Boundaries: The Social Organization of Culture Difference.* Boston: Little, Brown.

Bennett, John W.
1969 *Northern Plainsmen: Adaptive Strategy and Agrarian Life.* Chicago: Aldine.

Conklin, Harold C.
1961 Some Aspects of Ethnographic Research in Ifugao. *Transactions*, Ser. 2, Vol. 30, No. 1. New York: New York Academy of Sciences. Pp. 99–121.

Esher, Lord
1966 Air Photographs and Contemporary Planning. In J. K. S. St. Joseph, ed., *The Uses of Air Photography.* New York: John Day.

Fals Borda, Orlando
1968 *Subversión y cambio social: el dedo en la herida.* 2nd ed. Bogotá: Ediciones Tercer Mundo.

Firth, Raymond
1951 *Elements of Social Organization.* London: Watts.

Fluharty, Vernon L.
1957 *Dance of the Millions.* Pittsburgh: University of Pittsburgh Press.

Gutiérrez, José
1964 *La revolución contra el miedo.* Bogotá: Ediciones Tercer Mundo.

Guzmán, Germán, Orlando Fals Borda, and Eduardo Umaña Luna
1962 Bibliografía colombiana sobre la violencia. *La violencia en colombia.* Vol. 1. Colección "El Hombre." Bogotá: Ediciones Tercer Mundo. Pp. 427–30.

Hotchkiss, John C.
1967 Children and Conduct in a Ladino Community of Chiapas, Mexico. *American Anthropologist* 69(6):711–18.

Lievano Aguirre, Indalecio
1968 *Los grandes conflictos sociales y económicos de nuestra historia.* 3rd ed. Bogotá: Ediciones Tercer Mundo.

Morrill, Richard L.
1970 *The Spatial Organization of Society.* Belmont, Calif.: Wadsworth.

Payne, James L.
1968 *Patterns of Conflict in Colombia.* New Haven and London: Yale University Press.

Ramsey, Russel W.
1973 Critical Bibliography on La Violencia in Colombia. *Latin American Research Review* 8(1):3–44.

Schorr, Thomas S.
1965 *Cultural Ecological Aspects of Settlement Patterns and Land Use in the Cauca Valley, Colombia.* Ann Arbor, Mich.: University Microfilms.

1968   Cauca Valley Settlements: A Culture Ecological Interpretation. *Actas y Memorias*, Vol. 1. Thirty-seventh Congreso Internacional de Americanistas, República Argentina, 1966. Buenos Aires: Librart S.R.L. Pp. 449–66, Figs. 1–7.

1973a   Fighting and Killing Behavior Between Human Populations: A Reflection on the Current Controversies. *Actas y Memorias.* Thirty-ninth Congreso Internacional de Americanistas, Lima, Peru, 1970.

1973b   Aerial Ethnography in Regional Studies: A Reconnaissance of Adaptive Change in the Cauca Valley of Colombia. In Evon Z. Vogt, ed., *Aerial Photography in Anthropological Field Research.* Cambridge: Harvard University Press.

1973c   The Psychodynamic Motivations for Violence in Peasant Populations of the Central Cauca Valley, Colombia. Paper read at Seventy-second Annual Meeting of the American Anthropological Association, Nov. 28–Dec. 2, 1973, at New Orleans (mimeo).

Wagner, Philip
1960   *The Human Use of the Earth.* London: Free Press of Glencoe, Collier-Macmillan, Ltd.

Williamson, R. C.
1965   Toward a Theory of Political Violence: The Case of Rural Colombia. *Western Political Quarterly*, March:35–44.

Chapter 12

Adaptations to Crowded Space: The Case of Taos Pueblo

Pearl Katz

ABSTRACT   The manner in which a culture organizes its space may result in compacting people into small areas. In turn, the ways in which people seek relief from constant interaction may evolve into distinct cultural patterns. Studies of animals in crowded conditions have revealed that such animals display both hormonal and behavioral changes. These studies also suggest that reorganizing the space to decrease interactions can serve to alleviate stress caused by crowding. Some of these behavioral changes seem analogous to the cultural patterns that the Taos Indians employ to cope with their densely settled community and houses.

The Taos have the most compact settlement pattern of the eastern Pueblos. The Taos multistoried houses and plaza are grouped within an area surrounded by a four-foot wall. The area within the wall is one of high interaction. Interaction within the multistoried houses is particularly intense. Not uncommonly a family of six or more will eat, sleep, cook, and perform many other household tasks in one or two rooms 10 by 17 feet each. Other locations, such as the kivas and council rooms, also have high intensities of interaction.

Three cultural patterns have evolved in response to the crowding in the pueblo. One pattern encourages the maintenance of social distance among people through idealizing restraint, moderation, and noncompetitiveness. The second pattern consists of displays of aggressiveness, hostility, suspicion, and factionalism. The third pattern consists of a complex of mechanisms to maintain solitude and privacy; these are withdrawing from social (although not visual) contact, keeping secrets, and periodically traveling long distances from the pueblo.

Edward T. Hall has suggested that space is incorporated differently in different cultures and that, like language, spatial configurations may both organize a culture and be organized by it (1959, 1966). Hall also suggested that the concept of crowding varies among cultures, that a given density may seem crowded in one culture and may be comfortable in another (1968). I should like to report on ways in which some configurations of space, such as crowding and privacy, are incorporated in the social structure of a culture. Specifically, I will examine the ways in which the Taos Pueblo Indians structure their space and how, in turn, their space structures their culture.

The compact pattern of settlement and land use among the Taos is one which promotes high population density. This density provides potentials for frequent personal interactions. Among nonhuman mammalian populations high frequencies of interaction have been demonstrated to lead to a variety of responses. These will be reviewed. As to the Taos, three adaptive cultural patterns which relate to their crowded living arrangements will be suggested:

1. One pattern consists of attempts to encourage social distance among people by idealizing restraint, moderation, noncompetitiveness and avoiding involvement in others' affairs.

2. Another culture pattern consists of displays of aggressiveness, hostility, suspicion, and factionalism.

3. A third culture pattern consists of mechanisms for maintaining privacy, such as keeping secrets from others and traveling over large distances outside the pueblo.

I shall first report on some ethological studies on crowding. Secondly, I shall illustrate the settlement patterns and living arrangements among the Taos. Finally, I shall discuss some ways in which the Taos organize their space.

ETHOLOGICAL STUDIES ON CROWDING

There have been a number of ethological studies on rats, mice, hares, rabbits, muskrats, deer, voles, monkeys, guinea pigs, and dogs to determine their reactions to high population densities. It was discovered that, given an adequate amount of food, drink, and health standards, if crowding becomes too great, stimuli and interactions increase, producing stress.

The major physiological response to stress consists of the activation of pituitary-adrenal-cortical steroids. These may adversely affect growth, reproductive functioning, resistance to diseases, thymus functioning and may also increase aggression and tension, perhaps contributing to further stress (Calhoun 1952, 1962; Christian *et al.* 1961). The negative effect upon growth, reproductive capacity, and resistance to disease has direct consequences on the adaptation and survival of a dense population.

However, it should be noted that observed reactions to crowded conditions were not due to the density per se, but rather to the immediate proximity of other members of the population and, thereby, the high number of interactions that occur as a result of the density (Christian *et al.* 1961, pp. 431, 446). When the experimental environments were shifted to alter the frequency of contacts—by changing the design of a cage or changing the method of food distribution or allowing periodic emigration—without changing the total density of the population, some reactions to stress were alleviated (Calhoun 1952, 1962; Christian *et al.* 1961; Crowcroft and Rowe 1958; Snyder 1961; Southwick 1955).

J. B. Calhoun (1962) studied the consequences of greatly increased population density among Norway rats. He raised six populations of thirty-two to fifty-six rats from the time of weaning. The animals were evenly divided among males and females. They had an abundance of food and drink and lived in adequate quarters. They multiplied to twice the number which would normally occupy the same space. The living quarters for the rats were designed in a manner which would encourage the use of two pens (Pens 2 and 3) and discourage the use of two pens (Pens 1 and 4), by not allowing passageway through Pens 1 and 4 to each other (Fig. 12.1). This raised the probability of there being a higher population density and higher frequency of contacts in Pens 2 and 3 as compared with that in Pens 1 and 4. In addition, food was presented in pellet form which required a long time to consume. This encouraged, and eventually reinforced, the rats to congregate around the food hopper. Although each rat was compelled daily to make some kind of adjustment to virtually every other

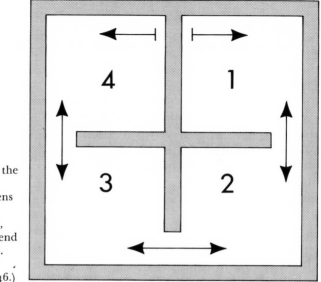

FIG. 12.1
Pen Arrangement in the
Calhoun Study of
Crowding in Rats. Pens
1 and 4 tend to be
relatively uncrowded,
while Pens 2 and 3 tend
to be highly crowded.
(Redrawn from Cal-
houn 1962, pp. 139–46.)

rat, the amount of stimulus experienced by the rats in Pens 2 and 3 increased exponentially, according to Calhoun.

Some of the results of Calhoun's experiment are:

1. One group of males in Pens 2 and 3 developed pathological withdrawal symptoms, sitting in the corner during the day and feeding early in the morning when no others were around.

2. The remaining males in Pens 2 and 3 developed grossly aggressive behavior. This manifested itself in fighting for status, tail biting, occasional cannibalism, and forming packs which relentlessly pursued females.

3. The females in Pens 2 and 3 tried to escape the constantly pursuing males. They did not build nests normally. They could not terminate pregnancy normally or nurture their young normally. Ninety-six percent of their progeny died.

4. The males and females in Pens 1 and 4 formed harems consisting of a dominant male with several females who nested and raised litters normally.

Calhoun reports that when a type of powdered food was introduced which could be consumed quickly, fewer rats were present at one time at the food hoppers, the numbers of encounters at the food hoppers decreased, and less social pathology was observed.

In other animal experiments it was found that clearly defined rank differences altered the physiological responses to density, allowing a greater population size than those in which rank differences were less well defined (Christian *et al.* 1961, pp. 431–32). These animal experiments demonstrate that high population density creates many opportunities for interaction and stimuli between the members of a population. These may cause stress, triggering the adrenal-cortical functions, which may, in turn, increase the stress and interfere with the growth, reproductive, and disease-defense systems. The increased opportunities for interaction and stimuli may lead to stimulus overload if the environment is not altered (Spitz 1964). In Calhoun's study we have seen how the environment was affected by the layout of the rooms, which offered differential access to other members of the population. It was also affected by the type of food which allowed for quick or slow consumption and, therefore, time around the food hopper (Calhoun 1962). In other studies, the differential ranking of members and opportunities for periodic emigrations limited the amount of stimuli and the numbers of interatctions (Christian *et al.* 1961; Crowcroft and Rowe 1958; Snyder 1961; Southwick 1955).

These studies not only demonstrate the range of pathologies—from extreme withdrawal to frenetic aggressiveness—which can result from stimulus overload; they also suggest that ways of organizing space to decrease interactions—rather than changing the overall size of the population—can serve to alleviate some pathological responses. Some of these results have analogies in ways in which the Taos Pueblo Indians organize their space.

SETTLEMENT PATTERNS AND LIVING ARRANGEMENTS IN TAOS

Taos Pueblo is the most northern of the pueblos (Map 12.1). It is situated on a high plateau northeast of the upper Rio Grande in New Mexico. This location places the Taos not only close to the other northern pueblos, such as Picuris, San Juan, and Santa Clara, but also close to some Plains Indians, such as Apaches, Utes, and Kiowas, all of whom they occasionally visit. The inhabitants of Taos are Tiwa-speaking and, as such, are linguistically related to the inhabitants of

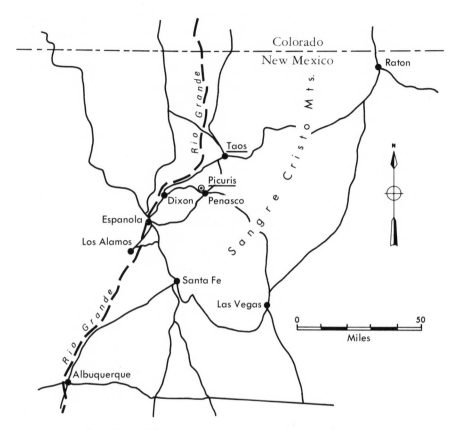

MAP 12.1   Location of Taos Pueblo, Northeastern New Mexico

Picuris Pueblo, which is fifteen miles south of Taos. They are similarly related to the inhabitants of the pueblos of Sandia and Isleta, near Albuquerque, New Mexico.

The pueblo consists mainly of two multistoried structures which are separated by a small river. The north side has five stories and the south side four stories. In addition, there are six underground chambers called kivas, which are used for ceremonial purposes by the men. There is an open space, or plaza, used for ceremonials by all the members. There are also a number of "summer houses," located on the outlying pueblo land, separated from the multistoried residences.

The surrounding land which belongs to the Taos is used for irrigation and agricultural crops, principally corn, wheat, peas, beans, oats, and squash. It is also used for hunting rabbits and herding small numbers of buffalo. There is a four-foot-high adobe wall which surrounds the area of the pueblo containing the multistoried houses, the plaza, and the kivas. The Taos distinguish the parts of their land as being "within the wall" or "outside the wall." Most of the daily interaction takes place within the wall.

The total population living on Taos land in 1968 was 1,471 (Bodine 1970). The ratio of men per land is not particularly high, but the nucleated residential settlement pattern is one in which each Taos has the opportunity of interacting with a very large number of other people in the course of a day. Of all the eastern Pueblos, Taos has the most compact settlement pattern (Spicer 1962, p. 182).

The reasons for the development of the nucleated settlement pattern may have been a technique to increase social control over the population to permit cooperation for irrigation. Or, it may have been useful for defense. For the purpose of this study, which is to clarify the cultural correlates of their dense living arrangements, the historical causes of the compact settlement pattern need not concern us.

The ground floor of each multistoried structure covers three hundred to four hundred feet; the second story recedes a bit, and the third and subsequent stories recede still more. The multistoried structures contain about 175 residential units. Most of the house units consist of one or two rooms. A number of the units contain three rooms, but this is considered spacious by the inhabitants. The size of a room is small, about seventeen feet square and ten feet high (Miller 1898, p. 20). Archaeological excavations and historical accounts indicate that in former times the rooms were even smaller and the residential density was higher than it is at present (Herold and Leubben 1968; Parsons 1936, p. 17; Wetherington 1968).

The families that live in these residential units are nuclear families with approximately three or four children, although six children is not uncommon. Often an aged parent or unmarried sibling is also included in the family. If a family has only one room, the family members eat, sleep, cook, and conduct many other tasks inside that one room. If there are two rooms, one would be used as a sleeping room and the other as an eating, cooking, and living room, as well as a sleeping room.

The traditional way of entering a room was by climbing a ladder, which leaned along the outside wall, leading to the roof, and descending a ladder to the room below. There were landings on each floor for ladders and doorways on top of each story. In recent times, however, there are doorways level with the ground or landing, so that one need only climb as far as the door. This means that, in the case of a ground floor entrance, no climbing is necessary. Since, in the past there were fewer ladders than house units, many people used the same ladders, and there were frequent opportunities for interaction while entering or leaving a house.

Inside a house, at mealtime, a family eats around a table, sitting shoulder to shoulder; at night, a whole family often sleeps in one room, children and adults together, with mattresses or beds laid side by side, and frequently with several children to a bed.

The house unit of one to three small rooms is used by a family of six to nine people for eating, sleeping, and cooking, as well as many additional household tasks and much socializing. Thus, the indoor living pattern in which each Taos participates is one in which many people are in close physical proximity to others for a large part of the day.

On the pueblo land, outside of the houses, there is also opportunity for frequent contacts, since most of the daily activities take place within the wall. The major activities in which the Taos are engaged are those of transporting wood from the land to the house, agricultural activities at selected times of the year, baking bread, attending kiva and council meetings, and sitting around gossiping. The compactness of the pueblo settlement provides frequent contacts with others, while engaging in all these activities.

There are six small kivas in Taos, twenty feet in diameter (Miller 1898, p. 25). They are dark underground rooms with a small overhead entrance. About once a day, fifteen to twenty men descend the ladder to gather in each kiva. They sit in a circle, practically touching shoulders, while conducting their ceremonials. There is also a council room in Taos in which once a day about twenty members of the governing council of forty members gather. The room is fourteen by twenty feet. These men, too, sit close together in a circle around the major officials.

As Taos Pueblo is so densely settled, with so many people in close proximity, it is interesting to note that there is no Taos word for *crowded*. If pressed to express the English word *crowded* a Taos will say, "There are too many people in a room." However, what a Taos regards as too many people in a room has more to do with providing for the immediate needs of the people than with the actual space used.

For example, a Taos may have forty people to dinner in a typical room (seventeen feet square) used for eating, a relatively common entertainment pattern. As long as there is sufficient food for the guests, a Taos would not consider this situation crowded. He would manage by allowing ten people at a time to sit at the table shoulder to shoulder. When a person finishes he gets up and sits on the outside perimeter of the room, as another person, who is already sitting on the outside perimeter, assumes his place at the table. In this way, the guests eat in four uneven shifts, with forty people finishing a complete meal in forty-five minutes. The relevant factor is that, although there are many people in the room and they are squeezed together while waiting to eat and while eating, no one feels crowded.

We have seen how the spatial structure in Taos Pueblo, both indoors and outdoors within the wall, promotes frequent contact in close proximity. Opportunities for physical privacy are rare and continuous personal interaction is unavoidable. Since it is rare for a Taos to be alone in a room, except for dressing, or to be alone for any length of time outdoors within the walls, it can safely be assumed that some cultural mechanisms would become necessary to minimize the effects of continuous personal interactions. There must be ways to cope with the kinds of "stimulus overload" noted in the ethological experiments, in which the continuous stimuli and interactions resulting from the dense environment activated the adrenal-cortical system. In turn, this resulted in the arrest of normal growth, reproductive, and disease-defense systems, as well as encouraging pathologically aggressive and withdrawal behavior. How is Taos culture structured to minimize the nonadditive responses to such stress? What are the adaptations of the Taos to this high density and the potentially high stimulus of continuous personal interactions?

THE POSTURE OF RESTRAINT

All the Pueblos have been well known for their idealization of moderation, restraint, standardization, and noncompetitiveness (Benedict

1934, pp. 52–119; Bunzel 1932, p. 480; Fenton 1957, p. 301; Goldfrank 1945, p. 527; Siegel 1949, p. 571). Any personal assertiveness is disapproved; unanimity in government decisions is assumed. A Taos who distinguishes himself in any way, in dress, speech, accumulation of wealth, or who seeks prestigious positions within the pueblo, earns disapproval and becomes the subject of sanctions such as gossip, accusations of witchcraft, whipping, vandalism of his property, or "accidental" death.

The posture of restraint also takes the form of restricting personal interactions, physical contact, and involvement in others' affairs. Although, in the crowded rooms and the outside area within the wall, there are numerous opportunities for verbal or gestural communication, such communication is minimized. When several people are together in a room, which is usually the case in a Taos house, there is no obligation to talk or interact. Similarly, there is usually no acknowledgment when anyone in a family enters or leaves a house, although there are usually several people in the house. A Taos man commonly leaves his house without saying farewell, without any indication of where he is going, without saying whether he will return in a few minutes, a few hours, or a few days.

Although the amount of space between people in the houses, kivas, or council chambers is minimal, physical contact between people is negligible. There is virtually no touch contact among adults that is observable to others in the pueblo. The physical contact between parents and children appears much less than one finds in most western European societies.

A Taos may be alone within the walls of the pueblo in two kinds of situations. He may be alone if he sits on a roof of the pueblo, situated away from the ladders and entrances and out of the mainstream of traffic. At any time of day it is quite common to see isolated men sitting silently for hours at a time on a roof of the pueblo. This scene bears some similarities to the withdrawal behavior of some of Calhoun's rats. There, too, individuals sat silently by themselves.

A Taos may also arrange to be alone if he wishes to dress or undress. To do so he must explicitly state, "I am going in this room to dress." This conveys the implicit command, "No one shall enter until I am finished." The Taos value modesty, and it is most unusual for a

Taos to see another adult, even of the same sex in the same family, undressed. Even though a number of people sleep together in close proximity in the same room, clothes, which cover much of the body, are always worn.

Although cooperation is idealized in Taos culture, a distinctive contrast is made between cooperation in community affairs and involvement in others' personal affairs. When a Taos child falls down outside his house, hurts his knees, and cries, no one is likely to pay the slightest attention to him, although there may be several adults very near him. He may have to walk across the pueblo grounds, crying and bleeding, past many others who know him, with no one acknowledging that he is hurt. The explanation given is that the child is his parents' responsibility.

Similarly, if a Taos hears a fight next door, in which a husband is severely beating his wife, threatening to kill her (and there is good reason to believe he might succeed), he would not interfere; it is none of his business. He believes that this is only the concern of the two people who are fighting. The screams begging for help from the wife are not sufficient cause to interfere. A Taos would consider getting involved only if the wife would come to his door and explicitly request that he interfere—an unlikely possibility under the circumstances. One Taos explained, "If there was a fight I wouldn't go in another person's home and butt in. If there's no complaint, well, that's the way they want it. It's none of my business, so I'll leave them alone."

Such noninvolvement in others' affairs in situations in which there are so many opportunities for having contact shows remarkable similarities to Western urban patterns in which incidences of anonymity and noninvolvement are common occurrences. It is reminiscent, for example, of events in New York a few years ago in which the repeated screams of Mrs. Genovese being stabbed to death brought no response from the many neighbors who heard her (Smith 1967, p. 185). The explanation of the neighbors was similar to that of the Taos: It was not their responsibility; they did not want to get involved. But there is one difference. In New York City one's neighbors are not kin; indeed, one barely knows one's neighbors. In Taos, however, one's neighbors are extremely familiar and are likely to be kin. In Taos, one is required to be in constant contact with the neighbors.

AGGRESSIVENESS

There are types of behavior in Taos which contrast sharply with the idealized behavior of restraint, moderation, and noncompetitiveness. Reference has already been made to incidents of beating—frequently with furniture or iron bars—and sanctions of gossip, accusations of witchcraft, vandalism of private property, and "accidental" deaths against transgressors of Taos norms. This type of behavior is quite common to all the Pueblos. Ellis (1951, pp. 177, 179) points out that "an underlying stratum of personal aggressiveness" exists in all the Pueblos. She believes that this is reflected in the importance of the institution of the war cult. Dozier (1956, p. 496) mentions the Pueblo Indian's "deep anxiety and suspicion toward his fellow man."

Taos Pueblo has been described by many anthropologists as being the most violent, rent with factionalism, and the most difficult to study of all the pueblos. It is interesting to note again that it is also the most compact of the eastern pueblos (Spicer 1962, p. 182). Trager stated in 1948, "It has long been evident that one thing that distinguishes Taos from other Pueblo groups is the recurrence of violence in many sets of behavior patterns" (303–304). Fenton stated in 1957 that "Taos had been a constant 'problem' to the Indian Service for several years; it is rent with factions, and tensions had reached a crisis in 1949" (303). Fenton also referred to the "almost schizoid character" of the Taos (312). The frequency and extent of aggressive behavior in Taos are striking. The violence and aggression in Taos show analogies to the aggressive behavior in the rats observed by Calhoun.

MECHANISMS FOR MAINTAINING PRIVACY

There is no Taos word for *privacy*. For a Taos, the concept of privacy does not apply to being out of the visual range of others or being in a separate room, except for the purpose of dressing. Privacy is more closely related to having secrets from others, preserving one's autonomy of thinking and acting in the routine matters of daily life. All the Pueblos, including the Taos, have been well known for their refusal to disclose information about their culture to outsiders (including members of other Pueblo tribes), for keeping secrets from anyone, and for maintaining a wall of reticence about most of their activities. They manage to do this by a variety of evasive techniques, such as changing the subject of conversation, not acknowledging that they understand what one has said, or by answering fallaciously. These responses are often interpreted by anthropologists as a form of restraint and non-assertiveness (Fenton 1957; Parsons 1936). I am suggesting that they can also be interpreted as mechanisms for maintaining social distance and privacy.

In one case, when a Taos has his son, daughter-in-law, and three grandchildren for three weeks staying at his home in which his own family of five lived, it never occurred to him to admit that they were crowded, nor did he wish that his guests would soon leave. When I persisted in questioning him about whether he felt that he wanted to be alone, he finally replied, as if to change the subject, "Sometimes I just stand up and decide, 'I'm going to Oklahoma,' and I just go to Oklahoma for several days."

This reply was not a usual Taos avoidance of a particular topic by abruptly changing the subject. It was, instead, a revealing rationale for another way in which the Taos adapt to their compact or crowded situation and obtain a measure of privacy. I am referring to their frequent traveling over long distances outside the pueblo. A Taos thinks nothing of traveling several hundred miles to visit an acquaintance. Frequently he will visit a Plains Indian whom he had briefly met at a ceremony in the past. The purpose of the journey is usually to renew acquaintances and promote reciprocal visiting invitations. In recent times transportation by car makes these trips manageable in less than a day one way, but it is likely that long-distance travel was common when the only means of transportation was by foot or horse.

One other way that the Taos use the space outside the wall is by retreating to their summer houses. Traditionally, there have always been a few one-room houses which were used by some Taos families for several weeks in the summer when their agricultural activities demanded a large part of their time. These houses were located within the pueblo land, but most were outside the wall. In the past fifty years, however, more and more Taos have used the land to build summer houses. Frequently these houses would be built with a larger number of more spacious rooms than existed in their residences within the wall. In the past ten years, it has become increasingly popular for some Taos to use these "summer" residences throughout the year, although they never relinquish their ownership in their original residences (Bodine 1970). This is being done in spite of the fact that a fine is imposed on those members who do not remain in their original residences in the winter.

By getting away from the densely packed area of the pueblo, either by traveling long distances to visit other Indians or by retreating to their summer houses, the Taos are avoiding the constant interaction present within the wall. This is another way in which a Taos may obtain privacy. This kind of adaptive response is somewhat similar to that in some experiments with mice in which emigration was allowed to relieve the stress produced by the crowded environment. In these experiments some stress was reduced as a result of emigration (Crowcroft and Rowe 1958; Southwick 1955).

CONCLUSION

In summary, this study has presented the view that living in a densely populated situation creates distinct cultural reverberations, and the culture, in turn, influences the way that people adapt to living in a densely populated situation. While the bulk of this chapter was concerned with the Taos Pueblo Indians, the chapter also summarized some studies on the effects of high population density on the behavior of animals. Although no direct replication of these ethological studies was done to a human situation, it is all too obvious that the animal findings offer highly tempting analogies.

The picture concerning the Taos is as follows: The Taos have the most compact living arrangement of all the eastern Pueblos. Three adaptive cultural responses to crowding were suggested.

1. One culture pattern consists of attempts to encourage social distance between people by idealizing restraint, moderation, noncompetitiveness, and avoiding involvement in others' affairs.

2. Another culture pattern consists of displays of aggressiveness, hostility, suspicion, and factionalism.

3. A third culture pattern consists of mechanisms for maintain-

ing privacy, such as keeping secrets from others and traveling over large distances outside the pueblo.[1]

REFERENCES CITED

Benedict, Ruth
1934   *Patterns of Culture.* New York: New American Library. Pp. 52–119.
Bodine, John J.
1970   Personal communication.
Bunzel, Ruth L.
1932   *Introduction to Zuñi Ceremonialism.* Forty-seventh Annual Report, Bureau of American Ethnology. Washington, D.C.: Smithsonian Institution. Pp. 467–544.
Calhoun, John B.
1952   The Social Aspects of Population Dynamics. *Journal of Mammalogy* 33:139–59.
1962   Population Density and Social Pathology. *Scientific American* 206:139–46.
Christian, John J., Vagh Flyger, and David E. Davis
1961   Phenomena Associated with Population Density. *Proceedings*, Vol. 47. Washington, D.C.: National Academy of Sciences. Pp. 428–49.
Crowcroft, P., and F. P. Rowe
1958   The Growth of Confined Colonies of the Wild House-Mouse (*Mus musulus L.*): The Effects of Dispersal on Fecundity. *Proceedings*, Vol. 131. London: Royal Zoological Society. Pp. 357–65.
Dozier, Edward P.
1956   The Values and Moral Concepts of Rio Grande Pueblo Indians. In Vegilius Ferm, ed., *Encyclopedia of Morals.* New York: Philosophical Library. Pp. 491–504.
Ellis, Florence Hawley
1951   Patterns of Aggression and the War Cult in Southwestern Pueblos. *Southwestern Journal of Anthropology* 7:177–201.
Esser, Aristide, ed.
1971   *Behavior and Environment: The Use of Space by Animals and Men.* New York: Plenum Press.

1   This is a revised version of a paper, "Inner Space and Outer Space in Taos Pueblo," presented at the 1969 meeting of the American Anthropological Association in New Orleans, Louisiana. Since the completion of this article in 1970, additional studies have been published on crowding and use of space, notably Esser (1971). In 1970, Gregor published a study of Mehinacu Indians of Brazil, which has striking analogies to the behavior observed among the Taos.

Fenton, William N.
  1957   *Factionalism at Taos Pueblo, New Mexico.* Bureau of American Ethnology, Bulletin 164. Washington, D.C.: Smithsonian Institution. Pp. 297–346.

Goldfrank, Esther S.
  1945   Socialization, Personality, and the Structure of Pueblo Society. *American Anthropologist* 47:516–31.

Gregor, Thomas
  1970   Exposure and Seclusion: A Study of Institutionalized Isolation among the Mehinacu Indians of Brazil. *Ethnology* 9:234–50.

Hall, Edward T.
  1959   *The Silent Language.* Garden City, N.Y.: Doubleday.
  1966   *The Hidden Dimension.* Garden City, N.Y.: Doubleday.
  1968   Proxemics. *Current Anthropology* 9:82–108.

Herold, Laurance C., and Ralph A. Luebben
  1968   *An Archaeological-Geographic Survey of the Rio Grande de Ranchos (Herold) Site TA 32: A Deep Pit House and Surface Manifestations in North Central New Mexico.* Papers on Taos Archaeology, No. 7. Taos, N.M.: Fort Burgwin Research Center.

Miller, Merton L.
  1898   Preliminary Study of the Pueblo of Taos, New Mexico. Ph.D. dissertation, University of Chicago, Chicago, Illinois.

Parsons, Elsie Clews
  1936   *Taos Pueblo.* General Series in Anthropology, No. 2. Menasha, Wis.: George Banta.

Siegel, Bernard J.
  1949   Some Observations on the Pueblo Pattern at Taos. *American Anthropologist* 51:562–77.

Smith, M. Estellie
  1967   Aspects of Social Control Among the Taos Indians. Ph.D. dissertation, State University of New York at Buffalo, New York.

Snyder, Robert L.
  1961   Evolution and the Integration of Mechanisms That Regulate Population Growth. *Proceedings*, Vol. 47. Washington, D.C.: National Academy of Sciences. Pp. 449–55.

Southwick, C. H.
  1955   The Population Dynamics of Confined House Mice Supplied with Unlimited Food. *Ecology* 36:212–25.

Spicer, Edward H.
  1962   *Cycles of Conquest: The Impact of Spain, Mexico, and the United States on the Indians of the Southwest, 1533–1960.* Tucson: University of Arizona Press.

Spitz, René A.

1964 The Derailment of Dialogue: Stimulus Overload, Action Cycles, and the Completion Gradient. *Journal of the American Psychoanalytic Association* 12:752–75.

Trager, George L.

1948 Symbol and Personality at Taos. *Southwestern Journal of Anthropology* 4:299–304.

Wetherington, Ronald

1968 *Excavations at Pot Creek Pueblo.* Papers on Taos Archaeology, No. 6. Taos, N.M.: Fort Burgwin Research Center.

Chapter 13

Social Structure as Reflected in Architectural Units at Picuris Pueblo

Donald N. Brown

ABSTRACT   Recent work in anthropology has stimulated a renewal of interest in the relationship between material and nonmaterial aspects of culture. Research at Picuris Pueblo, a small Tiwa-speaking community located in the mountains of northern New Mexico, suggests that architectural units reflect the major social units and that use or disuse of architectural units reflects many of the changes which have occurred during the last seventy years. Such research may aid in the construction of general models dealing with material culture.

An inventory of architectural units at Picuris Pueblo in 1967 indicated ten types, classified according to form, use, and ownership. These types of architectural units include residences, various ceremonial structures, storage units, the Catholic church, the day-school complex, recently constructed community buildings, and a prehistoric multistoried structure. Using census materials, photographs, and informant information, it was possible to reconstruct the settlement pattern and architectural units for the period immediately preceding 1900.

Analysis of this data revealed that several changes have occurred since then. With a shift in economic orientation from subsistence farming and hunting to wage work and welfare programs, summer field houses have been totally abandoned. The compact village settlement pattern which had been characteristic only of the winter months is now the sole pattern. Clusters of houses constructed with contiguous walls and inhabited by related families, common in 1900, are now rare as the importance of the activities of the bilateral kinsmen has diminished. Dual organization groups and several ceremonial associations formerly integrated the household groups. As the activities of these groups, primarily ceremonies for weather control and fertility, became of less concern with the shift to wage work, the groups disappeared and the architectural units associated with them became community property. The Council of Principales composed of the headmen of the ceremonial groups and headed by the cacique, the ceremonial leader of the pueblo, was the primary group of the political system. The council met in the cacique's kiva and annually appointed the civil officers. As these men became less influential, the council was replaced by a community council formed by all adult men. The cacique's kiva is no longer the focus of Picuris activities. It has been replaced by the modern cement-block community center.

The relationship between the material and the nonmaterial aspects of cultural systems has been a topic of interest within anthropology for a number of years. Lewis H. Morgan's study, *Houses and House-Life of the American Aborigines*, published in 1881, suggested a relationship between architectural forms and family organization. In recent years archaeologists have stimulated a renewal of interest in this topic in their attempts to reconstruct social aspects of prehistoric cultures through analysis of the material remains (Binford 1962; Longacre 1964; Deetz 1965; Binford and Binford 1968). The success of such reconstructions depends largely upon the availability of reliable ethnographic descriptions from which models of cultural systems can be constructed (Vogt 1956; Dozier 1965).

While conducting a program of field research at Picuris on the nature of the changes which have occurred within Picuris during the life-spans of the oldest living residents, a period of about ninety years, it became evident that architectural units within the pueblo reflected the major groups of the traditional social structure. It also became evident that the present use or disuse of various architectural units reflected many of the changes which occurred at Picuris following Anglo-American dominance of the region in the last decades of the nineteenth century.[1] This discussion is offered not only in the hope that it may contribute to the body of knowledge of the Rio Grande Pueblos, but also in the hope that it may provide insight into the pro-

1   The field research upon which this paper is based was sponsored by the following: the Comins Fund of the University of Arizona, the Doris Duke American Indian Oral History Project of the Arizona State Museum, Fort Burgwin Research Center, and the National Science Foundation. Without the interest and cooperation of the residents of Picuris Pueblo, such research would have been impossible. Grateful acknowledgment of their assistance must be noted.

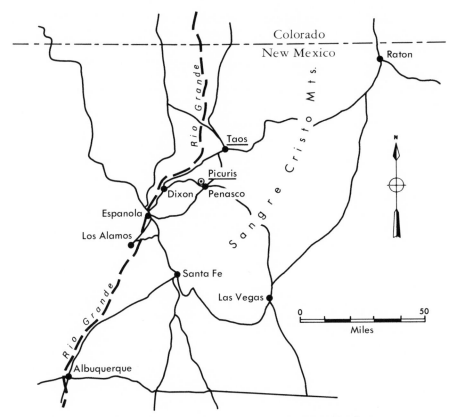

MAP 13.1   Location of Picuris Pueblo, Northeastern New Mexico

cesses of culture change in northern New Mexico and that it may be useful in constructing models of the relationship between the material and the nonmaterial aspects of cultural systems.

THE PUEBLO OF PICURIS

The pueblo of Picuris is a small Tiwa-speaking community located on the Rio Pueblo in the mountains of northern New Mexico. Although several small Spanish-American communities are located within three to five miles from Picuris, the nearest urban centers are Taos, twenty-one miles north; Espanola, thirty miles south; and Santa Fe, fifty-one miles south (Map 13.1). Throughout its history Picuris has been one of the most isolated Rio Grande pueblos. Today it remains one of the least studied, ethnographically, Pueblo Indian communities. The primary ethnography is the seventeen-page article by Parsons published in 1939. Although the population may have been as great as 2,000 in the early historic period, for the last century the resident population has never been greater than 127, and the present population is about 75.

In the last seventy years the pueblo of Picuris has been transformed from a self-contained community with few ties to the outside world into a community totally dependent on the outside world for its survival. The economy, traditionally subsistence farming, hunting, and gathering, is now based on welfare programs supplemented with only a minimal amount of wage earning. The political system, once centered in a council of ceremonial leaders which appointed the civil officers, consists now of a community council composed of all adult men which annually elects a set of civil officers. Law and order which was maintained through such traditional sanctions as fines, community work, public whippings, and banishment is now possible only with the assistance of federal and state law enforcement agencies. Except for a dim reflection in the activities of the annual feast day on August 10, the ceremonial system, the heart of the traditional community, has disappeared, leaving only elements of the introduced Spanish-Catholic system, and these in a weakened form. In spite of these dramatic changes, the residents of Picuris continue to speak their own language, along with Spanish and English, and are able to maintain an identity independent of their Spanish-American neighbors and an orientation separate from the surrounding dominant Anglo-American culture.[2]

ARCHITECTURAL UNITS: 1967

An inventory of the architectural units at Picuris in 1967 includes the following types based on the criteria of form, use, and ownership (Map 13.2, Fig. 13.1):

1. Thirty-nine enclosed surface structures of one to five connected rooms, each room ranging in size from about one hundred to

2   Two articles by Siegel (1959, 1965) deal with the nature of the change occurring within Picuris. I believe, however, that his reconstructions for Picuris social structure are not completely accurate, especially his interpretation of the ceremonial organization.

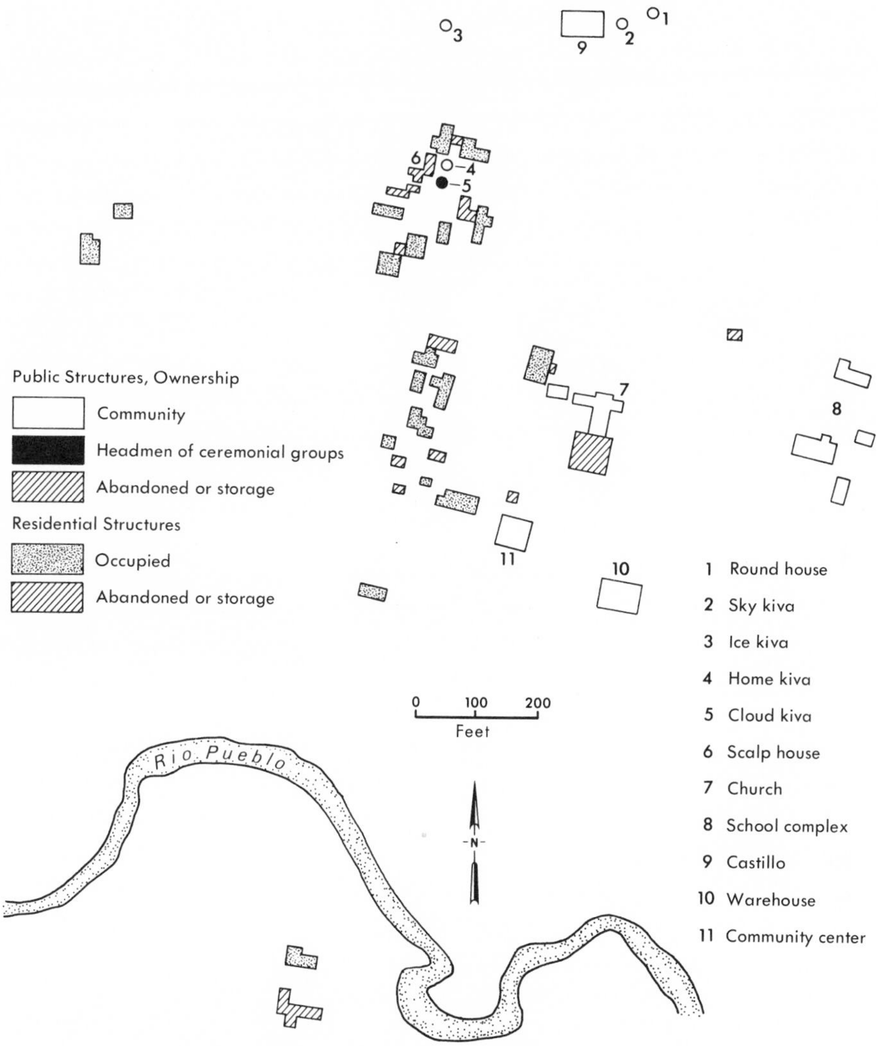

Public Structures, Ownership

Community

Headmen of ceremonial groups

Abandoned or storage

Residential Structures

Occupied

Abandoned or storage

0   100   200

Feet

Rio Pueblo

-N-

1 Round house

2 Sky kiva

3 Ice kiva

4 Home kiva

5 Cloud kiva

6 Scalp house

7 Church

8 School complex

9 Castillo

10 Warehouse

11 Community center

MAP 13.2   Picuris Pueblo, 1967

two hundred square feet. These structures are rectangular in shape, single story, and generally made of adobe bricks with flat roofs. Several log-and-tie structures with adobe plaster and one wooden frame structure with a pitched roof are also included. Thirty-three of these structures are located in the pueblo, while six are located in the fields surrounding. In 1967 twenty-one of these structures, all in the pueblo,

FIG. 13.1   View from the South of Picuris Pueblo in 1967

were in use as residences for households. The remaining structures were used for storage. Ten of these structures share at least one wall with a similar structure; they have contiguous walls. At least ten of the twenty-one structures now in use as residences were constructed since 1900, while thirteen have been abandoned. Ownership of these units is by individuals as household heads.

2. One enclosed surface structure, circular in shape, about fifteen feet in diameter, made of adobe bricks with a flat roof (Fig. 13.2). Entrance is by ladder through an opening in the roof. It contains a Spanish-style wall fireplace on the east wall, but no other features. This structure is located north of the present pueblo in a location believed by residents to be the center of the prehistoric pueblo. In Picuris this structure is referred to as *tolewene*, or as the Round House in English. Until about 1940 the structure was used for a series of three summer rain ceremonials conducted by ceremonial associations in June, August, and September. It was owned by the headman of the Summer People, one of the ceremonial associations. In 1967 it was

considered to be owned by the community. No activities have been associated with this structure since the ending of the summer rain ceremonials.

3. Four subterranean structures, circular in shape, about eighteen to twenty feet in diameter, entered by a ladder through an opening in the flat, ground-level roof (Figs. 13.2–13.4). Each of these units is named and was associated with a ceremonial group. *Apukuma* (sky place), located near the Round House, and *measeakema* (cloud place), located in the upper plaza of the present pueblo, are associated with the dual organization groups of Picuris, the Northside People and the Southside People. *Apukuma* was owned by the headman of the Southside People and is no longer in use. *Measeakema* is still used for dance rehearsals and as a dressing room for dancers and foot racers. It is no longer associated exclusively with the activities of the Northside People, but is considered to be the appropriate place for any "Indian doings." *Measeakema* is considered to be owned by the son of the last

FIG. 13.2   Round House (*Tolewene*), 1967. In the foreground is Sky Place (*apukuma*).

headman of the Northside People, although he no longer conducts ceremonial activities within the structure. *Achikuma* (ice place) is the third subterranean structure and is located northwest of the pueblo. It was associated with the Winter People, a ceremonial association, whose headman owned the structure. It is no longer used. The fourth subterranean structure, *ahupa* (home place) located in the upper plaza area north of *measeakema*, was owned by the cacique. It was primarily used as the meeting place of the Council of Principales, the major political group at Picuris composed of the headmen of each of the ceremonial groups and headed by the cacique, the ceremonial leader of the pueblo. It was also used by ceremonial associations without a specific meeting place. With the death of the cacique in 1967, this structure was no longer in use and, along with *apukuma* and *achikuma*, is considered to be owned by the community.

    4. Various open surface structures of logs and poles, such as corrals, pens, coops, and ramadas (Figs. 13.3, 13.5). These structures were primarily used for maintaining livestock and poultry and for storing

FIG. 13.4   Upper Plaza Area, 1967. The Cloud Place entrance (*measeakema*) is in the center foreground, the Home Place (*ahupa*) entrance is at right background, and the ruins of the Scalp House (*pilituone*) are at the left background.

FIG. 13.5   Log and Pole Corrals Located North of the Pueblo, 1967

FIG. 13.6   Catholic Church, 1900. (Photograph by A. C. Vroman, Bureau of American Ethnology Collection, Smithsonian Office of Anthropology.)

forage and farming equipment. Many of these structures are located north of the pueblo, especially the corrals, while several pens and coops are located within the pueblo. In 1967 only four of these structures were in use for maintaining horses and pigs. Each of these structures is owned by an individual as head of a household.

5. The Catholic church, constructed about 1770 and remodeled most recently in 1921 and 1955, is a large adobe structure in the shape of a cross with a flat roof and an enclosed courtyard (Fig. 13.6). It is considered to be owned by the community, and all expenses for repairs or maintenance come from community funds.

6. Four large single-story adobe structures, three of which contain several rooms, located east of the pueblo form the day-school complex. This complex was constructed by the Bureau of Indian Affairs in 1929. The school remained in use until 1953, not only as classrooms and teacher residences, but as a community center for meetings and social dances. In 1967 it was used by HELP, an adult educational program sponsored by federal funds for Picuris residents. Since 1957 when

FIG. 13.7   Sheet-Metal Warehouse, 1967. Structures in the left background are part of the day-school complex.

a quitclaim deed assigned this property from the Bureau of Indian Affairs to the pueblo, this complex has been owned by the community.

7. A large sheet-metal structure constructed in 1938 with federal funds for use as a storage shed for community-owned farming equipment (Fig. 13.7). It is located southeast of the pueblo and is considered to be owned by the community.[3]

8. A large, single-story, cement-block structure constructed in 1963 with federal funds for use as a community center (Fig. 13.8). It contains a modern kitchen, rest rooms, showers, detention rooms, and two meeting rooms. It is located south of the Catholic church and is considered to be owned by the community.

9. A large coursed-adobe, multistoried structure located north of the pueblo near the Round House and *apukuma* (Fig. 13.9). This structure, referred to as the *castillo* (Spanish, "castle"), is now largely in ruin. The few remaining rooms have been sealed recently and re-plastered. The structure is the remains of a large multistoried house block of the prehistoric period. Until recent years, parts of this structure were used as pens for livestock. In 1967 the sealed rooms con-

3   The sheet-metal warehouse was moved during the summer of 1969 to a location west of the day-school complex. It was moved in order to build a parking lot for a large museum complex which was constructed in 1969 with federal and tribal funds.

FIG. 13.8   Community Center, 1967

FIG. 13.9   Architectural Units at Picuris Pueblo, 1900. On the left is the *castillo*, on the right the Round House (*tolewene*), and in the center the entrance to the Sky Place (*apukuma*). (Photograph by A. C. Vroman, Bureau of American Ethnology Collection, Smithsonian Office of Anthropology.)

tained ceremonial paraphernalia no longer in use. This structure is considered to be owned by the community.

10. A complex of log, pole, and brush structures located about one and one-half miles north of the pueblo in a small canyon (Fig. 13.10). This complex includes a large open structure used for ceremo-

FIG. 13.10   Ceremonial Structure and Lean-Tos Used During the Annual Fall Ceremonies, 1967

nial activities during an annual three-day ceremonial in late August or early September. There are also eleven lean-tos of poles and brush east and south of the large ceremonial structure. These are occupied by household groups during the ceremonial. In past years the large structure was owned by the headman of the Mountain People, the ceremonial association which sponsored the fall activities. This large structure is now considered to be community owned, while each of the lean-tos continues to be owned by a separate individual as head of a household.

ARCHITECTURAL UNITS: PRE-1900

In the summer of 1881 John G. Bourke, then a lieutenant in the U.S. Army, visited Picuris. His notes include mention of the corrals and pens, the *castillo*, the Round House, and the Pueblo architecture in general:

Their houses are all of adobe, but the stables for burros and ponies are of log and the pens for the pigs of "jacal." ... The old pueblo itself is a veritable relic of antiquity; built of "cajon," it must at one time have been of large dimensions, but at this date only three stories remain and these are rapidly going to pieces. The workmanship was extremely crude, the wood used being split with axes and put together in a clumsy way. There were no windows opening on the outside; presumably, there must have been openings upon an interior court of small size, but this I could not determine exactly, there being no ladder and the ediface being in such a tumble down condition that my guide said it would not be prudent to attempt to climb about it. ... The "estufa" of Picuris is a circular tower, 9 paces in diameter, about 8 or 10 ft. high ¾ of which is above ground; it is built of adobe and is now much dilapidated. It is entered by ascending to the roof by a crazy ladder of cottonwood and thence by another equally crazy to the damp, dark and musty interior. ... The number of houses in Picuris cannot be much, if any, over thirty; they are about equally divided between one-storied and two-storied, but there are none higher than the latter. The Pueblo has a slouchy, down in the heel look, greatly at variance with the neat, trim and cleancut look of the Mexican settlements in the neighboring valleys. There are no accommodations for man or beast (Bloom 1936, pp. 280–81).

By 1900 the two-story houses mentioned by Bourke were no longer in use. The only two-story structure maintained was used for the display and storage of enemy scalps and belongings. It was referred to as *pilituone* (scalp house; Fig. 13.11). It was owned by the Scalp headman, a ceremonial leader. As late as 1910 M. C. Stevenson noted this structure: "Another interesting feature observed at Picuris was the hanging of scalps to a rafter in an upper chamber of a house, the eastern side of which was open in order to expose the scalps to view" (Hodge 1916, p. 15). In 1967 this structure was in ruin (Fig. 13.4).

With the exception of the large community-owned structures constructed in the last forty years and the newer residences, Picuris in 1900 (Fig. 13.12) was very similar to the inventory listed for 1967. Additions would be sixteen structures used as residences which have now disappeared or are in ruins and eleven summer houses located in the fields surrounding the pueblo. In 1967 only four of these summer houses remained, and all were used for storage only. Using a series of photographs taken about 1900 and a census of Picuris dated 1904, it

FIG. 13.11   Upper Plaza Area, 1900. In the background, the two-story structure is the Scalp House (*pilituone*), in the center foreground is the entrance to Cloud Place (*measeakema*), and at the right is the entrance to Home Place (*ahupa*). (Photograph by A. C. Vroman, Bureau of American Ethnology Collection, Smithsonian Office of Anthropology.)

was possible to reconstruct the settlement pattern of Picuris for 1900 (Map 13.3).

SOCIAL STRUCTURE AND ARCHITECTURAL UNITS

The relationship between the major groups of the social structure and the architectural units at Picuris can now be examined. The basic group within the social structure was the household (*naitoe*, "all living in that house"), composed of a nuclear family or a nuclear family modified by the loss of a member or the addition of a near relative. In 1900 two places of residence were maintained by many households, a house within the pueblo occupied during the winter months and a second house in the fields occupied during the farming season. This settlement pattern, compact for the winter and dispersed for the summer, reflected the economic activities of the community. With a shift in emphasis from subsistence farming and hunting to wage work in the 1930s, many of the summer houses were abandoned and only the residences in the pueblo were maintained. With the growing importance

FIG. 13.12   View from the South of the Pueblo Looking Toward the Northeast. (Photograph by A. C. Vroman, Bureau of American Ethnology Collection, Smithsonian Office of Anthropology.)

of the welfare programs since 1948, the few summer houses which were occupied between 1930 and 1948 have been abandoned also and are only used for storage today.

The bilateral kinship system of Picuris is also reflected in the settlement patterns. Residence in the summer houses was usually neolocal, while residence within the pueblo was ambilocal with a tendency toward a patrilocal bias and neolocal as an alternative. Ownership of residences also reflects this bilateral emphasis. Generally the household head was the father of the nuclear family. Widowed women, however, also acted as household heads and owned houses. Houses could be inherited by either sons or daughters. According to a 1904 census, twenty-four household heads were men and three were women. In 1967 thirteen household heads were men and eight were women.

Kinships groups larger than the nuclear family of the household were only weakly developed at Picuris. The Picuris term *kemamoyo* refers to "all of one's relatives," both consanguineal and affinal, a kindred as defined by Murdock (1960, p. 4). These relatives might be called upon for assistance in fieldwork or house construction or for contributions of food and help for such activities as weddings and funerals. In terms of the residence patterns, there was a tendency to establish a new residence near kinsmen, so that clusters of houses of related individuals were common in Picuris in 1900. Houses of several

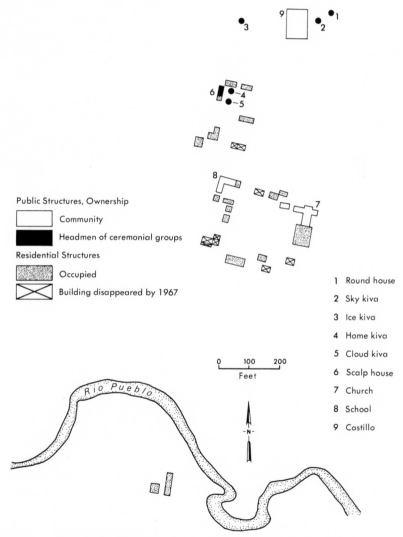

Public Structures, Ownership

Community

Headmen of ceremonial groups

Residential Structures

Occupied

Building disappeared by 1967

1   Round house

2   Sky kiva

3   Ice kiva

4   Home kiva

5   Cloud kiva

6   Scalp house

7   Church

8   School

9   Castillo

0   100   200

Feet

-N-

Rio Pueblo

MAP 13.3   Picuris Pueblo, 1900

of these clusters shared contiguous walls, but no common entrances. In 1967 such clusters were rare, with neolocal residence being the preferred residence pattern. Only five houses occupied in 1967 shared a common wall. As a functioning group the *kemamoyo* has disappeared from Picuris.

Integrating the various household groups was a series of ceremonial groups. The dual organization groups, the Northside People (*huota*) and the Southside People (*hukwita*), based affiliation generally on patrilineal descent although an individual could change his affiliation. Both men and women belonged to these groups. These were ceremonial rather than kinship groups since affiliation could be changed, and activities were limited to ceremonial activities. As listed above, a circular subterranean structure was associated with each of these groups.

Crosscutting the dual organization groups and further integrating the household groups in the traditional system was a series of ceremonial associations. Membership in these groups was through selection by the association membership. These associations included four seasonal groups—Spring People, Summer People, Fall People, and Winter People—which were primarily concerned with weather control and fertility of plants and animals. The Round House was used by the Spring People, Summer People, and Fall People for ceremonial retreats during the summer rain ceremonials. The Winter People used *achikuma*, one of the circular subterranean structures. Other ceremonial associations included the Clown association, which used *ahupa* for ceremonial activities, and the women's association, which apparently met in a private home. The complex of log, pole, and brush structures north of the pueblo and used for the annual fall ceremonial was associated with the Mountain People.

Each of these structures associated with a ceremonial group was considered to be owned by the headman of that group. The Round House, which was used by three groups, was owned by the headman of the Summer People. Ownership of these architectural units by the headmen might more correctly be termed custodianship. The headman of each ceremonial group was the member with the greatest seniority. He held this position until his death, when the next eldest member of the ceremonial group assumed the position. The headman was responsible for directing the maintenance of the structure, but the membership of the group, aided by the women's association, carried out the needed repairs.

About 1910, the ceremonial groups began restricting initiation of new members, probably due to the number of young men leaving the pueblo for school and wage work. In the 1930s with the shift from a subsistence economy to a wage work economy, the activities of the ceremonial groups—weather control, crop and animal increase, and so forth—lessened in importance. With the deaths of the remaining members, the ceremonial groups began to dissolve. As the last member of each group died, ownership of the structure associated with the group passed to community ownership. In 1967 only *measeakema* remained owned by an individual, the son of the last headman of the Northside People.

The subterranean structure associated with the cacique, *ahupa*, reflects the nature of the political system within the pueblo. The cacique (*tolapiane*, "head of the tribe") was the ceremonial leader of the pueblo as well as the head of the Council of Principales, the primary group of the political system. The Council of Principales was composed of the headmen of each of the ceremonial groups. They met in *ahupa*, which is similar in details to the structures associated with the ceremonial groups. This council appointed a set of civil officers, offices apparently introduced by the Spanish, including a governor, lieutenant governor, sheriff, and fiscal, as well as a war chief and assistant war chiefs. These civil officers carried out the policies of the council and maintained order within the pueblo. When meeting without the council, these civil officers did not meet in *ahupa*, but held their meetings in the residence of the governor and later in the school buildings and the new community center. There appears, then, to have been a council with a ceremonial orientation and a set of civil officers with a secular orientation. These two orientations were reflected in the meeting places of the two groups.

With the deaths of the ceremonial leaders, the Council of Principales began to disappear. In 1940 the authority of the council was challenged by a group of younger men who successfully sought the impeachment of the appointed governor. In 1950 the Council of Principales was replaced by a community council composed of all adult men residing in the pueblo. The community council annually elected the civil officers. Council meetings were no longer held in *ahupa*, but at the day school. With the construction of the community center in 1963, the meetings of the community council and the civil officers both took place in the new structure.

In the traditional system the cacique was considered to be the leader of the pueblo and responsible for the welfare of all residents. In the present system the elected governor is the responsible leader. As the various architectural units passed from ownership by individuals acting as ceremonial headmen to community ownership, the governor, as head of the community, had to assume a growing number of new responsibilities. His responsibilities are no longer those defined by the traditional system only, but now include those that are associated with the various ceremonial leaders as well as the cacique. Inability to successfully meet these requirements and responsibilities or mismanagement of community-owned property are frequently used arguments during the impeachment proceedings which are brought against governors almost annually.

CONCLUSION

In conclusion, then, on the basis of form alone a distinction can be made between architectural units associated with ceremonial groups and those associated with secular groups. Ceremonial architecture is circular; secular is rectangular. Except for the Round House, which may be a relatively recent replacement of a subterranean structure, ceremonial architecture within Picuris is subterranean. The Scalp House may be an exception to this generalization.

In terms of changes within the social structure as reflected in architectural units, the household, the basic group, remains as do the single family residences. There is now a tendency for neolocal residence within the pueblo rather than the traditional ambilocal pattern, but neolocal residence was an alternative even within the traditional pattern. The households and the architectural units associated with them have changed the least.

The integrating groups, the ceremonial groups, have disappeared, and the architectural units associated with them are no longer in use. The Council of Principales is no longer present, and the structure associated with the cacique is no longer used. In the self-contained community of seventy years ago, the cacique and his Council of Principales represented the community. Today, the governor and his officers represent the community and also act as the integrating mechanism between the household groups and the surrounding non-Indian world of which Picuris is now a part. *Ahupa* (home place), the structure associated with the cacique, is no longer the focus of Picuris activities. It has been replaced by the modern cement-block community center as the center of Picuris activities today.

REFERENCES CITED

Binford, Lewis R.
  1962 Archaeology as Anthropology. *American Antiquity* 28:217–25.

Binford, Sally R., and Lewis R. Binford
  1968 *New Perspectives in Archeology*. Chicago: Aldine.

Bloom, Lansing B.
  1936 Bourke on the Southwest, X: Chapter XIX, the Northern Pueblos. *New Mexico Historical Review* 11:245–82.

Deetz, James
  1965 *The Dynamics of Stylistic Change in Arikara Ceramics*. Illinois Studies in Anthropology, No. 4. Urbana: University of Illinois Press.

Dozier, Edward P.
  1965 Southwestern Social Units and Archaeology. *American Antiquity* 31: 38–47.

Hodge, F. W.
  1916 *Report of the Ethnologist-in-Charge*. Thirty-first Annual Report, Bureau of American Ethnology. Washington, D.C.: Smithsonian Institution, 1909–10.

Longacre, William A.
  1964 Archaeology as Anthropology: A Case Study. *Science* 144 (3625): 1454–55.

Morgan, Lewis H.
  1881 *Houses and House-Life of the American Aborigines*. Contributions to North American Ethnology, Vol. 4. U.S. Geographical and Geological Survey of the Rocky Mountain Region. Washington, D.C.: Government Printing Office.

Murdock, George Peter
  1960 Cognatic Forms of Social Organization. In George Peter Murdock, ed., *Social Structure in Southeast Asia*. Viking Fund Publications in Anthropology, No. 29. New York: Wenner-Gren Foundation. Pp. 1–14.

Parsons, Elsie Clews
  1939 Picuris, New Mexico. *American Anthropologist* 41:206–22.

Siegel, Bernard J.

 1959   Some Structure Implications for Change in Pueblo and Spanish New
        Mexico. In Verne F. Ray, ed., *Intermediate Societies, Social Mobility,
        and Communication*. Proceedings of the 1959 Annual Spring Meeting
        of the American Ethnological Society. Seattle. Pp. 37–44.

 1965   Social Disorganization in Picuris Pueblo. *International Journal of Com-
        parative Sociology* 6:199–206.

Vogt, Evon Z.

 1956   An Appraisal of "Prehistoric Settlement Patterns in the New World."
        In Gordon R. Willey, ed., *Prehistoric Settlement Patterns in the New
        World*. Viking Fund Publications in Anthropology, No. 23. New York:
        Wenner-Gren Foundation. Pp. 173–82.

Chapter 14

Settlement Patterns as Artifacts of Social Structure

Milton B. Newton, Jr.

ABSTRACT   As exemplified by the Upland South culture of the piney woods section in east Louisiana, the various aspects of settlement patterns reflect different social components. In the typical Upland South county (parish, in Louisiana), the two principal aspects, the rambling patterns of the countryside and the more compact county-seat nucleus, express the two major social components: the rural peasantry and the urban elite.

The rural-peasant component is further subdivided into "settlements," a cluster of kinsmen and their allies loosely identified with a church, and "communities," small service centers, each normally having a few stores, service stations, churches, a school, and a post office. These are not static units, but wax and wane in response to varied pressures. Although whites and blacks are culturally nearly indistinguishable (both share in the syncretic Upland South peasant culture), the politics of race dictate that settlements, in particular, be racially homogeneous.

The nucleus of the county is the courthouse town, the center of civic life, of legal order, and of the literati. The roads of the county flow into it, and there are located the chief judge, the county agent, the sheriff, the newspaper, the library, lawyers, and doctors. In response to population growth and to the shift from agriculture to industry of varying magnitude, some courthouse towns have developed into larger centers. A schematic model is proposed to account for the sequence of development in racial residential patterns.

Underlying both the settlement patterns and the social structure of the Upland South is a basic cultural configuration centered around familistic egal-

339

itarianism, individualism, personal honor, and "action seeking." This core
configuration accounts for much of the Upland South landscape, social structure,
and behavior.

Settlement patterns are the largest and most complex of the artifacts
in material culture. Their heroic proportions stem from at least two
sources. First, the individual structures (houses, fields, roads, churches,
clinics) are the greatest material accomplishments of both men and
their institutions. Second, the complete settlement pattern is the largest tangible expression of the configuration of the culture. As is the
case with many aspects of material culture, the settlement pattern is a
complex structure, acting as both cause and effect at several levels of
the man-to-man, man-to-technology, and man-to-land relations of the
culture; the various aspects of settlement reflect different social facts.

The piney woods sections of south Mississippi and east Louisiana
can serve as a convenient and instructive specimen for observing the
relations between social structure and settlement patterns. This region
pertains to the Upland South culture (Kniffen 1965), the Frontier-
Appalachian South (Arensberg 1955) originating in a complex hearth
in Pennsylvania and the Piedmont (Wertenbaker 1938) and spreading over the region in question by the 1820s.

Search for the culturally significant unit of settlement and social
structure which is representative of the Upland South leads repeatedly
to the county (parish). Because the Upland South frontier movement
included both elite and peasant segments,[1] and because only the

1 That the small agriculturists of the South, or "plain folks" (Owsley 1949), should
   be termed "peasants" rests upon the following definition obtained by synthesizing
   Redfield (1960, p. 19), Evans (1956, pp. 220–21, 237), Pfeifer (1956, pp. 242 ff.), Wolf
   (1966, pp. 2, 8–9, passim), Warriner (1939, pp. 1–42), Kroeber (1948, p. 248), Foster
   (1967, pp. 2–13), and Diaz (1967, pp. 50–56): A peasant is a member of a rural
   community of rustic agriculturists, horticulturists, or stockmen, who individually
   or collectively have sufficient control of the land to carry on largely traditional methods of producing mainly customary crops. Such a community supports its labor-
   supplying households importantly from the land and produces certain specific
   staples demanded by the dominant sections of the larger society and culture in which
   they participate only partially. Partialness stems from a historic status, occupied by
   the peasant with regard to historic nobility, if the latter shares title to the peasant's
   land, and from the equally historic relations to the elite of the market town where
   originate external economic, political, and religious demands upon the peasant, his
   community, and his produce. Peasant farming is part of a way of life involving a
   series of historically derived man-land relations which have value in themselves
   beyond their potential for profit. In the partial conflict between these rustic life-

county includes the minimum personnel to represent both parts of Upland South society, a study of settlement social relations must deal with the county as the culturally meaningful unit. A smaller social group will lack the important courthouse-town elite; a larger one will introduce unwieldy complications.

To obtain a model of the role of social structure in forming settlement patterns of the Upland South, a county should be selected which was settled early and predominantly by Upland South people and which has been little altered by urban and industrial development. At the same time, the specimen county should not be so isolated, retarded, or depopulated as to mark it as deformed; it should be representative of functioning, rural, Upland South counties in general. With a model derived from such a specimen, the functionally subsequent urban, commercial, and industrial developments of the Upland South can be seen in terms of their cultural background.

ST. HELENA PARISH: AN UPLAND SOUTH COMMUNITY

St. Helena Parish, Louisiana (Map 14.1), can serve as a representative Upland South county (Newton 1967). It was settled between 1800 and 1820 by people whose main immediate origins lay in the southern Appalachians and the southern Piedmont—the eastern parts of Tennessee and Kentucky, the western parts of Virginia and the Carolinas, and the northern parts of Georgia and Alabama.[2] Most of their current family connections lie in southern Mississippi, nearby Louisiana parishes, Louisiana towns, and East Texas (Succession Records n.d.). St. Helena (420 square miles) has about ten thousand people; its parish

---

ways and the demands and values of the elite of the market town lies the source of hostility toward commercial culture and cities.

2   A major stumbling block to cultural interpretaion of life in the South has been the failure to realize that states do not form adequate units of observation. Some studies (such as Lathrop 1949) have produced excellent beginnings; however, others (notably, Jordan 1967, but also to an extent, Meinig 1969) lose much of their potential by continuing, two decades later, to treat each state as a homogeneous culture area. Quite clearly, there are important differences between eastern and western parts of the south Atlantic states; just where the boundary ought to lie is not agreed. Nevertheless, recent research has left the Lowland (Tidewater) South restricted to a narrow coastal band in Maryland, Virginia, the Carolinas, and Georgia, with small enclaves in Alabama, Mississippi, Louisiana, and Texas; the interiors of these states are largely Upland South in culture (Kniffen 1965; Kniffen and Glassie 1966; Gordon 1968; and Zelinsky 1951).

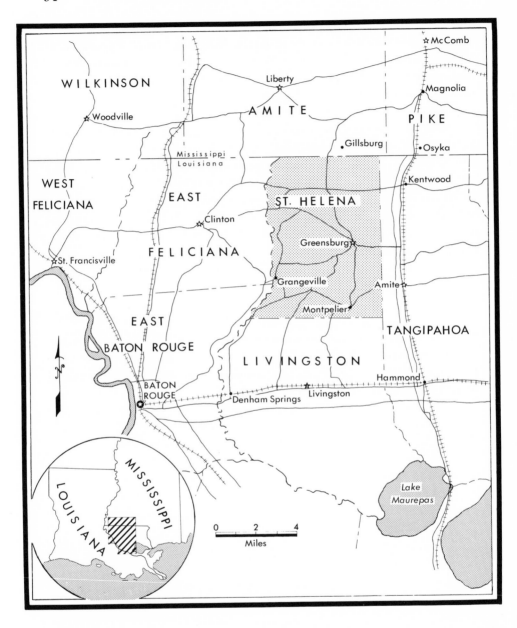

MAP 14.1   General Location of St. Helena Parish

seat, Greensburg, about seven hundred. Households average 4.25 persons, and almost none live in multifamily houses (only 25 persons in 1960). The people are about 55 percent black, nearly totally Protestant, all rural (in census terms), and mostly workers in primary economic activity (agriculture and forestry), government, or commuters to Baton Rouge wage work.

Seen from a great height, the paved roads and highways stand out as two contrasting patterns, one centripetal pattern focusing upon the courthouse town and one through-flowing pattern articulating with the larger statewide network. The state-oriented highways, one north-south and three east-west, coincide in part with the centripetal system, though they serve different primary purposes. The larger network is aimed at connecting the parts of the state to the capital and knitting the region to the political and economic structure of the nation.

The smaller, courthouse-centered system has been from the beginning an expression of the political power and dominance of the elite of the courthouse town over its domain. Among the very first acts of the St. Helena Parish Police Jury (county commissioners) was an effort to connect effectively all parts of the parish to the parish seat (Prichard 1940). Without this system, the citizens could not be expected to meet the political, economic, and social demands required to support the courthouse-town elite. Conversely, without this system, the officers of the parish could not effectively carry out the will of the police jury over its area of jurisdiction.

A collateral function of the centripetal system lay in its usefulness to local commerce. Merchants and their customers, factors and their patrons, and professionals and their clients require a reasonably complete road system for their transactions. Roads that served the parish also served the merchants, factors, and professionals and in serving them generated more income for the parish. To a large extent, these relationships still function (although the automotive material complex has made people less dependent upon the services of the courthouse town), and certainly they are still to be seen in this grossest of the settlement patterns. Subsequent modifications of the centripetal system have appeared in other counties with the rise of railroads, national highways, urbanization, and industrialization. But, even in the more developed counties and parishes, the functionally anterior elements still play significant roles (Newton 1970).

Moving closer, one of the most striking social traits becomes noticeable: the unusually high frequency of churches and cemeteries, as well as their scatter throughout the parish (Map 14.2). St. Helena has more than fifty small churches dispersed widely and seemingly randomly. Typically, these congregations are small and the church buildings in fair-to-poor condition. While some are well kept and have permanent, full-time ministers, many are in distressed condition, some even abandoned. Being completely evangelical-fundamentalist Protestant (Baptist, Methodist, African Methodist Episcopal, Pentecostal, and the like), the congregations are locally autonomous and may split over quite small points of doctrine or over social conflicts among the members. A maximum average membership of about two hundred is greater than actual average membership because of the customary lack of participation, especially by young and middle-aged men.

RURAL-PEASANT COMPONENT

Factionalism and extreme local autonomy, however, do not leave the church element chaotic in the landscape. On the contrary, among the strictly rural (peasant) people of the Upland South, it is the cluster of families surrounding and affiliated with the "little brown church in the wildwood" that is the functional social unit. In spite of the folklore concerning the sanctity and autonomy of the family farm, such is not fundamental or self-sufficient. The unit which can sustain the individual and the family through hardship and can reproduce the culture in subsequent generations is not the family, but the local group—in folk terms, the "settlement" (Arensberg 1955, p. 1144; Newton 1967). Church-related settlements (Map 14.3, for example) scattered loosely over the parish constitute the major fabric of the peasant section of the Upland South settlement social pattern. Each settlement, though loosely identified with a church, correlates as well with a cluster of kinsmen and their allies. As such, settlements are usually known by family names (Butler, Crier, Day, Bridges, Venable), though few of these appear on maps as place-names. Settlements form the unit from which are drawn associations, work groups, and mutual assistance. Neighbors are scarcely within "hollerin" distance, but fieldwork and large-scale (1:1200) air photos reveal a fine-grain complex of roads, lanes, and trails, some of the smallest material expressions of

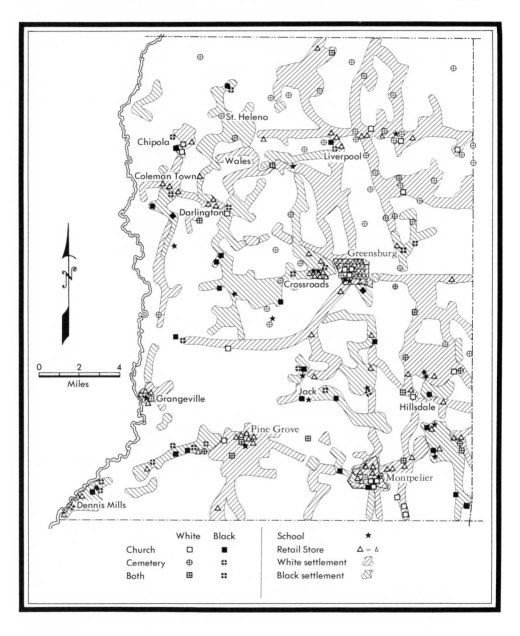

MAP 14.2   Races and Service Points

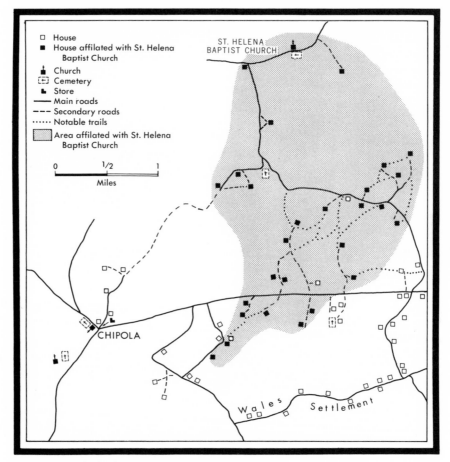

MAP 14.3   St. Helena Baptist Church Settlement

social arrangements. So, the meaningful settlement unit is the meaningful social unit as well.

Not all settlements function well, nor do they share the same degree of functional coherence; some are more populous or richer or
better led; some are black, some white. The more favorably situated
(in terms of transportation, commerce, and so forth) or those with better leadership (frequently in the church or school) tend to rise in dominance to the status of a higher-order central place—in folk terms, a
"community" (Map 14.4). Commonly, the names of communities are
topographic (Crossroads, Rocky Hill, Planer Mills), though others are

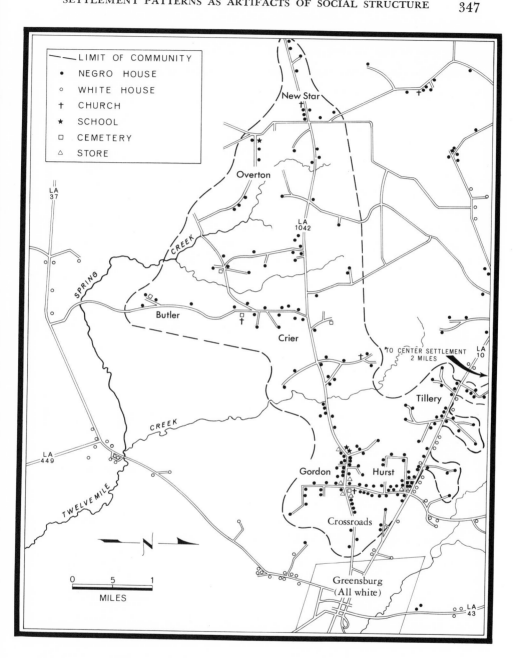

MAP 14.4   Crossroads Community

patronymic or named for some other place (Liverpool, Grangeville); only some of the community names appear on regular maps. If settlements can be termed dispersed hamlets, communities should be termed dispersed villages. The various settlements tributary to the community function as open, country neighborhoods, the inhabitants owing dual allegiance to the settlement and to the community.

At or near the core of the community, a slight increase in the concentration of service points gives the community some of the character of an urban place. In addition to a number of schools and churches, there are usually one or a few stores, cemeteries, scout troops, service stations, post office, fraternal halls, and such. These are seldom densely concentrated or arrayed along a pattern of streets, except as the community grew up around a crossroad. Indeed, any one of these service points may appear at any place throughout the community and are frequently associated with the settlements. With the rising influence of the automobile and the drive toward school and church consolidation, the community has increased its influence over the settlement. Nevertheless, the settlement is still there—as a unit in both settlement and social patterns—and continues to exert its influence.

But neither the settlement patterns nor the social structures represented by these units are static. The numerous cemeteries (more than eighty), like the churches, settlements, and communities, are generally racially homogenous. But there are many white cemeteries in black-settled areas, many are peripheral or remote to any settled area, and many are abandoned cemeteries. In this Upland South region, cemeteries are generally associated with settlements, though some are small, family burial grounds (Jeane 1969). The graveyards, like the settlements they serve, generally orient around a large family and its allies. But families and settlements rise and fall in their fortunes and even disappear, especially with rural exodus and the rising importance of more central places. But the cemeteries remain as necropolitan social structures, and the now-scattered remnants of families occasionally bury a kinsman who had sought his fortune far away (Delambre 1969).

The peasant segment of the settlement pattern, then, is made up of slowly waxing and waning settlements responding to many and varied pressures and demands. Knitting together the settlements, an intricate network of routes both reflects and influences social structure. Old settlements decline slowly as the member families age and die for lack of interested heirs. While the old decline, new settlements appear, usually taking their main character and organization from one or a few vigorous individuals.

Depending upon the location of inherited or purchasable land, new families tend to locate on the kind of land that they see as best meeting their needs and desires. One of the more important variables, the availability of good roads, helps determine the ultimate location and importance of the new potential settlement focus. As new, vigorous settlement leaders appear, the peripheral remnants of declining settlements reorient toward the new center. A dynamic example of such a process is to be seen in the black St. Helena Baptist Church settlement (Map 14.3). With the aging of older leaders (the seventy-to-eighty bracket) and the rise of younger leaders (the forty-to-fifty group), the focus of the settlement is shifting toward the northwest and closer to the church. The church building had been purchased from a white settlement that gradually declined and shifted its residences elsewhere and whose families sold most of their land either to blacks or to paper companies. The developing settlement includes older persons from the old settlement, children of the old settlement, and migrants (chiefly from Mississippi), along with spouses who have married into the settlement. The rising peasant leader gradually attracted a large number of clients and, though a Negro, achieved a measure of respect as a citizen and farmer, even from whites.

Current parishwide paving projects, because they are strictly local and independent of state control, respond to local wishes by paving the existing roads. By this means, the peasant-oriented routes serving peasant interests, expressed through the police juror of each of six wards, are being enhanced and made more permanent. Unlike the state highways which ignore folk values and patterns, the new projects interconnect all places that people live, neutralizing the attraction of the few state highways as sites of settlement growth (Newton 1970). The new system facilitates travel within and among the peasant settlements rather than through and away from the parish. Greater reliability of roads, reduced wear on vehicles, greater ease of going to market or the clinic, reduced travel time for school children, and many other amenities have suddenly increased the attractiveness and permanence of farm life and thereby reinforced the peasant settlement as an element in the social structure of St. Helena Parish.

In the case of St. Helena Baptist Church settlement, the new road project has not only facilitated the new patron's development of his system of clientage, but also helps assure that vigorous families will not migrate to seek opportunity. The cases of this and other settlements show that peasant life is still functional and that any governmental project that supports the culturally meaningful settlement-social unit will reinforce the cultural development of that unit.

Though communities may be slightly racially heterogeneous, settlements are homogeneous. Minor lanes and trails, the rural equivalent of over-the-garden-wall relations, are less notable between white and black settlements. To the south of St. Helena Baptist Church settlement lies white Wales settlement; it lies on the "other" side of Joiner Creek (Map 14.3). Air photos made in 1940 show a large number of small routes crossing Joiner Creek and, though most families in Wales settlement are affiliated with Center Church three miles to the east, the family graveyard lies north of Joiner Creek and in the periphery of Negro St. Helena Baptist Church settlement. Currently, the net of small lanes and trails has all but disappeared. Clearly, the black settlement has expanded at the territorial expense of the white, and the more detailed elements of the settlement pattern responded quite sensitively to the changed social arrangements.

The cardinal rule underlying racial segregation is the insistence that blacks and whites may not enter intimate associations as equals; all other sanctions flow from this value and from reactions to thwart real and imagined challenges to the ascription of dominant status to whites in all intimate relations. Such seems to be the cause of the particular ways in which the settlements of whites and blacks articulate to form the larger settlement pattern of the parish. Negroes either live in separate settlements or as dependent elements on white farms. The latter is becoming nearly nonexistent as renters of all kinds become infrequent in St. Helena Parish (only 10 percent in 1964). Where a few individuals of one race are found living within the territory of the other's settlements, it most frequently represents a transitional period in the evolution of the neighborhoods of each.

The separation of blacks and whites is fundamentally social and political; the separation is bridged, however, by a common cultural origin, a largely common history, much shared ancestry, many common values, and a broadly common inventory of material culture (Newton 1967). The significant point is that there is a rural settlement social pattern staffed by white Upland South peasants (WUSPs) and black Upland South peasants (BUSPs). They cannot be separated on any but politically supported social definitions of "white" and "black." The settlement pattern and material culture again reflect social reality: there is no objective means of distinguishing white from black farms and settlements without seeing the people themselves. The one qualification of this statement is also represented in the settlement pattern. The Negroes of St. Helena Parish are, as a group, about one generation behind the whites in responding to cultural change. Archival materials representing whites of two generations back show by the content and by their phonetic misspellings that rural Negroes today perpetuate social, linguistic, and material traits common to whites of that time[3] (Anderson Papers n.d. and Lewis Diaries n.d.). The settlement pattern reflects this one-generation lag in the earlier and greater abandonment of rural life by the whites, their total dominance of dairying, their greater role in stock farming, their greater dependence upon wage labor and rural nonfarm residence, and in the frequency of their cemeteries in black neighborhoods.

URBAN-ELITE COMPONENT

But both BUSPs and WUSPs together, as with peasants generally, make up only part of society, part of culture (Kroeber 1948, p. 248); their settlement social relations explain only part of the settlement pattern of a parish or county; both occupy positions subordinate to the elite of the courthouse town. Here, around the courthouse square, appears the first semblance of civic life, of legal (rather than customary) order, of a literati. Here, real streets appear along with hierarchical buildings of distinctive function and found nowhere else in the county.

Here also is—or was—"culture," the cultivated or polished life. Any courthouse town can point with pride to a number of proofs of its

3   This is temporarily avoiding the issue of the origins of the many traits shared by the Upland South; a number of important ones are certainly African.

claim to culture, such as, among other things, distinguished graduates of its old "academy" or "institute." Another part of the culture of the courthouse town is clustered around what might be termed Anglo-Saxonism, a distorted conception of "our Anglo-Saxon heritage." Anglo-Saxonism is fed by both a very few actual settlers from the aristocratic Tidewater (Lowland) South families of eastern Virginia and eastern Carolina and by an almost-conscious effort by some of the more successful Upland South people to ape prestigious groups—until recently Tidewater South. Most of the families from, say, North Carolina must be traced to western (not eastern) sections of the state—to a nest of WUSPs, not WASPs. The myth of Anglo-Saxonism leads not only to white columns and southern belles, but to a greater feeling of solidarity among the elite.

The courthouse in its square, emblem of the latter-day preindustrial city,[4] spreads its power throughout the county along the roads that repeatedly ramify outward from the grid around the courthouse; reciprocally, the political, commercial, and social tribute is drawn in toward the four streets that outline the courthouse square. Until quite recently, it was difficult to travel through a county without being required by the route system to pass before the courthouse. While Greensburg can be avoided by two direct and several circuitous routes, most roads and highways lead quite easily to the courthouse and to the businesses and offices surrounding the square.

Some of the importance of the courthouse square has been captured recently by Price (1968, pp. 58–59):

The [land use] returns of the square are not only from private profit but also from government and government services placed in a spot of maximum accessibility, esteem, and scrutiny; from its esthetic charms, even caught in the midst of mundane errands; from its promotion of social contact; and from an increased sense of civic pride for residents of town and county alike. The true intensiveness of the land use is the whole made up of all the economic, political, esthetic, and social gains, each evaluated in its own currency.

4 Though Sjoberg's definition (1955) of the preindustrial city specifically excludes cities and towns of the United States, the courthouse town resembles the preindustrial city; it is not, but it is quite similar. The ordinary county town has lost most of its literati; and what is more important to Sjoberg's definition, the county town now has inanimate energy. Nevertheless, electrical power wired in, but controlled elsewhere, has little effect on the social structure; if the arrival of inanimate energy produces little change in the social structure, why change the classification?

In short, the importance of the functions and people arrayed around the square is impressed upon all travelers, but most importantly upon the citizens.

Anyone raised in such a setting came to expect to know—without prior specific experience—where in any county to find the offices of the chief judge, the county agent, the health officer, the sheriff, the newspaper, the library, various lawyers, some of the doctors, and several churches; he knew that he could find these and more within two blocks of the courthouse, if not within it. Interspersed among these sources of power, justice, and help are the merchants who offer the tangibles of material well-being. It is in and around the courthouse square that the network of client-patron relations becomes thickest and most interwoven; it is here that the weak seek the aid of the strong to deal with the strong, where the strong guarantee their support from, and acceptance in, the peasant hinterland. The routes and buildings reflect this elite-dominated clientage and such has been noted by many, many observers (Price 1968).

EVOLUTIONARY MODEL OF THE UPLAND SOUTH SETTLEMENT PATTERN

Greensburg, typical of smaller courthouse towns in this part of the Upland South, is all white; blacks live on the periphery, in "quarters" scattered along the main roads leading into the courthouse square. Actually, each of the four small towns (Greensburg, population about seven hundred; Montpelier, about two hundred; Pine Grove, about two hundred; and Grangeville, about one hundred) all are exclusively white (except for six Negro households at the edge of Montpelier), and each has one or more black settlements along one or more of its main roads. The first, developmental stage (Fig. 14.1) of town evolution— unincorporated or recently incorporated—shows the clear pattern of a white core with one or more black spurs or spokes appended. In the second developmental stage, the corporation limits are extended beyond the black spokes to include growing white clusters (settlements and subdivisions) which desire urban services: water, gas, police, fire protection, and the like. In addition, the black settlements are brought under direct police control of the white-elite town. A major change results: the little towns are no longer entirely white. If the town grows

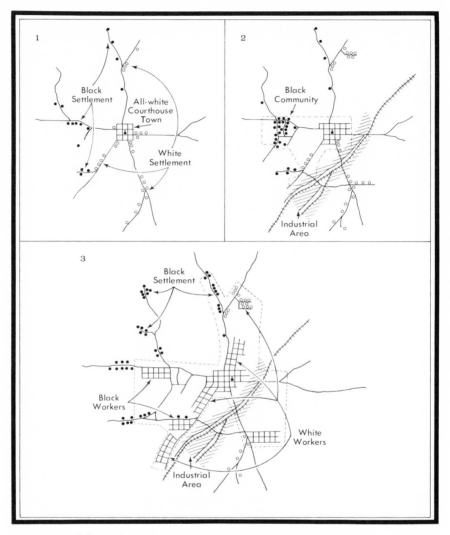

FIG. 14.1   Schematic Evolution of an Upland South County Seat

rapidly away from its old core, the small black neighborhoods remain in their original spoke positions as islands in a mainly white city; new black neighborhoods tend to grow first along the highways just beyond the new corporate limits, later also in the inner-city core.

Inspection of the small county-seat towns of the Upland South—in this case, Greensburg—shows the basis for this model. Such a historically obtained model explains the neighborhood patterns of larger cities such as Baton Rouge, Louisiana. A comparison of the map of Baton Rouge in 1908 with the present arrangement of Negro neighborhoods shows simply that the historical model explains the arrangement. At the turn of the century, Baton Rouge was as importantly a parish-seat town as any other character. Off center to the parish because it was also the head of deepwater navigation, it was (and is), nevertheless, the focus of routes, and along the rays of the centripetal system of roads were scattered the Negro neighborhoods, positions that they still occupy even though—as the model would have it—the limits of the white city were extended beyond them. Subsequent developments have seen, first, new Negro settlements grow up beyond the newer limits and along the main arteries, and second, a movement of Negroes into the former white-elite core of the old city (Brill 1963, especially Maps 12, 13, 18, 25).

Other dimensions of Upland South town development are also historically obtainable. If, unlike Greensburg, industrial development became important to the city, neighborhoods of laboring whites—like most of the Negroes, derived from the surrounding rural settlements—also grow along the main routes and close to their work. In Baton Rouge, one such neighborhood is Istrouma, almost a separate city having its own churches, schools, shopping centers, voting patterns, social arrangements, and a separate settlement area (Brill 1963). Lacking any industrial development (other than a brief and passing railroad period), Greensburg lacks almost completely any such laboring section; craftsmen and laborers are either members of the old-town families or are blacks and whites from the surrounding peasant countryside who go to town daily to work.

Today, still another trend has added complexity to the social-settlement patterns. The efforts to deal with the difficulties of pluralism and to develop the status and participation of Negroes have also made an impression upon the settlement pattern of St. Helena Parish. The once-small settlement of Gordon. occupying one of the westward spokes of Greensburg's road system, has grown steadily to become the community of Crossroads, generally recognized as the black parish seat. Its importance was enhanced by school consolidation, by increased mobility resulting from automotive travel, and by its proximity to Greensburg, the functional center of the parish. There are focused, not only the traditionally dominant church, school, cemetery, fraternal order, scout troups, and the like, but also such agencies as CORE, NAACP, and OEO. Drawing support from the tributary settlements of Gordon, Hurst, Crier, Butler, Overton, New Star, Tillery, and Center, the community of Crossroads has been the focus of change in the black population of the parish. Initial success in school and church consolidation led to the development of a federally sponsored community water project and to efforts toward incorporation as a city (Delambre 1969). A new and second elite has arisen and with it, not only trappings of political power, social prestige, slightly increased economic importance, and a devotion to the literate life, but also the appropriate settlement changes to house these new conditions. In this instance, the reciprocal mutual influence of society and settlement should be clear; a situation produced by one makes possible changes in the other which result in changes in the first.

While complete black separatism is a staggering demand in cities where black neighborhoods are scattered among whites, it is an accomplished fact of both society and settlement in rural areas such as St. Helena Parish, even before the demand was raised. Consolidation of segregated schools and transportation development set a separate stage in heavily rural areas for a separate focus of black elitism and power, adjacent to the old elite centers.

Under current conditions, though WUSPs share a considerable background with BUSPs, they also accept the first tenet of segregation: white dominance of intimate relations. As a result, WUSPs move closer to the white elite and even come to deny any similarity or connection with the customs and backgrounds of the BUSPs. Most of the poorer rural whites have already moved away or taken up wage work so that former earthy traits are more easily lost; most, at any rate, are seen by the people as resulting from the difficulties of the Great Depression. WUSPs now find it quite easy and convenient to take up the cloak of Anglo-Saxonism used by the elite for so long and to forget their rural past as completely as possible.

CULTURAL CONFIGURATIONS AND SETTLEMENT PATTERNS

Dispersal of central-place functions and a resulting poorly developed central-place hierarchy have marked the history of the Upland South

(Mitchell 1969, p. 111; Evans 1965, 1966, 1969; Arensberg 1955). Such was the character of the historic European antecedents of the Upland South (Evans 1964; Arensberg 1963; Geddes 1955; Powell 1958); such also was the character of its descendant and successor, Texan culture (Vogt 1955; Meinig 1969, pp. 118–19). Dispersed settlement and diffuse settlement functions should be explained by (and to some extent, produce) social traits, both of which are to be understood as manifestations of some central cultural values of the Upland South. Several scholars with different viewpoints have found causal correlations between cultural values of the Upland South and both settlement and social patterns. The central configuration has been described as represented by a "loose, open, country neighborhood" and by a "loose, open, Dionysian, kin-based, *famille-souche* . . . egalitarian through isolation and personal honor rather than through conscience and congregational control" and, it is frequently concluded, "this culture and this community were and are a match" (Arensberg 1955, pp. 1157–60). In terms of settlement, such a configuration explains, not only the spatial and temporal patterns of houses, settlements, and communities, but also the many small, fundamentalist, locally autonomous, Protestant churches; the scattered cemeteries; the scattered schools; the many small country stores and shops—in short, the dispersed central-place function.

In human terms, the configuration controlling settlement patterns seems also to dictate the distinctive male mystique common to a large degree to both WUSPs and BUSPs: an "action-seeking" (Gordon 1968) behavior model followed by men and boys and which involves, among many other things, respect for Robin Hood figures (Jesse James, Sam Bass, Bonnie and Clyde), a passion for guns, the love of hunting and fishing, hunting in groups, hunting and herding with dogs, an exaggerated dislike for excise taxes, an uneasiness about working regularly for others, a high valuation of the ruthless fighter, a tendency to sudden rage, a "Presbyterian" ethic which sees all issues in black and white, a preference for country-western music, and an increasing use of western clothes.[5] There is, of course, a racial difference

5   Much of this personality characterization is based—in addition to field observation and interview—on discussions arising from a seminar led by Fred B. Kniffen and E. Estyn Evans concerning Ulster-Upland South relations. The seminar was held during the spring of 1969 at the Department of Geography and Anthropology,

in the acceptance of western music and clothes, especially since the rise of black consciousness; nevertheless, some BUSPs have accepted even parts of this complex.[6]

The model Upland South county, then, consists of a territory inhabited by six rather distinct social-settlement groups, all using much the same terrain, but with differing objectives. These six are the white and black elites, the WUSPs and BUSPs, and the growing black and white rural, nonfarm workers. Because of the dispersed, diffused character of the culture and society, many central places have developed with only a limited central-place hierarchy. Where industrial and urban development has been slow, segregation in settlements and communities has been maintained into the present period of rising black expectation and power. Where development has been rapid, both white and black settlements and communities have been engulfed, but remain rather distinct, while the interstices are filled in by subdivision development, housing either the children of older residents or migrants from other areas. In time, the new subdivisions tend to take on some of the character of older communities and become identifiable on a variety of social-settlement criteria.

Comparative and historical evidence, then, seems to support the contentions that settlement patterns are, in part, artifacts of social structure, that settlement and social patterns interact, and that material culture (represented by settlement patterns) is a vital part of culture, not the discarded shuck of a social process.

REFERENCES CITED

Anderson, Mollie E., Papers
    n.d.   File B–16–1, Archives Room, Louisiana State University Library, Baton Rouge.

Louisiana State University. Kniffen and Evans, however, are not to be held responsible for the present summation of the personality.
6 Country-western music is, of course, generally rejected by Negroes though a few perform and consume it. Nevertheless, the difference between the "Nashville sound" and the "Memphis sound" is not an unbridged chasm. The history of country music has been detailed by Malone (1969), who called research attention to Nashville-Memphis similarities.

Arensberg, Conrad M.
  1955 American Communities. *American Anthropologist* 57:1143–62.
  1963 The Old World Peoples: The Place of European Cultures in World Ethnography. *Anthropological Quarterly* 36 (3):75–99.

Brill, Deter
  1963 *Baton Rouge, La.: Aufstieg, Funtionen und Gestalt einer jungen Grosstadt des neuen Industriegebiets am unteren Mississippi.* Schriften des Geographischen Instituts der Universitat Kiel, Vol. 21, No. 2. Kiel, Germany.

Delambre, Jules W.
  1969 Brokership in a Rural Subcommunity: A Study in Group Relations. Master's thesis, Louisiana State University, Baton Rouge.

Diaz, May N.
  1967 Economic Relations in Peasant Society. In Jack M. Potter *et al.*, eds., *Peasant Society: A Reader.* Boston: Little, Brown. Pp. 50–56.

Evans, E. Estyn
  1956 The Ecology of Peasant Life in Western Europe. In William L. Thomas, Jr., ed., *Man's Role in Changing the Face of the Earth.* Chicago: University of Chicago Press.
  1964 Ireland and Atlantic Europe. *Geographische Zeitschrift* 52 (3):224–41.
  1965 Cultural Relics of the Ulster-Scots in the Old West of North America. *Ulster Folklife* 11:33–38.
  1966 Culture and Land Use in the Old West of North America. *Heidelberger Studien zur Kulturgeographie.* Wiesbaden: Franz Steiner Verlag.
  1969 The Scotch-Irish: Their Cultural Adaptation and Heritage in the American Old West. In R. R. Green, ed., *Essays in Scotch-Irish History.* London: Ruteledge and Keegan-Paul.

Foster, George M.
  1967 What is a Peasant? In Jack M. Potter *et al.*, eds., *Peasant Society: A Reader.* Boston: Little, Brown. Pp. 2–14.

Geddes, Arthur
  1955 *The Isle of Lewis and Harris: A Study in British Community.* Edinburgh: University Press.

Gordon, Michael H.
  1968 The Upland Southern-Lowland Southern Culture Areas: A Field Study of Building Characteristics in Southern Virginia. Master's thesis, Rutgers University, New Brunswick, N.J.

Jeane, Donald G.
  1969 The Traditional Upland South Cemetery. *Landscape* 18 (2):39–41.

Jordan, Terry G.
  1967 The Imprint of the Upper and Lower South on Mid-Nineteenth Century Texas. *Annals of the Association of American Geographers* 57:667–90.

Kniffen, Fred B.
  1965 Folk Housing: Key to Diffusion. *Annals of the Association of American Geographers* 55: 549–77.

Kniffen, Fred B., and Henry Glassie
  1966 Building in Wood in the Eastern United States: A Time-Place Perspective. *Geographical Review* 56 (1):40–66.

Kroeber, Alfred L.
  1948 *Anthropology.* New York: Harcourt, Brace.

Lathrop, Barns F.
  1949 *Migration into East Texas, 1835–1860.* Austin: Texas State Historical Association.

Lewis, Jones, Diaries
  n.d. Microfilm Room, Louisiana State University Library, Baton Rouge.

Malone, Bill
  1969 *Country Music, U.S.A.* Austin: University of Texas Press.

Meinig, D. W.
  1969 *Imperial Texas: An Interpretive Essay in Cultural Geography.* Austin: University of Texas Press.

Mitchell, Robert D.
  1969 The Commercial Nature of Frontier Settlement in the Shenandoah Valley of Virginia. *Proceedings of the Association of American Geographers* 1:109–12.

Newton, Milton B., Jr.
  1967 The Peasant Farm of St. Helena Parish, Louisiana: A Cultural Geography. Ph.D. dissertation, Louisiana State University, Baton Rouge.
  1970 The Routes of St. Helena Parish, Louisiana. *Annals of the Association of American Geographers* 60:134–52.

Owsley, Frank Lawrence
  1949 *The Plain Folk of the Old South.* Baton Rouge: Louisiana State University Press.

Pfeifer, Gottfried
  1956 The Quality of Peasant Living in Central Europe. In William L. Thomas, Jr., ed., *Man's Role in Changing the Face of the Earth.* Chicago: University of Chicago Press.

Powell, T. G. E.
  1958 *The Celts.* Ancient Peoples and Places Series. New York: Frederick A. Praeger.

Price, Ed T.
  1968 The Central Courthouse Square in the American County Seat. *Geographical Review* 58:29–60.

Prichard, Walter, ed.
  1940 Minutes of the Police Jury of St. Helena Parish, August 16–19, 1813. *Louisiana Historical Quarterly* 23:405–27.

Redfield, Robert
   1960   *Peasant Society and Culture.* Chicago: University of Chicago Press.

Succession Records
   n.d.   Parish Clerk of Court, Greensburg, La.

Sjoberg, Gideon
   1955   The Preindustrial City. *American Journal of Sociology* 60 (5):438–45.

Vogt, Evon Z.
   1955   American Subcultural Continua as Exemplified by the Mormons and Texans. *American Anthropologist* 57:1163–72.

Warriner, Doreen
   1939   *The Economics of Peasant Farming.* New York: Oxford University Press.

Wertenbaker, T. J.
   1938   *The Founding of American Civilization: The Middle Colonies.* New York: Scribner's.

Wolf, Eric
   1966   *Peasants.* Englewood Cliffs, N.J.: Prentice-Hall.

Zelinsky, Wilbur
   1951   Where the South Begins. *Social Forces* 30:172–78.

Notes on
Contributors

DONALD N. BROWN is Assistant Professor of Anthropology at Oklahoma State University. He received his B.A. degree from Harvard University and his M.A. and Ph.D. degrees from the University of Arizona. His extensive fieldwork among the Pueblo Indians dates back to 1958. He has also worked with Navaho women patients in a sanatorium in Colorado and has excavated historical sites in Nashville, Tennessee. Among his wide interests are music and dance of the Rio Grande Pueblos, and in 1965 the Society of Ethnomusicology awarded him the Jaap Kunst Prize. As extension coordinator of the Oklahoma Indian Programs at Oklahoma State University, he teaches special courses on the cultural adjustment of urban Indians and on continuity and change in rural Indian communities.

GEORGE F. CARTER is Distinguished Professor of Geography at Texas A & M University. Dr. Carter received his Ph.D. degree in geography from the University of California, Berkeley, where as an undergraduate he had majored in anthropology. He has continued to maintain an interest in both disciplines, and through his voluminous and innovative publications, he has become one of the foremost authorities on the subject of cultural movements between the Old World and the New World prior to Columbus. He writes, "I have vast files on subjects from art to zodiacs, for the Atlantic and the Pacific. The evidence of diffusion is overwhelming. I publish mainly the biological data since it circumvents the independent inventionists. You can't invent a chicken!"

WILLIAM N. FENTON, Research Professor of Anthropology at the State University of New York at Albany since 1968, was educated at Dartmouth College and at

Yale University (Ph.D. degree, 1937). He began fieldwork with the Iroquois in 1933 and has continued his interest in that tribe ever since. He stayed thirteen years at the Bureau of American Ethnology of the Smithsonian Institution (1939–1952) and spent equal time as Assistant Commissioner for the New York State Museum and Science Service at Albany (1954–1967). From 1965 until 1972 he was chairman of the Committee on Anthropological Research in Museums (CARM) of the American Anthropological Association. In connection with Iroquois studies, his main interests lie in ethnohistory, the history of anthropology, material culture studies, and political anthropology. He has in press a critical edition of Joseph François Lafitau's *Moeurs des sauvages amériquains* (2 vols.; Paris, 1724), which was prepared with Elizabeth L. Moore for the Champlain Society of Canada, and he is currently preparing a new version of his *American Indian and White Relations to 1830* (1957). He is also contributing to the forthcoming *Handbook of North American Indians* being sponsored by the Smithsonian Institution.

BILL HOLM received his B.A. and his M.F.A. degrees from the University of Washington in 1949 and 1951, respectively. He has continued his association with his alma mater and is now Associate Professor of Art and Adjunct Associate Professor of Anthropology at the University of Washington. He also holds the position of Curator of Northwest Coast Indian Art and is chairman of the Education Division at the Thomas Burke Memorial Washington State Museum in Seattle. Since 1957 he has been doing fieldwork among the Kwakiutl, and this unusually extensive field experience accounts for his close familiarity with Kwakiutl art and artists. Among other publications, he is the author of *Northwest Coast Indian Art* published by the University of Washington Press.

PEARL KATZ is presently Research Associate in Anthropology at Tel-Aviv University, Israel. She has previously been Research Associate in Anthropology at the State University of New York at Buffalo. In addition to her fieldwork in the American Southwest, she has also conducted research on immigrants in Israel. Her interests include acculturation, social networks, and educational anthropology.

FRED B. KNIFFEN is Boyd Professor Emeritus of Geography, Louisiana State University, Baton Rouge. Trained in both geography and anthropology at the University of California, Berkeley, Dr. Kniffen has written on geomorphology, archaeology, ethnology, and cultural geography. His work on settlement geography has drawn worldwide attention. He is presently writing a volume on the ethnography of Louisiana's Indians.

ARTHUR G. MILLER worked at Teotihuacan during the summers from 1966 to 1969 and for an intensive six-month period in 1970–1971. Dr. Miller, who received his Ph.D. degree from Harvard University in 1969, recently finished a book on the mural paintings at Teotihuacan, and for the past three years he has been working on recording the pre-Columbian murals of the Yucatan Peninsula. In cooperation with the Departamento de Monumentos Prehispánicos of the Instituto Nacional de Antropología e Historia, Dr. Miller is now directing intensive excavations of the Maya site of Tancah in Quintana Roo, Mexico.

DOLORES NEWTON received her Ph.D. degree in anthropology from Harvard University, and in her dissertation she looked at the social and historical dimensions of Timbira material culture. She supplemented her fieldwork among the Timbira Indians of Brazil with work in museums in Brazil, the United States, and Europe. Dr. Newton is presently Assistant Professor of Anthropology and Curator of the University Museum at the State University of New York at Stony Brook.

MILTON B. NEWTON, JR., received his Ph.D. degree in cultural geography from Louisiana State University, Baton Rouge, where he is now Associate Professor in the Department of Geography and Anthropology and Director of the Museum of Geoscience. His principal topical interest is the geography of settlements (both prehistoric and historic); his regional interests are the southeastern and southwestern United States, particularly the Upland South and the frontier. He has done fieldwork in Louisiana, Mississippi, south Texas, New Mexico, and northeast Mexico. In addition to preparing an atlas of Louisiana and working on the concept of cultural preadaptation, Dr. Newton is directing the collection of ethnographic and cultural geographic materials for LSU's Museum of Geoscience.

RICHARD B. POLLNAC is Assistant Professor of Anthropology at the University of Rhode Island. He received his Ph.D. degree in 1972 from the University of Missouri, Columbia, where he was an NDEA and Woodrow Wilson Fellow. In 1969 he was a research associate at the Makerere Institute of Social Research, Makerere University College, Kampala, Uganda. In 1971 he returned to Uganda to do additional fieldwork. Earlier in 1968 Dr. Pollnac worked in highland Guatemala on market systems. To a degree rare for an anthropologist, he has special expertise in statistical analysis and quantitative research design.

MICHAEL C. ROBBINS is Associate Professor of Anthropology at the University of Missouri, Columbia. He received his Ph.D. degree in 1966 from the University of Minnesota. A speaker of Swahili and Luganda, Dr. Robbins has considerable field experience in Africa: Tanzania in 1959–1960, Uganda in 1967, 1969, 1971, and again in 1972. He has published extensively in the professional journals, such as *Human Organization* and the *American Anthropologist*, on psychological anthropology, Africa, and modernization.

RALPH M. ROWLETT, presently Associate Professor of Anthropology at the University of Missouri, Columbia, received his Ph.D. degree from Harvard University, where he specialized in European prehistoric and protohistoric archaeology. He has also studied at the Institute of Archaeology, University of London, and in 1968–1969 he was a postdoctoral fellow at the Seminarie voor Archeologie at Gent University, Belgium. Dr. Rowlett's main interest is in the reconstruction of synchronic cultural activities and processes through the use of quantitative analysis.

MARY JANE SCHNEIDER received her M.A. degree from the University of Missouri, Columbia, where presently she is Research Assistant at the Museum of Anthropology. In pursuit of her studies of material culture, Ms. Schneider received a grant from the Wenner-Gren Foundation for a descriptive and historical study of Kiowa beadwork designs. With funds from the National Science Foundation she is directing an inventory of ethnological collections in the museums in Missouri.

THOMAS S. SCHORR obtained his A.B. and Ph.D. degrees in anthropology at Tulane University, New Orleans. He is currently Associate Professor of Anthropology at the University of Pittsburgh, having moved there in 1967 from the International Center for Medical Research and Training, Universidad del Valle, Cali, Colombia, where he was Assistant Professor and Research Coordinator of the Sociology-Anthropology Unit. For more than five years, he has resided and done ethnographic fieldwork in Colombia on the adaptive responses of peasant populations in the Cauca Valley to programs of regional development. His interests include ecology and system analysis, cognitive organization, medical anthropology, prehistory, anthropological film making, and aerial ethnography.

AUGUSTUS SORDINAS was born on Corfu, Greece, and thus has the advantage of an intimate acquaintance with the island's culture to go with his objective perspective gained through broad and extensive studies: economic history at the Graduate School of Economics in Athens, languages at the Institute of Languages and Linguistics, Georgetown University, and cultural anthropology at Harvard University (Ph.D. degree, 1968). He has excavated prehistoric sites in France, Greece, and West Africa and has spent several field seasons on Corfu. Dr. Sordinas is the author of *Old Olive Oil Mills and Presses on the Island of Corfu, Greece,* published in 1971 by Memphis State University, where he is presently Professor of Anthropology.